REGIONAL THEATRE The *Revolutionary Stage*

REGIONAL THEATRE

The Revolutionary Stage

JOSEPH WESLEY ZEIGLER

UNIVERSITY OF MINNESOTA
PRESS • Minneapolis

© Copyright 1973 by the University of Minnesota.
All rights reserved. Printed in the
United States of America at Napco Graphic Arts, Inc.,
New Berlin, Wisconsin. Published in
the United Kingdom and India by the Oxford
University Press, London and Delhi, and
in Canada by the Copp Clark
Publishing Co. Limited, Toronto.

Library of Congress Catalog Card Number: 73-75795

ISBN 0-8166-0675-7

For Alison

Foreword

Once upon a time groups of theatre people met and talked and dreamed about something we called, for lack of a better phrase, the tributary theatre. At that point we thought of ourselves as serving the once-flourishing theatre in New York City as a river's tributaries serve the mainstream by sending their most sparkling waters surging into it. Then the tributary theatre became the regional theatre, a phrase which nobody liked and everybody used, and the regional theatre eventually came of age or at least began to fill the growing vacuum of Broadway. As our theatre kept dying in one place and springing up in new forms and new rhythms in lots of other places, we came to think of it as resident professional theatre, although it was too rarely resident and too often not nearly professional enough. Repertory theatre, we called it in shorthand, although it usually wasn't repertory either and we knew it wasn't. And noncommercial or nonprofit theatre, which it usually was and we didn't want it to be. Progressively inaccurate descriptions for the same geographical and psychological phenomenon: the spread of the American theatre outside the steadily-growing-colder canyons of Times Square—or at least the growth of a theatre not bound up in New York's traditional processes and attitudes, what Zelda Fichandler has labeled the "whaddaya-call-it" theatre.

A million years ago—as Beckett's Vladimir would have described it—by the light of my idealistic youth, I came to compose a somewhat visionary article for the National Theatre Conference *Bulletin* entitled "One Theatre," a call for one American theatre instead of a theatre hopelessly separated into worlds which were even more hopelessly antagonistic: New York and the provinces. Little did I dream that I would live to see the day—and the nights (six of them weekly and two matinees)—when the vision would become a reality. In the theatre, as everywhere else, there are only two things that can happen to one's hopes: they can fall, or they can get there—to confound you.

For most of my hoping life in the theatre, I have had the fortune and often the misery of being a small wave in the shifting yet persistent tide toward one theatre. I have watched that tide swell with achievement as it surmounted confusion and doubts, seeking to establish and assert its identity. I happened to be on hand, for example, when a curiously likable though inexperienced band of zealots set out to open a theatre on a showboat floating up and down the Potomac River and wound up instead on a seamy street in an ex-burlesque house which they renamed Arena Stage. In later years I was to direct the opening productions in two of Arena's subsequent physical manifestations, choking with cement dust on both occasions.

I wandered into the Alley Theatre in Houston in its early days and watched it survive and grow. And I worked with the Playhouse in the same city and saw it fade away and die. I've directed in whatever regional theatre location or theatrical setup offered an opportunity—in San Francisco, Minneapolis, Chicago, Milwaukee, and Boston and heaven-knows-what whistlestops in between. And in places where I haven't had the opportunity to direct, I have frequently been on hand to see and listen and care and blame a bit and hope and gnash my teeth and wait for Godot. Always, I trust, with the sympathy and understanding of a true believer—even when Broadway or off-Broadway was absorbing my major energies. Now that I am once again back on some sort of sustained basis with my first love, Washington's Arena Stage, what is more obvious than ever is that theatre in America has gloriously and permanently penetrated the hinterlands. If indeed the American theatre's very existence as an art form has been threatened by the changing values and consciousness of the frenzied '60s and '70s, the new Dark Ages may sooner and more likely descend upon 44th and 45th streets or the Lincoln Center Plaza than upon the myriad camping grounds where Margo, Nina, Zelda, good Sir Tony, and all their fellow Johnny Appleseeds have succeeded in scattering their largesse.

Not that the centrifugal theatre (as it has been called by Joe Zeigler, my friend and once-colleague in a regional resident repertory nonprofit theatre which failed before it opened) is without its problems, its limitations, and its critics galore. The best evidence of its durability, in fact, lies in the number and grievousness of the faults ascribed to it even by those of us who have had a part in its development. Had the regional theatre lost its generation-long struggle to survive, we would all have shed tears like mad and soon would have forgotten where the body was buried. But because it won—that is, it survived—we could begin to knock hell out of it, knowing full well that it could weather our sneers just as it had managed to outlast our hosannahs.

The regional theatre, everybody always said, might be regional but it rarely, if ever, belonged to its region. Whenever a regional theatre sought deliberately to become regional, either in its choice of play material or in its personnel, it was too provincial or too folksy. When it wasn't doing new plays, we blamed it for timidity and conventionality. When for varying reasons and under varying pressures it started to do that and when the new plays increased in both quality and quantity, we said it was just interested in doing tryouts for New York. When companies of actors began to stick around for a season or even two at a time, we criticized the theatres for merely imitating their European antecedents or for encouraging mediocrity. When companies succumbed to casting for individual productions, we accused them of selling out to the Broadway system. At a time when theatres were doing the classics, we were sure they were just playing safe; when they weren't doing the classics, they were afraid. If a theatre failed, it failed because it wasn't much good; if it happened to survive, that was only because it was too conservative. Because the regional theatre, after its first decade or two, had not produced world-shaking talents, scintillating personalities, and absolutely original production styles, it acquired a reputation for being dull and unimaginative. When after another decade it did produce such exciting phenomena, we observed that it lost them almost at once to New York and Los Angeles. Nevertheless, despite the criticisms from the world at large and from within its own ranks, the theatre outside New York has been holding its own with the theatre on the "right" side of the Hudson. And as we enter a new decade it is astoundingly clear that the regional theatre may be pulling away to new heights of artistic leadership and responsibility.

Mr. Zeigler's record of the regional theatre's pioneering age is a chronicle of its origins, struggles, failures, strengths, uncertainties, concerns, and triumphs. He not only traces the regional theatre's roots and historical line but digs deeply and fundamentally into its causes, its inner reasonings, and its interconnections with American life and American values. Things change so fast in the theatre world as elsewhere that in addition to the facts we need to know the basic truths which underlie them. In time, some of Mr. Zeigler's facts will surely be outdated, but it seems to me that many of the truths he has brought to light will live on to intrigue us. I do not know of another work more carefully analytical of those forces and currents which have shaped our present-day potential for a national theatre or at least a nationwide theatre. While I do not necessarily agree with all of Mr. Zeigler's premises or with certain of his conclusions, I consider his account both truthful and penetrating in the major thrust of its argument. I am pleased to share his optimism about the future of this exciting phenomenon of regional theatre, and I am most grateful for the breadth of knowledge which he couples with perspective and objectivity in dealing with an exceedingly subjective process.

The future determines the past, as one of my playwrights once taught me. And I have come over the years more and more to appreciate this apparent enigma. A successful revolution needs historians not merely to chronicle its triumphs but to make those who participated and those who come after understand what it is that has happened. The more vital the theatre comes to be in our lives and the more these "small islands in a sea of Babbitry" (again Zelda Fichandler's phrase) expand and flourish, the more our descendants will ask how we came to do this with our theatre and why we waited so long and labored so confusingly.

Plato observed that "when the mode of music changes, the walls of the city shake." Well, the mode of the music of our time is surely changing, and the walls of our cities are shaking to their foundations for all sorts of reasons and in all sorts of ways. The pages that follow provide us with a glimpse of how stronger walls, more appropriate to our newer music, can be built.

Alan Schneider

Washington, D.C.
November 1972

Preface

A written history of an art form is inevitably a secondary statement. The primary statement is the art itself. I want it to be clear from the start that this book covers the story of the regional theatre through the 1960s and into the 1970s, but it does not cover the art of it. The reader, I hope, will go to find that for himself.

This is as it should be, for I am neither a critic nor a student of the stage. Instead, I am interested primarily in culture and sociology as joint forces—"culturology," if you will. One definition of culture is "the concepts, habits, skills, art, instruments, and institutions of a given people in a given period"; another is simply "civilization." As a "culturologist," I am fascinated by culture as a reflection of its society and as potentially a changer of it. Therefore, in telling the story that follows, I have concentrated on the creative tension between the cultural impulse of the regional theatre and the larger American society around it.

For all that, this is a personal book, and it comes out of a decade of direct involvement in the regional theatre movement. From 1962 to 1966, I worked as an administrator in several theatres in Washington,

Regional Theatre: The Revolutionary Stage

San Francisco, and upstate New York. Then, from 1966 to 1969, I gained an overview of the movement and came to know its leaders through my work in Theatre Communications Group, a national service organization for regional theatres throughout America. Many of the impressions and ideas developed here are the legacy of that overview.

In 1969, I was invited to teach a graduate seminar at Brooklyn College on the development of the regional theatre, an assignment that continued over three years. This book represents a substantial amplification of the material presented in the seminar. It incorporates in addition the results of research which I undertook in conjunction with my subsequent activities in the field: my editorship of *Theatre Today*, a small quarterly published by the City University of New York; various consulting assignments over the last four years for individual theatres, for the Business Committee for the Arts, and for the National Endowment for the Arts; and the publication of several articles in *Theatre Today*, the *Arts Reporting Service*, and *Cultural Affairs* (a quarterly published by the Associated Councils of the Arts).

Nevertheless, any analyst must eventually stop the research and put his observations and conclusions into words. This is particularly sobering with a subject as various as mine; theatres come and go and change with surprising frequency and speed. Therefore, the reader should bear in mind that the stories and personalities of individual theatres may be changing even as he reads—which is all the more reason for the reader to go to see for himself.

I have known directly all the theatres represented in this book and most of their leaders; and I have seen their work with some regularity over the last ten years. Still, there are some theatres outside New York which I have not treated. For instance, except for the Stratford Shakespearean Festival in Ontario, I do not discuss the numerous regional theatres which have developed in Canada during the same period because the book is a study of an American cultural and social phenomenon. Also, I have omitted professional theatres sponsored by universities; while these have grown in numbers in recent years and have become important in American theatre, I believe that the university support behind them has made their basis and their development significantly different in a "culturological" sense. Similarly, I have not dealt with the many and vital experimental theatres or the black and other ethnic theatres which have enhanced the theatrical palette in major cities in recent years.

The kind of theatre I discuss in this book has been called by many names, most frequently (and sometimes interchangeably) "repertory," "resident," and "regional." Of these, I have chosen to use the term "regional," partly because it is the most inclusive term but mostly because it reflects the anti-capital philosophy which is at the core of the story. For the "acorn" and "oak tree" terminology, I am indebted to the board of directors of Theatre Communications Group, who started using it as a convenient kind of shorthand in the middle years of the 1960s.

Indeed, I am indebted to many people who helped to stimulate and then to refine my study. The first debt is of course to those who created and sustained the theatres; certainly the story of each and every theatre quickly surveyed here could fill a book by itself. More particularly, I am indebted to Michael Mabry, cohort and buffer at Theatre Communications Group; to Eldon Elder, Glenn Loney, and Wilson Lehr, who called on me for the Brooklyn College seminar; and to the students of that course, who further stimulated my thinking, sometimes by disagreeing with it. I am especially grateful to Bradley Morison, who introduced me to "culturology" and who continues to fight with me for it, and of course to my parents who, faced with a culture-prone young son, had the great good sense not to push it but who enabled him to do so.

Finally, to my wife Alison, a salute for her willingness to live a life in which the theatre has been my mistress. She has given many evenings to listening and understanding, and she has spent many others alone. This book would not have been possible without her.

Joseph Wesley Zeigler

New York, N.Y.
March 1973

Contents

1. Defining a Revolution   1

2. Antecedents: A World Elsewhere   6

3. Margo Jones: Legacy and Legend   17

4. Acorns: Theatres before 1960   24

5. Oak Trees: The Guthrie Theater
   and What Came After   62

6. Saplings: Small Theatres of the 1960s   88

7. Stabs at a National Theatre   118

8. To Save the World: The Actor's
   Workshop Moves East   142

9. Up against the Marble Wall: The
   Loss of The Actor's Workshop   156

10. The Establishment Theatre   170

11. New Plays and New Ploys   188

12. The Regional Dilemma   199

13. Storming the Citadel: The Theatres
    Go to New York   210

14. A More Suitable Dream   234

Notes   255

Suggestions for Additional Reading   262

Index   265

Photographs between pages 140 and 141

REGIONAL THEATRE The *Revolutionary* *Stage*

1 Defining a Revolution

Revolution: n. 1. The course or motion of a body around another body or central point or axis considered as fixed. 2. A complete or drastic change of any kind. 3. The overthrow of one form of government or social system and the setting up of another.

After decades of urging by leaders and visionaries, there is finally in America an alternative to the theatre of Broadway. It is the regional theatre, a network of professional groups located in major cities around the country: Washington, Baltimore, New Haven, Providence, Cincinnati, Milwaukee, Minneapolis, Seattle, San Francisco, Los Angeles, Houston, and many others. Actors' Equity Association, the professional actors' union, now lists approximately forty such theatres, while a scant two decades ago there were fewer than a dozen. *Variety*, the theatrical trade newspaper, was forced to admit as early as 1966 that there are more professional actors working outside New York than on Broadway. In fact, a new theatrical generation has chosen the regional route rather than the "bright lights" of Broadway. These theatre people are settling down in regional cities, buying houses, raising families, joining the PTA, becoming politically active, and in general taking responsible places as citizens of their communities.

Their commitment has been matched increasingly by the communities themselves. Each year, hundreds of thousands of people across America subscribe in advance to entire seasons of plays. Their children

1

are being bused from school to theatre to see Faustus damned, Caesar stabbed, and Kate tamed, rather than merely reading about such horrors in class. In theatres fashioned out of old factories and warehouses, nightclubs, churches, and movie palaces—and in more and more new multi-million-dollar buildings—American audiences are getting a first-hand acquaintance with what otherwise might seem musty dramatic literature. Shakespeare is a summertime star; Sunday night post-performance symposia reveal the secrets of Brecht, Beckett, Albee, and Pinter; and the work of new playwrights is being tested on increasingly aware and demanding audiences. Like symphony orchestras and art museums, regional theatres are now accepted as fixtures of their communities. In short, in the words of *New York Times* drama critic Clive Barnes, "The scene is moving."

The rise of regional companies depends upon the concept of theatre as an institution rather than as the entrepreneurial phenomenon that it is on Broadway. Each theatre is structured as an entity unto itself, with an identity and standing of its own, like a business corporation; but there is one essential and major difference—the theatre institution is eleemosynary and nonprofit because it cannot break even on its operation, let alone make money. Being nonprofit, its income benefits no individual stockholders. Being tax-exempt, it can and must seek contributions to sustain itself, calling upon private citizens, corporations, local and national foundations, and civic, state, and even federal governments. While proud and independent, the theatre as an institution is technically a charity. This status places upon it a responsibility to serve the public, which it does not only by presenting plays of merit but also by allying its program with those of the schools and other institutions of the community.

As I see it, the regional theatre has several constituencies, both internal and external. Its most intimate constituency is its community of artists—the actors, directors, artisans, and administrators who form its working family. All of these people are professionals who earn their living at the theatre. They have banded together out of a belief that theatre is best when created through group effort, each person's talent complementing and enlarging that of all others. Working as a unit, they present plays each year that are chosen and performed to relate to each other as a body of work.

Another small constituency in each regional theatre is its most formal one—its governing board of directors or trustees. Again like the symphony orchestra or museum, or like a college or hospital, the theatre institution is governed by general policies approved by a board whose members are chosen from among powerful lay leaders within the community. The board has the ultimate civic and financial responsibility for the theatre. Financially, the board members are charged with finding the support to sustain the theatre; civically, they are charged with representing (and sometimes defending) the theatre to its community and the community to the theatre. The board is the theatre's link with its public.

The public, of course, represents the primary constituency of the regional theatre institution. Through its interest in attending performances and its support in the form of contributions, the public determines whether or not a theatre will survive, and its interest and support are directly proportional to the theatre's commitment and ability to serve the public.

The concept of public service is partly an insurance policy for the regional theatre institution. By serving, it hopes to provide for itself and its public an alternative to the "hit-or-miss" psychology of the commercial theatre. Regional theatres are out to prove that professional theatre in America can be created on an institutional bias and can grow and survive on it.

Institutionalism is the official basis of all regional theatre. I believe that the more compelling basis, however, is individualism—the essential need in each situation for a single, messianic leader to give it character, spirit, direction, and inspiration. The leader must be willing to abnegate himself for his theatre while fulfilling himself through it. He must have what W. McNeil Lowry, vice-president of the Ford Foundation and in that capacity a prime benefactor of regional theatres, calls "the drive or fanaticism or whatever of the person who has made his choice, and will eschew anything else—money, the elite identification of a university degree, even health—to develop the talent he hopes he has."[1] The leader must also be willing to function in isolation from a large concentration of similar minds and spirits, often in a relatively hostile environment. How he relates to that environment determines not only the theatre's personality but also its destiny. And that relationship is not always or even usually smooth; as noted by Nan Martin, an actress frequently appearing in the regional theatre, most important theatres are the "result of one person's incredible belief in the face of all odds, one person's vision and drive. Such a man is seldom a weather vane swinging with every breeze. Either he has his theatre on his terms or he doesn't want a theatre at all."[2] It seems to me that in any theatre of major importance, the individual is generally the master of the relationship, and the institution is an extension of his (or her) personality.

Beyond institutionalism and individualism, there is a third basis of the regional theatre, and that is decentralization. The regional theatre phenomenon has been a major and determined attempt to spread American culture throughout the country and even more to create a new basis of theatre not dependent on Broadway. The purpose of decentralization has been less to spread the wealth than to triumph in an ideological war between the institutional theatre and the commercial theatre. Those in the forefront of the regional theatre movement see it as a way to strip Broadway of its power. The primary force of their crusade has been centrifugal.

That force has now been active for twenty-five years—for a generation. Yet only a few theatres are that old; most have been operating less than ten years. The leaders of these theatres maintain that the theatres have not yet reached their majority and that individual theatres should not be judged by the standards applied to older and more firmly established arts institutions like symphony orchestras and museums, which have had more time to develop and cement themselves into their local societies. In the words of the late Sir Tyrone Guthrie, founding artistic director of The Guthrie Theater in Minneapolis, "An experiment of this kind simply cannot be judged in short term. It is essentially an attempt to apply longer-term policies and a more serious, though not I hope on that account pompous, approach to the theatre than is implicit in the frantic pursuit of the Smash Hit."[3]

Guthrie was right. His theatre, on its own, should not be judged in any final, absolute way; like its sisters, it is still evolving, still a specific experiment. Nevertheless, in fast-changing modern America, a generation is a long time, and so the regional theatre phenomenon as a whole can be assessed. In fact, I feel that it must be assessed because the phenomenon, unlike most individual theatres in it, is in middle age and has become one of the pillars of American culture. The regional theatre is in its prime; it is being seen—and is seeing itself—as a national solution. One of its most persuasive advocates in this is Zelda Fichand-

4

ler, producing director of the long-standing and venerable Arena Stage in Washington: "The impulse, then, was to remedy a grievous fault and reverse a direful trend—the contraction and imminent death of the art of the theatre. This goal has been, to a large degree, accomplished. . . . The American theatre has begun to have a tradition: a past, a present, a future, a somewhat coherent way to look at itself and to proceed."[4]

If the goal has been accomplished, it has been through revolt, and so this is the story of a revolution—not a bloody rebellion, or a quick mutiny, or a treasonous sedition, but a long and even accidental revolution, one that came about almost in spite of itself. It has been a revolution full of dedication and folly, grandeur and confusion, success and suffering. And it has been a revolution endangered, almost overwhelmed, by a secondary but obsessive purpose: the creation of a single American National Theatre to rival any in the world. America has long had to live with the embarrassment of having no one theatre that could stand beside France's Comédie Française, Russia's Moscow Art Theatre, Germany's Berliner Ensemble, and England's Royal Shakespeare Company and National Theatre as an ultimate expression of the art of the stage. The creation of such a company has long been a primary dream of all who work in the institutional theatre in this country. To be the answer to that dream became the self-imposed responsibility of the regional theatre, and so any assessment must concentrate on whether the larger revolution has survived that detour of purpose.

2 Antecedents: A World Elsewhere

"Broadway will be a mecca; it will remain a standard of reference; its nod of approval will set the stamp. . . . But as the nation grows up, as each state and region awakens to fuller self-consciousness, as the migrations cease and roots begin to grow deep into the soil, there will spring forth on the way to Mecca 1,000 oases. That is what I mean by decentralization of the theatre."

Norris Houghton, Advance from Broadway

When teacher-critic Norris Houghton called in 1941 for a serious, professional, and permanent decentralization of the American theatre, he was renewing a plea which had often been voiced in the theatrical world. In fact, at the turn of the century, there had been decentralization of a sort: hundreds of legitimate professional theatres in the United States, many in small, out-of-the-way communities. Those were the days when even minor towns boasted elegant opera houses; when James O'Neill, Eugene's father, was squandering his considerable talent in endless tours of *The Count of Monte Cristo*; when J. Forbes-Robertson, Richard Mansfield, Joseph Jefferson, and Sarah Bernhardt, among others, were robustly traveling the breadth of the nation to provide living theatre for all within reach (and a most lucrative living for themselves).

For such actors—and for their managers and the theatre chain owners like Abraham Ehrlanger, Charles Frohman, and later the Shubert brothers—these forays into the regions beyond the Hudson River did not arise from anything so noble as dreams of decentralization; they were simply attempts to cash in on individual stardom and the mystery and glamour of theatre itself. Still, what grew from the need of theatre people to keep working afforded for a curious public a series of live experiences otherwise unmatched. At the turn of the century, there were simply no other distractions to compete with in-person performances; and the public eagerly accepted individual performers and made them their own. The accessibility of the theatrical occasion was also served by professional stock companies in the early years of our century. Howard Taubman, in his book *The Making of the American Theatre*,[1] points out that by 1910 there were two thousand companies throughout the country rehearsing one play while presenting another, changing their bills usually every week, and above all providing for new actors and other talents the nuts-and-bolts experience that would stand them in good stead when they went on to more fertile grounds.

The birth of the movies changed all this, starting in the period of World War I and climaxing with the advent of "talkies" just before the Great Depression. Now the public could find even more mystery and glamour in the larger-than-life stars of the "silver screen"—and at reasonable prices. The now too-familiar actors of the stock companies could not compete with movie stars for the public's affection; through the magic of film, people everywhere could share Charles Chaplin, Mary Pickford, and Douglas Fairbanks, rather than bearing with their hometown actors and wondering if they were as good as those in the next town over.

What movies did not satisfy, radio did. The new home entertainment provided even more mystery—faceless entertainment in which the imagination of the listener could collaborate with the actor and engineer for new effects. Also, after the initial purchase, this entertainment was virtually free.

By the start of World War II and Norris Houghton's nationwide study of the scene, the earlier thrusts toward decentralized theatre had dwindled to almost no professional activity. Former theatres had been turned into movie palaces, radio was king, and the thousands of legitimate theatres throughout the country at the turn of the century had dropped to under two hundred—and nearly one-fourth of this number were Broadway houses in New York. It is no wonder that Houghton, like others before him, despaired over the lack of professional theatre outside New York and dreamed of the day when this lack could be dynamically redressed.

Regional Theatre: The Revolutionary Stage

Houghton's call for a new and professional decentralization arose partly from his disenchantment with another thrust toward a regionalized theatre, the Little Theatre movement of the 1920s. In the number of theatres created and the number of amateur talents working in them, the Little Theatre movement was the farthest-reaching homegrown theatre in American history. It was also the most self-consciously noble; it is no accident that even now we speak of the phenomenon in capital letters. The Little Theatres issued high-sounding manifestos on their purposes, and they stressed what was then avant-garde in the drama. Essential in their creation and operation was the belief that the simple amateur talent of community citizens could provide a body of work at least equal to Broadway, touring companies, and stock companies. People who had never seen Shubert Alley were convinced that theirs was the only true theatre; this self-righteousness fostered condescension toward the theatre world beyond them, which in turn limited the horizons of the Little Theatres.

Still, so widespread was the movement and so enthralling were its manifestos that many historians throughout the country attributed to it a potential which could not be justified upon close examination. Augustus Thomas, writing in *Variety* at the height of the movement, went so far as to predict that "the Little Theatre rebellion will have the 'legit' theatre by the throat ten years from now"; and Edith Isaacs, Stark Young, and others at *Theatre Arts* saw the Little Theatres as pure rivers refreshing the mainstream of the American theatre.

Nevertheless, the Little Theatres failed. By the end of the 1930s, their high-flying quest had run its course. Houghton realized that their revolution had failed: "Many of these theatres have lost their experimental character, their youthful idealism. . . . They appear middle-aged, realistic, quasi-commercial. . . . They are no longer artistic pioneers; they are now cautious followers in the ruts of Broadway."[2]

The Depression itself was one villain in the collapse of the Little Theatres. Another problem was that in most cases the lay leaders of the Little Theatres lacked the sophistication, expertise, and above all the time to transform their ringing manifestos into continuing specific programs. The high-minded amateurs had gamely taken a big bite of avant-garde and serious theatre, but they could not assimilate it sufficiently for it to become the basis of a lasting revolution. The Little Theatre movement did not die, of course; it changed into the commu-

8

nity theatre movement, with lowercase letters and lowercase ideas. With increasing emphasis on theatre as a social pastime, and concentrating on warmed-over recent Broadway light comedy successes, most community theatres now have the insular goal of providing pleasant evenings for unquestioning, ingrown audiences.

The Depression that helped to stifle touring, stock companies, and the Little Theatre nevertheless fomented two major attempts at non-commercial theatre which are still fondly remembered as models for today's regional theatre: the Federal Theatre and the Group Theatre.

The Federal Theatre Project, inaugurated by Congress in 1935 as part of the New Deal's Works Progress Administration, was designed to provide jobs for unemployed theatre artists and administrators. Hallie Flanagan, head of the Experimental Theatre at Vassar College, was chosen to lead the project. She took as her challenge the belief that "Now, for the first time, the professional theatre might also be considered regionally. Under a federal plan, could not all of these various theatres, commercial, educational, and community, in the East, West, North, South, work together?"[3] By creating production units in major cities around the country, the Federal Theatre was able to give work to more than fifteen thousand professionals at peak periods; and it had mounted more than a thousand productions in forty cities by mid-1939, when the ultra-right witch-hunting of the Dies Un-American Activities Committee forced a cancellation of its appropriation and thus killed the project. So died a theatre which had crossed regional lines to speak to an entire nation in crisis. Evidence of this success was the protest from the public when the project was facing extinction in Washington. In addition to fulfilling its primary responsibility of providing theatre jobs, the Federal Theatre had also accomplished two more subtle feats: it had stimulated the growth of a sizable body of theatre practitioners who were familiar with American theatre as a whole, and it had identified an audience for serious and socially committed drama.

Where the Federal Theatre failed was in not moving far enough in decentralizing itself. Six of its twelve production units were based in New York, where the vast majority of the talent was, leaving only six units for the rest of the country. So few could hardly provide the necessary muscle for broad-based regional development. Still, as with the Little Theatre movement, the heart of the Federal Theatre was in the right place, and unlike the Little Theatres it had enough expertise and talent to be truly effective—which makes its demise (one might almost say its murder) all the more tragic.

The other antecedent of the 1930s, the Group Theatre, was a distinctly New York phenomenon, not a regional one, but it helped to pave the way for regional theatres in its orientation toward group effort. While the Federal Theatre was largely unjustly accused of Communist leanings, the Group, as described in Harold Clurman's autobiographical *The Fervent Years,* was consciously communistic in spirit. It was a theatrical commune, and the spirit of joint life and effort which distinguished the Group has inspired countless theatre talents since its day. That this spirit disintegrated can be blamed on the commercial Broadway theatre as it existed then and as it exists now. Members of the Group were constantly invited to leave the commune to work for commercial managements or to act in films on the West Coast. Eventually they began to heed such Sirens, and the Group collapsed shortly after the Federal Theatre. Its legacy was assured, however, particularly through the reputation of its primary playwright, Clifford Odets; it was enhanced further by the Actors' Studio founded later by Group leaders Lee Strasberg, Elia Kazan, and Cheryl Crawford and by Clurman's book. New young talents continued to look to the Group as proof that communal effort could create a more advanced theatre.

There were other antecedents: the Provincetown Players, featuring the work of Eugene O'Neill and Robert Edmond Jones; the Washington Square Players, which evolved into the Theatre Guild; Eva Le Gallienne's valiant attempts to maintain repertory operations—first the Civic Repertory in the 1920s and later the American Repertory Theatre in the mid-1940s; and Orson Welles's and John Houseman's radical Mercury Theatre, a stepchild of the Federal Theatre which veered off on its own and produced innovative work in the late 1930s and early 1940s. While these attempts were all New York based and so not regional, they were still models in their belief that good theatre could be created on the institutional bias.

Another federally sponsored project that was supposed to support the concept of a decentralized theatre—but in my view a thorn in its side—was the American National Theatre and Academy (ANTA). Founded by congressional charter in 1935, ANTA, as described in its preamble, was designed to be "a people's project, organized and conducted in their interest, free from commercialism, but with the firm intent of being as far as possible self-supporting. A national theatre should bring to the people throughout the country their heritage of the great drama of the past and the best of the present, which has been too frequently unavailable to them under existing conditions." Senate Bill 2642, which established ANTA as a nonprofit corporation, also outlined its purposes: the presentation of theatrical productions; the stimulation of public interest in drama; the advancement of interest in drama through the United States by furthering production of plays; the development of the study of drama; and the sponsorship, encouragement, and development of the art and technique of the theatre through a school within the American National Theatre and Academy.[4]

While ANTA's charter did specify that it should serve people throughout the country, the organization did little to work toward that goal. The board of directors was packed with reactionaries who were either die-hard commercial theatre people or others who wanted to mingle with them. ANTA saddled itself with a large Broadway theatre that bore its name and was a drain on funds, and in it the organization occasionally tried to function as a producing unit on Broadway. (The most noteworthy series of productions was during the late 1940s and early 1950s—John Garfield in *Peer Gynt*, directed by Lee Strasberg; Katrina Paxinou in *The House of Bernarda Alba*; Arlene Francis in Edmund Wilson's *The Little Blue Light*; and, most successfully, José Ferrer and Gloria Swanson in *Twentieth Century*.) At other times, ANTA was little more than a landlord housing other commercial offerings in its theatre. Basically, ANTA was oriented too much toward the New York scene to accomplish what it could have or should have for the country as a whole. Its National Theatre Service (created by Elizabeth Burdick and later managed by Ruth Mayleas) was generally successful in providing known talents for short periods in college and community theatres, but that too was alien to the outlook of ANTA as represented by its entrenched New York leadership. The program was a sop thrown to Cerberus, and when it did not find funds to continue itself, ANTA discarded it.

I shall discuss later how ANTA restructured itself with the help of the federal government and tried to associate itself with the rise of the regional theatre it had done so little to foster. However, by then it was too late to change the narrow outlook that had so seriously hampered the organization. Whatever ANTA does in the future, its historical

11

importance at this point appears minimal; when it was needed most to help in decentralizing the American theatre, it was too busy marveling at itself in New York.

When Norris Houghton set out to tour the country in the early 1940s, there was virtually no professional institutional theatre activity outside New York. Several theatres sat in loneliness beyond the Hudson River. One of the more original was the Hedgerow Theatre near Philadelphia, founded by Jasper Deeter in 1923. The Hedgerow maintained a large repertoire of classics and regularly offered festivals of plays by Shakespeare, Shaw, and Chekhov. It was like the Group Theatre in its communal spirit, with some dozen actors co-owners in the Hedgerow Theatre Partnership. The training of actors formed a key element of the theatre's activity, and Ann Harding, Van Heflin, and Richard Basehart, among others, got their start there.

Another theatre which came into existence during this period was Robert Porterfield's Barter Theatre in Abingdon, Virginia. In 1932, Porterfield, himself an actor, found a more immediate and more modest answer to the work problem than the WPA's: He took some twenty of his fellow actors to the tiny town of Abingdon in southwest Virginia, opened a summer theatre, and allowed his audiences to attend the plays in exchange for hams, potatoes, or whatever other produce they could muster in the midst of the Depression. From this came the name of his theatre, which later became the official state theatre of Virginia. Unfortunately, hams and potatoes were the most original element of the Barter Theatre, and as a whole it has not developed beyond a pleasant and competent theatre (although it is hard to imagine how it could develop far in a remote and small town like Abingdon).

By far the most venerable early theatre outside New York was the Cleveland Play House, begun in 1916 by "serious amateurs" and still going strong to this day. In fact, the Play House started as a Little Theatre and was one of the very few to change to professional status, which it did in 1921 with the hiring of Frederic McConnell as director. The goal of the Play House during the 1920s was to create a professional theatre to complement a major urban community, making the Cleveland Play House the first American regional theatre of any size, scope, and continuity.

For its day, the Play House was a large institution. It operated first two and then three theatres in downtown Cleveland plus a restaurant-club which has bestowed on the organization more than $80,000 in subsidy in some years. The company numbered nearly forty when Houghton visited Cleveland in 1940; by the start of the 1960s it had grown to seventy-five, and by 1971 to over a hundred. Of this number, many have been members of the group for long periods, and this tenure of personnel has been vital in the Play House's maxim that only by banding together permanently could a professional theatre outside New York develop itself into a distinctive institution. Total fealty was the rule. It appears that the Play House has offered enough to keep many of its most talented artists working together and not yearning for wider vistas. Of course the theatre has not kept all its people (Paul Newman and Joel Grey are two who started in the Play House's youth theatre and left to conquer a wider world), but in general there has been such stability of employment that actors and actresses who appeared as young lovers in productions of the 1940s are now playing those lovers' parents in the same plays on the same stage. In this kind of longevity, the Play House resembles the Habimah Theatre of Israel or the Moscow Art Theatre (which the Play House had very consciously taken as its model). It is clear, however, that the Cleveland Play House was not destined to equal the Russian company; while sedulously copying the Moscow Art's continuity, the Play House has not been able to match its level of production, and so the Cleveland company achieved an inbred narrowness like the Moscow Art's but not its importance in world theatre.

Nonetheless, the history of the Cleveland Play House has been significant in the annals of American regional theatre, and its fate is ironic. When the Play House started, it was decidedly avant-garde in its choice of plays, and over the years it undertook a number of innovative programs. Its largest theatre, which opened in 1949, boasted one of the first "open" (non-proscenium) stages in the country. During the 1950s, with the help of an early Ford Foundation grant, the Play House toured classics like *Hedda Gabler, Ghosts, Arms and the Man,* and *Candida* through forty states over a five-year period. Yet by the 1950s and 1960s, when other regional theatres were being born, the Cleveland Play House was getting old and stagnant, losing its earlier adventurousness. Through these two decades, the Play House and particularly its director K. Elmo Lowe (who had come with McConnell in 1921) played the role of old fogey, generally disregarded or scorned by

13

younger converts for seemingly shallow and antiquated ideas. Neither Lowe's nor the Play House's imperturbability was shaken by this, and the only real losers were those who were denied the lessons to be learned from the Play House's success in garnering community support, in mounting productions in three theatres simultaneously, and particularly in holding onto an acting company for decades. Actress Nan Martin, who visited Cleveland twenty years after Houghton, shared the impatience but accorded Lowe the respect due one who had mastered the institutional aspects of regional theatre:

K. Elmo Lowe is the Barry Goldwater of the American theatre. If I wanted to have a very, very bad nightmare, I would dream up a party in which the members of The Living Theatre of New York [a radical company] had to spend a week together with K. Elmo Lowe and associates of the Cleveland Play House. . . . What can you say against a man who has for 30 years run not one theatre, but three theatres, full tilt, with repertoire ranging from *Oedipus Rex* to *Getting Gertie's Garter*; has employed I don't know how many hundreds of people consistently; has given their first look at the theatre to I don't know how many talents—hundreds of them; who started out originally to have a Moscow Art Theatre; who knows more about the practical side of the theatre than I suspect anybody I'm going to meet on my travels; who knows the knack of getting audiences and holding them?[5]

Lowe himself was an institution. He had left a promising career as an actor (and potential matinee idol) to come with McConnell to Cleveland in 1921, and he was prominent in the direction of the Play House for forty-eight years (also serving as the director of a five-state Federal Theatre installation in the 1930s). He retired in 1969 (and died two years later); this opened up the possibility for the Cleveland Play House to enter the modern age of regional theatre. His successor, William Greene, was the first leader chosen from outside the Play House's inner family, but he died several months after assuming the post. Rex Partington, another outsider who had joined the company with Greene, took the reins in 1970–71. Midway through that season, Partington resigned, claiming that he was "not getting the full support of the board of trustees."[6] I suspect that the community leadership of the Cleveland Play House found it difficult to support the ambitions of the new breed of regional theatre leaders. They turned back to their own family, engaging actor-director Richard Oberlin as the new director. Oberlin had been in the company for sixteen years before his accession; he knew not only the insides of the institution but also its

14

limitations. Since Oberlin's assumption of leadership from within, the Play House has ironically taken new forward steps. The English director Peter Coe came to Cleveland to stage an adaptation of the film *Woman in the Dunes* in the 1971–72 season—one of a number of guest directors engaged to bring ideas from the outside world to the Cleveland stages. Premieres of new plays have taken a more prominent place in the theatre's repertoire, among them the first American production in 1972 of Christopher Fry's new play *A Yard of Sun,* directed by José Ferrer. And, perhaps most tellingly, the budget of the Play House has doubled since 1963—making it a deficit operation like all modern regional theatres.[7] The Cleveland Play House has put a foot forward into the new age, and it may take larger steps in the future. It will do so as a follower, of course, outstripped by others who came later but ran faster. Still, I believe that the Play House can run with its head held high. It was the first soundly created permanent American regional theatre, and in our fleeting world that is a major achievement.

This, then, was the scene at the end of World War II: one full wintertime professional theatre in Cleveland; small professional theatres in Pennsylvania and Virginia, with other resident summer theatres mainly in the East; a decaying touring situation and almost no activity among stock companies; the late and lamented Federal and Group Theatres; a Little Theatre movement of unfulfilled promise and a community theatre movement of no promise and no distinction; and, as the only official and federally recognized national theatre fulcrum, an ANTA that never really played the role originally conceived for it.

After World War II, there was no logical reason to believe that any "advance" was possible, but the new generation coming into its maturity had no time for logic or old rules. They had more education than any generation before them; thanks to the ugly war they had just won, they had seen more of the world; they were young and vital, and the future seemed to be theirs. They were a generation, like all generations, which wanted above all to exist and prosper as and for themselves. To work in the theatre—any theatre—was far more important to them than where their theatre might be located. A theatre could come not only where they happened to be at the time but, more importantly, *from within themselves.* In an earlier age, they would have formed Little Theatres, orienting their work to the avant-garde and writing manifestos as noble and abstract as any of that former era. In the more sophisticated postwar world and in a less isolated country, their ambitions were not so Little, though their means clearly were. Their only means were themselves. They had studied Broadway, and I assume they loved it from afar. But it appeared no place for them to make their marks as quickly as they wished. They were young and anonymous; had they sought work at the time as directors in New York, they would almost surely not have found any. If they wanted to work as directors of plays, they would have to create their own situations where they could try their wings, where their lack of tough sophistication would not be noticed and used against them. Why go to Broadway when at home there was a more familiar and less forbidding world, untapped and apparently ripe?

Creating their own theatres may have been a second choice, but it soon became a crusade. Like the Little Theatres before them, the first regional theatres became a way to say "no" to what their creators saw as the commercial values of Broadway—quick success, star power, the businessman's literature, and money as a god. The first regional theatres after World War II became a new world dedicated to the establishment of new theatrical values—permanence, the ensemble company of actors, classics on the stage, and art as a goal. This was to be the new alternative; and Broadway, the theatrical capital of the country, was to be stripped of its ideological power. There may have been only a few anonymous young people at the start, but they were boldly saying to their capital, like Coriolanus, "I banish you! . . . There is a world elsewhere."

Having banished Broadway, they were very much alone on the cultural outskirts, and they did not even know each other. But each of them had heard of one other person, a visionary and prophet who had accomplished the seemingly impossible and who was now beckoning others to follow in her adventure. To those who found Margo Jones's little book called *Theatre-in-the-Round*, the call to arms was clear: "My dream for the future is a theatre which is a part of everybody's life. . . . This is the goal towards which we must now strive, for which all of us who love the theatre must give our energy, our ideals, our enthusiasm. We can, if we will, create a golden age of the American theatre."[8]

16

3 Margo Jones: Legacy and Legend

"I want our age to be a golden age. . . . I want to be a part of a civilization which is constantly being enriched. I like living in the age of the airplane and television, and I want to live in an age when there is great theatre everywhere."

Margo Jones, Theatre-in-the-Round

The modern American regional theatre began with Margo Jones in Dallas in 1947, and through its history until her death in 1955 Margo served as high priestess of the movement and a measure for all others. Even those of us who never knew her think of her on an affectionate, first-name basis. As critic Brooks Atkinson has noted, "Everyone agreed on one thing about Margo Jones. She was a dynamo. She was a vivid woman. She energized everyone and everything she came in contact with. Margo's vision, skill and vitality stimulated not only her audience but resident theatres in other parts of the country."[1]

Margo achieved her eminent position not only through her life and her work, which were one and the same, but also through her book *Theatre-in-the-Round*, published in 1951. The book is the nearest thing to a bible in the regional theatre world—an extraordinary self-testament which makes awesome reading because it is prophetic and above all pure.

Margo came out of nowhere, out of total anonymity. She grew up near Dallas, and she attended the Texas State College for Women (which was so small that it did not have a drama department—she had to major in psychology instead). She did further work for a brief summer at the Pasadena Playhouse in California, worked in community theatre in the West, and traveled in Europe during the early years of the Depression. Upon her return, she was hired to be the assistant director of the Houston Federal Theatre, an attempt to establish a Federal Theatre installation in that city. However, as revealed by Hallie Flanagan in her book *Arena*, "Texas was a hard nut to crack, and we failed to crack it." The Houston unit was stillborn and Margo's job ended, but she stayed on with the Houston Recreation Department (which had cosponsored the unit), directing plays for children under the city's banner. This program soon grew into an adult group called the Houston Community Players (1936). The Players mushroomed from nine members at the start to over six hundred in the early 1940s, and soon Margo convinced the Recreation Department to pay her a salary so that she could devote full time to the group. After that, apparently almost single-handedly, Margo was able to propel the Players as well as herself. She became involved on a national level with educational and professional theatre leaders—for instance, during World War II, she worked with people like Tennessee Williams.

It was during the years of the Community Players that Margo found and introduced what was to become her special stamp—the arena stage form. The style had been introduced to America in 1914 in a production at Columbia Teachers College in New York, and it was also used by Gilmor Brown at the Pasadena Playhouse in the 1920s; but it was not used steadily until 1932, when Glenn Hughes adapted a ballroom in Seattle into a theatre-in-the-round. In 1939, at a conference in Washington, Margo saw an arena production by a Portland (Oregon) group which had been established by a disciple of Hughes. Margo reacted strongly: "Their performance . . . impressed me so much that I felt I could do something similar in Houston. I remember that on the train on my way back to Houston, I shocked the girl sitting next to me by springing up from my seat all of a sudden and exclaiming, 'Why not!' "[2]

Margo installed an arena theatre on the mezzanine of a Houston hotel. By the early years of the war, the group had mounted more than sixty plays. The vicissitudes of the war years stunted the growth of the Community Players, however, and Margo was no longer satisfied with volunteer actors who were unable to devote their full time and energies. She was interested in producing theatre on a grander scale. She moved to university theatre, where the demands of the war were not so keenly felt. During two years on the faculty of the University of Texas, she staged more plays and also took leaves of absence to direct several Tennessee Williams plays at the Cleveland Play House and the Pasadena Playhouse. Margo was broadening her horizons.

During her university years, the idea of forming a permanent professional theatre took hold in Margo's mind. Searching for an ideal location, she settled upon her native Dallas, where the local drama critic encouraged her. She appealed to the Rockefeller Foundation and in 1944 received a grant to develop her plan and to do research on the few professional theatres of that time. Margo's plan was very carefully formulated and full of never-say-die enthusiasm. Its prologue sets the tone:

This is a plan for the creation of a permanent, professional, repertory, native theatre in Dallas, Texas: a permanent repertory theatre with a staff of the best young artists in America; a theatre that will be a true playwright's theatre; a theatre that will give the young playwrights of America (or any country, for that matter) a chance to be seen; a theatre that will provide the classics and the best new scripts with a chance for good production; a theatre that will enable Dallasites to say twenty years from now, "My children have lived in a town where they could see the best plays of the world presented in a beautiful and fine way"; where they can say, "We have had a part in creating theatre and working in it"; a theatre to go beyond the dreams of the past—and they have been wonderful; a theatre to mean even more to America than the Moscow Art meant to Russia, the Abbey to Ireland, or the Old Vic to England; a theatre that will carry on, but adapt to our country and time, the ideals of the Stanislavskis, the Copeaus, the Craigs; a theatre of our time.[3]

Margo worked long and hard on the realization of her dream during her Rockefeller grant and after it. However, I find it interesting that she was deterred several times during the formative years by calls to work on a national level—for instance, to co-direct Tennessee Williams's *The Glass Menagerie* in 1944 and later to stage Maxwell Anderson's *Joan of Lorraine*, starring Ingrid Bergman, on Broadway.

Finally, on June 3, 1947, she opened her theatre in Dallas. She called it Theatre '47, and each year the theatre used the year in its name (Theatre '48, Theatre '49, and so on). The full history of this theatre is contained in *Theatre-in-the-Round*: how to establish a company, what to look for in actors and directors, how to choose a repertoire, even how to build a stage and create scenery for that space. Yet *Theatre-in-*

19

the-Round is more than a handbook; it is also an apocalypse. The faith expressed in the book stays with the reader and must have strongly impressed the early admirers and disciples of Margo Jones. She was a romantic, and her book is dreamlike in its enthusiasm. Her primary rules are as ingenuous as they are noble: "One fundamental piece of advice to any theatre person who undertakes the establishment of such a theatre: the word DISCOURAGEMENT must be eliminated from his vocabulary before he goes to work. . . . If no substitute will be good enough, if no compromise is effected, if standards are not lowered, the objective will be accomplished. . . . I have learned that if you have a million-dollar idea, you can raise a million dollars." Throughout the book, Margo is involved in a dream that overwhelmed her compatriots, inspired her supporters, and consumed her.

Yet Margo recognized that dreaming, by itself, is a cheap pastime. One area in which she combined dreaming with action was her emphasis on new plays by unknown playwrights. No automatic detractor of Broadway, Margo realized that the greatest strength of the commercial theatre of her day was the ease with which it could introduce important new playwrights to the nation as a whole. She considered Broadway "an experimental theatre in the sense that it will risk its all on new plays and unknown playwrights. For this alone Broadway deserves the respect and attention of every theatre person in the country."[4] Yet she insisted upon this same experimentation for her own theatre, concentrating her creative energies on the search for and production of new plays. She considered the search for new plays a great adventure, and her attitude toward new plays was one of wonderment. She was instrumental in the development of writers like Tennessee Williams and William Inge. Inge's play *Farther Off from Heaven* was her inaugural production at Theatre '47 (later, when Inge had become a famous Broadway playwright, he revised this play and retitled it *Dark at the Top of the Stairs*). Williams's *Summer and Smoke* was brought to Broadway from its debut in Dallas, and *Inherit the Wind* moved directly from the theatre to Broadway in 1955. Today, the Margo Jones Award is given each year to the person or theatre in America displaying the most initiative in uncovering and producing important new works of dramatic literature in that year. The award is devotedly maintained by Jerome Lawrence and Robert E. Lee, authors of *Inherit the Wind*, whom Margo discovered.

20

Margo's emphasis on new plays created a constant uphill struggle for her. Like the theatres that came after hers, Margo's theatre produced new plays in spite of a basic disinterest in them among the members of her audience. John Rosenfield, in an article in *Theatre Arts* the year Margo died, pointed out how Margo was able to make an end run around Dallas's apathy: "The aspects of trying out a script, of providing a showcase for talent, of influencing commercial theatre trends, never have meant much to Margo's home constituency. Since she always has been solvent, the refusal of Dallas to participate in national career-making is testimony of something. It means that on the whole, Margo's discovered scripts have entertained the public and have kept it wedded to the living theatre."[5]

In short, Margo had an uncanny ability to reconcile her insistence on new plays with her audience's reluctance. I think it is important to realize that her passion was for new plays as a *genre*, not for any particular form of play or for any one theme or philosophy. Therefore she usually chose plays which could be tolerated by a regional consciousness; *Inherit the Wind* is perhaps the most notable example of the popular and accessible kind of play that Margo premiered. (This ability to sense what a general public would accept also made it more likely that the plays Margo premiered would find later success on Broadway.) Margo was willing to juggle her new plays for the public, but she would not be denied. According to director Adrian Hall, who worked with her in the 1950s, "Margo would not be put down. An audience member would say, in the lobby, 'Margo, that was a terrible show, just terrible!'—and Margo would say, 'Oh, baby, you'll enjoy next week lots more. I'm glad you're coming next week, 'cause you're gonna love that!' "[6] Margo always had the last word.

For all her dedication to her theatre in her native Texas, Margo was still a woman of far wider horizons. She saw her Dallas theatre as the beginning of a trend, and she also recognized the urgent importance of establishing a National Theatre in America. Her book begins with the statement that "The dream of all serious theatre in the United States in the middle of our twentieth century is the establishment of a national theatre."[7] Her emphasis upon new plays also reflected this wider horizon, for she saw her role as the discovery and introduction of new work for the nation. Her propulsion of herself into national forums and her direction of plays on Broadway even though it took her away from

Dallas attest to her recognition of the power of a national stance in her art. Indeed, there is frank self-propulsion in her ambition to make the Houston Community Players "the most exciting theatre in America."[8]

Relating decentralization to the concept of a National Theatre, Margo formulated what seems to me to be the most awesome idea in the history of the regional theatre—awesome precisely because it came true: the creation of a network of professional theatres in major American cities. Margo climaxes her book with a "grand conception"—a "plan to create twenty resident professional theatres modeled after Theatre '50."[9]

Margo insisted that each of the theatres would belong to its specific community and would grow out of its society, but she also made it clear that there would be a central office and policy-maker for the entire network. She left no doubt that this policy-maker would be either herself or someone chosen by her and that the entire project would be a duplication of her own in Dallas: "While the locations of the twenty theatres are being determined, I will also talk to and correspond with the people who can become the managing directors of these theatres. . . . I will find those who are in a position to do it more than anything else. . . . It will be necessary for me to go into these twenty cities and create in each one of them a nucleus for a board of directors. . . . With proper instructions—which I will draw up, using the experience in Dallas as a basis. . . ."[10] Margo's plan for a network of theatres like hers was more than a wish to share her experience. I believe that it was also, at least subliminally, a need to duplicate her dream and so to corroborate it. This is a natural human need, for all creative people seek constant proof that they are moving in the right direction. By urging others to imitate her work, Margo formulated her legacy; and that legacy is obvious and concrete. Through her work, ground rules were set down for the establishment of professional regional theatres throughout the country. Margo's book was undoubtedly read by all in the new generation of regional theatre leaders, and several enjoyed the added benefit of going to Dallas to learn directly from her or having her come to them to help. Through what she did and how she recorded it, Margo became a literal basis of the regional theatre.

Yet she was also a philosophical basis, and this constitutes the legend of Margo Jones which grew out of the purity of her dream, her almost mystical faith, and the sometimes mythical stories about her. Part of her legend is the story of how she died. It is known that she had a habit of reading new plays while sitting on the floor in her home. The rug had recently been cleaned with a toxic fluid; apparently Margo fell asleep while reading, inhaled the poisonous fumes, and died. While true, this story is also the stuff of which legends are made: this woman sat on the floor and read and read and read (fact) and so was consumed by her dedication to new plays (legend).

The legend also feeds on our wondering what would have happened to Margo and to her theatre had she not died prematurely. She says in her book that a nonprofit theatre can make ends meet and may even have surpluses from its seasons. How would she have adjusted to today's world, in which the inevitability of deficits is assumed? Or did Margo have some secret that would have saved her theatre from deficits? Would she have adjusted to the consuming institutionalism of the modern regional theatre? Would it have destroyed her purity, or would her purity have humanized it? The legend thrives on such questions.

Most of all, the legend of Margo Jones rests on the fact that when she died, her theatre also perished; it could not survive the loss of her leadership. I believe that at least subconsciously Margo structured her theatre so that it could not survive the one who had willed it into being. For Margo's disciples, the possibility that the individual leader has absolute power and that the theatre is an extension of his or her ego is the most compelling and attractive part of her legend and a theme constantly repeated in the history of the regional theatre.

Margo was fortunate to die at a time when her story could be told without any parentheses at the end. Had she lived longer, she might have grown tired and sour; had she moved permanently beyond the contained and controllable world of Dallas into the nation at large, her purity might have been crushed. Or are these assumptions we must make in order to absorb Margo into our cynical age? Today, Margo's faith may seem naive, and her purity may be embarrassing; but at the beginning of the revolution, it was inspiring and essential.

4 Acorns: Theatres before 1960

"*Let us, from the start, be quite clear that this was a revolt. . . . They were out to create something their own, something of substance.*"

Alley Theatre, Thresholds

"*Irving and I each plunked down about eighteen dollars a month and rented a loft behind a judo academy and went about our ingenuous business.*"

Herbert Blau, The Impossible Theater

"*We forged a better way, we scratched it out, hacked it, ripped it, tore it, yanked it, clawed it out of the resisting, unyielding, nose-thumbing environment. . . . We taught ourselves how to survive.*"

Zelda Fichandler, Theatre 3

The handful of leaders who immediately followed the example of Margo Jones created the theatres which were to form the backbone of the regional theatre revolution. For such people, in the words of critic Martin Gottfried, "the theatre was hardly more than a dream held together by half-a-shoestring."[1] In each case, the theatres created by this select group started out being small, highly personal, and essentially private. Despite the group effort involved, there were few ties to the community at large and none to the nation as a whole. The theatres did not turn into public phenomena or become formal institutions until later crises, usually of a financial cast, forced their leaders to seek broader constituencies and support. The early theatres were indigenous, rising from the energies within particular communities rather than from outside forces, and they were often conceived and led by homegrown talents. Lacking the resources which could assure permanence and constantly being forced to combat public apathy and misunderstanding, the early theatres were tentative, insecure, poor, and always on the brink of extinction. In later years, the theatres created before 1960 came to be called "acorns," signifying the fact that they had been planted in shallow soil with no assurances that they would grow into mighty oak trees.

Except for the professional status of some of their actors, the first acorn theatres were very much akin to the Little Theatres. Yet the new leaders were experienced enough to understand why that movement had disintegrated and so could guard against its pitfalls from the start. Perhaps the most significant difference between the Little Theatres and the early acorns was in the structure and dynamics of the group: in the Little Theatres, control was in the group as a whole, and the decision-making process was a democratic one, whereas in the acorns there was always one person who either began the group or quickly took control. Decisions were more a matter of decree, even when they appeared to be arrived at by the group. That one person's rule was absolute, if not despotic. The first regional theatres were expressions of the very real ambitions of their leaders.

Yet I believe that it would be wrong to attach to those ambitions any significance beyond the strictly personal one. In the beginning, there was really only one reason for the new talents to create their own thea-tres—to provide forums for their own work and places to test the talent they hoped they had. There were no theories of institutionalism or decentralization, let alone dreams of a National Theatre; the early leaders had no time for such abstractions, and they would not have felt confident in expounding them anyway. As in other human endeavors, reasons were later appended for which there was no room (and no need) in the first days of struggle. For example, Arena Stage's Zelda Fichand-ler, speaking for the regional theatre as a whole and looking back twenty years, appends these reasons: "Some of us looked about and saw that something was amiss. What was essentially a collective and cumu-lative art form was represented in the United States by the hit-or-miss, make-a-pudding, smash-a-pudding system of Broadway production. What required by its nature continuity and groupness, not to mention a certain quietude of spirit and the fifth freedom—the freedom to fail— was taking place in an atmosphere of hysteria, crisis, fragmentation, one-shotness, and mammonmindedness within the 10 blocks of Broadway."[2]

It is important to note that in seeking their new world, the early leaders were banishing an old world they did not know. Unlike Margo before them, they were people whom Broadway had not chosen any-way. There was no one saying "no" to Broadway who had had significant experience with it—and therefore there was no one leaving the central situation disgusted with it and revolted by it. This lack of a taste of what they were rejecting would come to haunt the earliest leaders, but that is a later story.

The first of the early energetic group was Nina Vance, who had worked with Margo Jones in the days of the Community Players in Houston. In 1947, the same year Margo began her theatre in Dallas, Nina began the Alley Theatre in Houston. The story of the genesis of the Alley is interesting because it is prototypical of the acorn genre:

In 1944 Vivien Altfeld was asked to teach some children's dancing classes at the Jewish Community Center. Mrs. Altfeld already ran a highly successful studio at 3617 Main. She agreed to give the classes. Did she happen to know someone who might teach some adult classes in drama? She knew Nina Vance. She would see if Mrs. Vance was interested.

Mrs. Vance said she was interested in *directing* plays; not in teaching. If she was allowed to direct, she would be happy to help the Center. They agreed. Fine. . . .

Groups of interested people, which usually included Nina and Milton Vance, got together and talked for hours about the possibility of doing plays on their own. The upshot was usually: "Why not? What have we got to lose?". . . .

Bob Altfeld had a dream about founding a theatre. He woke his wife Vivien and told *her* about it. "Go back to sleep. You're crazy," she told him. But he took his dream to Nina. She was a little skeptical, but eventually said: "Let's do it." Vivien volunteered her dance studio on Main for the first meeting.

Mrs. Vance had $2.14 in her pocketbook. In those halcyon days penny post-cards cost a penny. The lady bought 214 postcards. She and several others addressed them and sent them out.

The postcards were postmarked October 3, 1947, at 11:00 A.M. They read, "It's a beginning. Do you want a new theatre for Houston? Meeting 3617 Main. Bring a friend. Tuesday, October 7, 8:00 P.M.—Nina Vance."[3]

From that gathering, attended by more than a hundred interested Houstonians, the Alley Theatre was born. Thirty-seven people gave twenty dollars each to begin production of a season of plays. A mere six weeks after the first meeting, the inaugural production, Harry Brown's *A Sound of Hunting*, opened and was performed for ten nights. Through 1948, the Alley—then a completely amateur group—presented five more plays: Jeffrey Dell's *Payment Deferred*; Lillian Hellman's *Another Part of the Forest*; Somerset Maugham's *Caroline*; Clifford Odets's *Clash by Night*; and Norman Krasna's *John Loves Mary*. It was natural that the Krasna play was the greatest success of the group because unlike the other offerings, it was the kind of play on which community theatres thrive. In its first years, the Alley Theatre did more than its share of such plays in an apparent attempt to please an audience slow to accept more esoteric offerings. Yet while community theatre plays like *John Loves Mary* (and *The Tender Trap, Anniversary Waltz,* and others) gave the Alley a wider acceptance, the theatre workers themselves did not care to think of theirs as an amateur theatre. Nina Vance has said, "I suppose we were a logical extension of the 'Little Theatre' movement; we were a do-it-yourself enterprise that was a reaction to the 'social' community theatres of the time."[4]

By the time (in 1949) that their first home was condemned by the fire marshal and the Alley found larger quarters in an abandoned fan factory, this question of amateur versus professional was becoming more serious. In the early 1950s, Nina felt beset by the impossibility of getting volunteers to work full-time and persuaded the new board of directors to permit the payment of some semiprofessional actors. This decision—and no doubt Nina's power to effect it—rankled the feelings of the many community talents who had worked for five years to make the Alley a success:

> The storm had been growing since the decision to pay actors. Many of the Alley's oldest members were bitterly opposed and said so. . . . A meeting was called. Anyone who'd paid his dime could vote. It was Nina or board control. Amateur theatre or full professional status.
> Nina was given full artistic control. This she had always had; what was at stake was the Alley's status. People who'd been there from the start left, hurt and embittered. Board members resigned. One actress thinks it was natural that some people resented the decision. "It left a gap in their lives," she says. "I think rather than self-aggrandizement Nina simply thought of the Alley as a theatre that needed to keep moving ahead. I think there were thresholds in her life when she realized that one goal had been achieved and another was waiting."
> Today, many years later, a couple who had much to do with beginning the Alley look back on the controversy with wisdom, but a certain conviction that a lot of people had had something that was *theirs* taken away from them. Still, it is important to remember that from the beginning Nina had never been satisfied, had pushed them on toward something better, burning with a deep need for establishment, for security, for an effort that didn't depend on theatre as an avocation. From the beginning it had been her *life.* . . .[5]

This story, too, is prototypical because it reflects the essential need for one person to reign supreme in the small and precarious acorn theatres. Nina, after all, had worked with Margo and had seen how the master operated. She must have known that without this ultimate sway within the group she could not hope to accomplish her personal goals. And so, "One wonders what held the group together. Part of it was Nina, of course. There was no doubt in anyone's mind that she was absolute."[6]

Nina's personality seems to me to be the most specifically regional of those who followed the lead of Margo Jones. Raised in the tiny town of Yoakum, Texas, she comes from a background boasting a pioneer spirit typical of the rigorous Depression life in the rural Southwest. She is very much of Texas—a southern country belle with a will of iron. Among many who have paid tribute to her indefatigable energies, former Alley design director Paul Owen found words most apt: "What are little girls made of? Nina Vance *is* made of sugar and spice and everything. . . . PLUS! It's that 'plus' that has separated her from the other little girls and has provided her with the stamina she sorely needed to arrive at this rather remarkable plateau."[7]

Nina herself has described another essential and more specific ingredient of her personality—her faith in the rightness of the regional, even anti-urban approach: "People always ask, why did you stay in Houston . . . why not New York? Now, there *is* a certain fear level there. I suppose I still think of it in a country way. It's those thousands of nameless faces and the anonymity of the buildings. When Paul Owen and I were attending all those building conferences in New York, the city wore us out; getting back here was regaining our sense of perspective. You lose it in New York; it jangles you. Here in Houston, there was a feeling of roots. It has never seemed as urbanized to me."[8] This hearty rural frontier spirit combined with Nina's large ambition in the creation of the Alley Theatre.

In Nina's assumption of the helm, several other talented people got lost. The key person who fades away from the history of the Alley is Bob Altfeld, who had the original idea for the theatre and, failing to excite his wife about it, "took his dream to Nina." While Altfeld (the first president of the group) worked in the theatre in its early years and found the fan factory that was its second home, he disappears thereafter from the theatre's recorded history. It is possible that Bob and Vivien Altfeld are the couple who "had much to do with beginning the Alley" and who look back on it with "a certain conviction that a lot of people had had something that was *theirs* taken away from them." One might get the impression that Nina Vance took Bob Altfeld's dream away from him. Yet this was not necessarily wrong or cruel; Nina no doubt had more ability not only as a director but also as a *leader*. She had the necessary drive, vision, and what became known as the "famous Alley chutzpah." Theatres do not come into being or survive through everyone being equal; someone must take control to give order and character to each situation. Nina took control of the Alley because she was most fit for it.

One of the few recorded instances of less than absolute power for her was the naming of the theatre in the beginning: "They called it the Alley Theatre. Nina voted against it. To her it was cute, Bohemian, precious . . . awful. But to the majority it was right. There was a poll and Alley Theatre led them all."[9] That may have been both the first and the last poll. People within the Alley may have thought they were voting, but never again would majority rule stand in the way of Nina's authority. Over the twenty-five years since its start, the Alley has become more and more a manifestation of her. Knowing this, I find it amusing and revealing to note the back cover of *Thresholds*, the theatre's 1968 souvenir book, which features a quotation from Nina and the title of the book itself. The quotation, from the opening night in the fan factory theatre, is Nina addressing the audience: "It is with humility and pride that I accept this applause . . . not for myself, but in the name of those people who gave their days and nights to make it possible. Ladies and gentlemen, this is your theatre." Below this quotation is the title of the book: *Thresholds: The Story of Nina Vance's Alley Theatre.*

In 1954, faced with mounting financial crises, Nina determined that only a star could save the Alley in Houston. When Albert Dekker agreed to guest-star in *Death of a Salesman*, the theatre was forced to "go Equity" and so became a fully professional company. In the ensuing years, other stars like Signe Hasso, Chester Morris, and Virginia "Ma Perkins" Payne worked with the company, and budding directors Alan Schneider and William Ball also came to Houston to further their careers on the Alley's "postage-stamp" stage.

In 1960, the Alley was chosen by the Ford Foundation as one of the first regional theatres to receive major financial help. It came in the form of a three-year grant of $156,000 to enable the theatre to attract better known actors away from New York by the promise of $200-a-week salaries over forty or more weeks each season. This constituted a major change from the usual minimum salary of $57.50 per week. Of the total money needed, the foundation's grant provided half (the first $100 per week per actor), and the theatre was required to supply the other half. The Alley was on its way to full permanence, with some national recognition, but still it was limited by the minuteness of its fan factory theatre. To grow significantly, the Alley needed larger quarters. Through most of the 1960s, this need motivated the Alley's primary thrust. In 1962, the theatre received the largest of a series of Ford grants to regional theatres: $2,100,000. The first million dollars was earmarked for construction of a new theatre; the foundation stipulated that it be matched locally dollar for dollar—and it was, by fifteen thousand Texans. The other $1,100,000 was to be set aside to sustain the theatre over the first ten years in its new building.

After an exhaustive search, Nina chose New York architect Ulrich Franzen, and together they set out to design and build a mammoth theatre with the "theme of marriage: of male and female, father and mother . . . a building that *sings* viewed from any point."[10] They succeeded, with a theatre building that looms above the Civic Center in downtown Houston on land donated by the Houston Endowment. It is a very successful statement of both theatrical and architectural values, cited in 1972 by the American Institute of Architects as "inside and out, a brilliant theatrical event." The Ford Foundation gave the Alley an additional $1,400,000 to complete the construction of the building which the foundation considered an important theatrical-architectural statement. However, the additional money was given not only to commend the design but also because the original money (including the funds earmarked for later general support) had to be used to get the theatre built. The new Alley Theatre, which opened in 1968, cost far more than its original estimate to complete.

Residence in the new theatre has brought major changes to the Alley: from half a dozen actors in the late 1950s to more than twenty today and from approximately 225 seats in the fan factory to nearly 1,100 in the new building (which includes a replica of the fan factory stage). Since the opening of the new theatre, the Alley's budget has tripled in size, but this jump has been complemented by a similar rise in the regular subscription audience to more than twenty thousand Houstonians.

Clearly, the Alley Theatre is an acorn no longer; it is now a big operation in a massive setting. The new building expresses the expansiveness of Nina Vance—authoritarian leader, able director of plays, and brilliant master of institutional propulsion—a woman who I think would have been aghast had she been told in 1947 that her Alley Theatre would mushroom into what it is today, but a woman who propelled herself and her theatre so that it did.

Supposedly, Nina once said that she "started her theatre as if she were going to church and wound up running the corner grocery store."[11] That is very apt—but since she first said it, the Alley has grown into an emporium.

The early leaders started their theatres in order to create places for themselves to direct plays. They saw themselves as artists, sitting in darkened rooms talking to actors about character interpretation. It is significant that today most of these people direct plays rarely if at all. Early in the life of their theatres they discovered that no one else wanted to do the "dirty work" of management, without which the theatre would collapse, and so the leaders themselves undertook this responsibility in order to secure their own opportunities. Soon, however, the dirty work began to get not only cleaner but also very interesting and often far more dynamic than the interplay of actors. In addition, as the institutions grew, there was more to protect, particularly in terms of local reputation, and no one could protect it better than the leaders themselves, or so they thought. Therefore the natural direction of the role of the early leaders has been from director to producer.

Nina Vance is an example of this pattern, and she is a good producer. An even more natural example, in my opinion, is Zelda Fichandler, co-founder and producing director of Arena Stage in Washington. With Nina, Zelda shares billing as the distaff power of the regional theatre revolution. Yet they are very different. Where Nina drawls, Zelda darts. Hers is a razor-sharp mind.

The inception of Arena Stage was like the Alley's in its modest scope but high ideals and also in the role that Margo Jones played in it. Asked recently to identify the person who had most influenced her, Zelda named Margo: "She showed the road. And in 1949 she took the time to talk to a frightened young girl to encourage her objectives and stiffen her right arm."[12]

Arena Stage began in 1950, during a time when Washington's only road-show theatre, the National, had closed its doors rather than inte-

31

grate. Its first home was in a dilapidated neighborhood in northwest Washington, in the old Hippodrome movie theatre with 247 seats. Both before and after Arena Stage's tenancy, the Hippodrome featured burlesque and blue movies. Like the Alley Theatre, Arena Stage was a group effort, and Zelda came into it after the idea had circulated around town awhile. She was just graduating from George Washington University, and her mentor there, Edward Mangum, impressed by the quickness of her mind, included her in his planning for a theatre. Zelda was the one, however, who had the time and the energy to work day and night on the idea. She found the old movie house, and she cleverly skirted antiquated Washington regulations which insisted that all theatres have a fire curtain (an impossibility in the arena form) and obtained a special allowance for the new theatre (which prohibited the use of the word "theatre" in its name). Like Nina before her, in the end Zelda took over the idea of others and made it her own—and for the same reasons: nerve, recognition of the necessity for one authority, and the ability to survive. Like Robert Altfeld in Houston, Edward Mangum disappeared from the story of Arena Stage, although Zelda has always been meticulous in saying that she "co-founded" the theatre.

Where Arena Stage differed from the Alley was in the fact that from its start it was professionally staffed and had an Equity company. Early members included Pernell Roberts and George Grizzard; for many years Alan Schneider, then on the faculty of Catholic University in Washington, was the resident director and sometimes the associate director (as he now is). The inaugural production was *She Stoops to Conquer,* followed soon by *The Glass Menagerie, The Hasty Heart,* and *The Importance of Being Earnest.* Arena Stage never produced plays as obviously commercial as the Alley's *Light Up the Sky* or *The Remarkable Mr. Pennypacker.* Zelda sometimes chose American comedy classics like *Room Service* and *Three Men on a Horse* but never American potboilers. The theatre also rediscovered and found success with plays which had been commercial failures on Broadway, most notably *Summer of the Seventeenth Doll, Epitaph for George Dillon, Mademoiselle Colombe,* and *The Disenchanted.*

In the first five years, Zelda forged ahead with Arena Stage despite incredible financial odds and difficulties. Like the Alley and all other early regional theatres, Arena Stage's greatest problems centered on its lack of precedent. The idea of a company of professionals banding together to perform seasons of serious plays was foreign to a public accustomed to think of theatre as a glamorous Broadway entity; so was the idea of operating such a company at a financial loss. In Washington, this problem was aggravated by other factors not as evident in other cities: the fact that many of the upper middle class are in government and so are not permanent residents over many years; the high proportion of black citizens whose cultural backgrounds do not orient them toward classical theatre; and the proximity of New York, which allows lovers of theatre to see Broadway plays with ease. Encumbered with the need to educate its public in the pleasures of serious theatre and the high cost of it, Arena Stage, like the other theatres, aimed simply to survive from one season to the next.

It did survive and it did grow. By the middle of the 1950s, the theatre had gross receipts of $121,000 and had outgrown its first musty home.[13] In the middle of a successful run of Agatha Christie's *The Mousetrap* in its American premiere, the theatre closed and the search was started for a new location. In 1956, it reopened in the abandoned Heurich Brewery in Foggy Bottom with an expanded version of Arthur Miller's *A View from the Bridge,* directed by Alan Schneider. The new theatre afforded not only double the number of seats but also the romantic charm of producing plays in an old beer factory. The brewery was affectionately christened the "Old Vat" and became the setting for Arena Stage's first coming of age.

Like the Alley Theatre and Nina Vance, Arena Stage and Zelda were early favorites of the Ford Foundation; as a result, they soon began to see significant financial help coming their way. Arena Stage was given money by the foundation in 1960 for the formation of an acting company of $200-per-week actors. Then, in 1962, it received another $861,000 from the foundation to erase the debt incurred by the theatre in building a new home, occasioned by its growing audiences and the demolition of the "Old Vat."

Designed by Chicago architect Harry Weese, the new facility was the first professional theatre in America built expressly in the arena style; it grew out of Zelda's decade of experience with the arena form and solidified her commitment to it. What had started from simple necessity had evolved into a philosophy of theatre for Zelda. In 1950, she had chosen the arena form because it demanded less costly scenery and was the only form that could be put into the movie theatre and still provide as many as 247 seats. Later, upon moving into her custom-built new theatre, Zelda expounded on the dynamics of the arena form, and particularly on the strong masculinity of her rectangular stage as opposed to the soft femininity of the circular arena. Again, philosophy followed necessity and legitimatized it. The new Arena Stage opened in 1961 with the first American professional production of Brecht's *The Caucasian Chalk Circle*, directed by Alan Schneider. It was an abstract and efficient building without embellishment—an expression of the mind behind Arena Stage, Zelda's mind.

Working at Arena Stage was my first experience in the regional theatre. Upon graduation from Harvard and while studying at the Yale School of Drama, I had become fascinated by the possibilities in the field of nonprofit theatre management—first at a small summer theatre in New Hampshire, then at Joseph Papp's New York Shakespeare Festival during a summer stint. I was sent to Arena Stage in the fall of 1962 on a grant from the Ford Foundation to improve my management skills as an "administrative intern." There could have been no better introduction to the field, for Arena Stage was the best managed of the acorn theatres. Thomas Fichandler, Zelda's husband, had left his job in the Washington office of the Twentieth Century Fund and had joined the theatre as its executive director during construction of the new building. By the time I arrived, the Fichandlers had mastered running their theatre to the point where they could do the job without a budget. They simply never spent more than the box office and grants brought into their coffers. Each year there was either a break-even situation or a surplus. In the early 1960s, Arena Stage was the only regional theatre in America with extra money in the bank (with the possible exception of the Cleveland Play House).

Since that time, however, the picture has changed. During recent years, Arena Stage has always incurred an "income gap"—commitments to creditors over and above funds brought in as earned income. It is characteristic, I think, that after moving into its new building, Arena Stage did not have income gaps until they became acceptable. Income gaps in the performing arts became acceptable with the publication of the Twentieth Century Fund's *The Performing Arts: The Economic Dilemma*, which proved their inevitability and opened up the possibility of deficit funding for theatres. The other justification for income gaps came from the establishment, at the same time, of the National

Endowment for the Arts, the federal government's first step in accepting support of the arts as a proper function. Arena Stage, with its extraordinary administrative savvy, saw that income gaps could be funded; from then on Zelda instituted additional programs which could be judged suitable for foundation assistance and which assured that Arena Stage would need help.

Arena Stage's new emphasis upon its income gaps was ironic, given the fact that unlike its sister theatre in Houston it began as a profit-making entity with shares totaling $15,000 sold (at 7 percent interest) to three hundred Washingtonians. Still, while there were occasional minor surpluses in the early years, they never benefited the stockholders because they were always plowed back into improving the organization. When the time came to build the new theatre, there was an acute need for funds, and the only way to obtain gifts was to be nonprofit. Arena Stage was therefore reconstituted into a nonprofit parent organization, the Washington Drama Society. The investors became members, and a board of directors was formed to address the need for money. When income gaps became acceptable, Arena Stage was therefore ready with a structure that allowed it to use philanthropic support to erase them.

While the structure was there, however, the lay leadership to manage the funding was not. The Arena Stage board, in the first fifteen years of the theatre's life, was not representative of the power structure of the city. This was Zelda at the helm of an acorn theatre, and this was Washington. Zelda chose her own board, and naturally, like any realistic administrator, she chose people who would complement her personality and not overturn her decisions. In this she was typical of the leaders of acorn theatres, who when they began were neither friendly with powerful people nor secure enough to create groups that could conceivably challenge their authority. Even today, while the Arena Stage board may technically employ Zelda and fix her salary, she controls the board. Arena Stage is a ladylike autocracy.

Since Zelda's board has not been particularly adept at raising money while Zelda has excelled at it, the board has naturally looked to her to do it. In the last half-dozen years, a regular stream of funding proposals has emanated from Zelda, who is the best writer of grant proposals in the regional theatre and an acknowledged genius of theatrical subsidy on the East Coast. These proposals have won support that has significantly increased the programming, influence, and budget of Arena Stage. (From a 1957 break-even level of $125,000, the budget has grown more than tenfold, and in 1971–72 it included an income gap of nearly $400,000.) For example, for the 1967–68 season, Zelda received a $250,000 Ford grant to institute a high-minded if not entirely successful experiment: an interracial company doing classic plays to point up the black-white tensions either inherent in them or read into them. More successfully and ultimately more meaningfully, smaller amounts of money have gone into training backstage talent and into the Living Stage, a more quietly integrated improvisational group that performs in schools, churches, stores, community centers, and anywhere else where young people gather and can participate. In general, the high level of support Zelda has captured has enabled her Arena Stage to become *the* major nonprofit theatre institution outside New York in the East and the master of the arena form in the nation. All this while Zelda continues to insist on viewing her work not as an ultimate statement but as a process. When asked recently if there is anything else (beyond theatre) that she would like to master, she replied: "I don't know whether there are other things I can still master, because I haven't mastered theatre. It's like what Vershinin says in *The Three Sisters*: 'If only you had another life. If only this one could be a rough draft.' It takes a long time. I don't presume to have mastered anything as malleable and as changing as a new form for an art."[14]

If it is true that Arena Stage's comings of age have been signaled by its moves into new quarters, then perhaps the theatre is due another—for since 1970, it has enjoyed still another new facility. Seeking a more traditional proscenium stage to complement her now familiar arena, Zelda commissioned architect Harry Weese to design a major addition to the 1961 building. Approximately $1,500,000 was raised—two-thirds of it from Ford and other foundations—for a 500-seat, fan-shaped theatre. Now, at times, Arena Stage offers productions in both of its theatres simultaneously. The new theatre bears the name Kreeger, after David Lloyd Kreeger, a Washington insurance magnate who gave $250,000 toward construction. His gift represents a major change in the funding of Arena Stage—the first large gift from a person. The money that Zelda has received to sustain her theatre has come most frequently from foundations and government and other agencies rather than from individuals, who need personal wooing instead of brilliant grant proposals.

The key to the future of Arena Stage may depend on whether there can be more wooing. For instance, the Ford Foundation, long the theatre's primary benefactor, has stipulated that the theatre must obtain more of its support from its local community; this is a difficult challenge in Washington, where there is little private wealth and very little industry to chip in. During the 1971–72 season, the theatre embarked on its first campaign to raise operating support, with a goal of $100,000. That goal was met, but just barely. Reflecting on the difficulty of raising money locally, executive director Thomas Fichandler has said, "Somehow people think that on the one hand we're very rich, and on the other hand that theatres should support themselves anyway. They haven't yet been educated in general to realize that theatres, just like symphonies and ballet, are a performing art; that they cannot save costs through labor-saving devices; and that they are not able to support themselves if they are theatres of quality."[15] Part of the difficulty in funding Arena Stage's major programs and high ambitions may lie in an internal discrepancy, for while Mr. Fichandler is trying to convince the community to give money, Mrs. Fichandler is waxing eloquent on the other side: "I am not very strong on community giving, except perhaps when it represents only a small percentage of the total. I think we could well do without the hand that rocks the cradle, for the hand that rocks the cradle will also want to raise it in a vote and mix into the pie with it. For while a theatre is a public art and belongs to its public, it is an art before it is public and so it belongs first to itself and its first service must be self-service."[16]

Zelda Fichandler's commitment to Arena Stage has been total, and she has personally carried it through the pangs of growth to its current major position. To accomplish this, she has had to remain cool; and her theatre, not surprisingly, still has what Washington critic Richard L. Coe once called a "faintly cold, intellectually striving atmosphere."[17] It is an atmosphere that people admire more than they relish or love. Whether Arena Stage can find the money to continue striving may well depend on how that atmosphere can be changed. Having known Zelda over the years, I trust that the atmosphere can be changed. There are small signs of it already; the many Washingtonians now giving money is one. Also, for the new addition to her building, Zelda programmed an "Old Vat" Room, in honor of former days—a place for the company and the audience to gather, and wonder, together. Also, something Zelda said ten years ago, soon after the new Arena Stage opened, has stuck in my mind. She said, "Of course I like my new theatre—it's what I wanted, and it works. But I keep thinking back to the way it used to be, and I miss having to duck." Perhaps for her next addition Zelda can program a private space where she can go to "duck" occasionally.

While Nina Vance and Zelda Fichandler took their lead from Margo Jones, other theatres created before 1960 used the Alley and Arena Stage as models. First was the Mummers Theatre in Oklahoma City, founded by local amateurs in 1949 under the direction of Mack Scism, who recalls the typical inception:

In the summer of 1949 there was a small group just out of the service or just out of school with nothing to do and wanting to go to New York or to the Coast. We wanted to be anyplace except Oklahoma City; we decided we would try to put on some plays and see if we couldn't get through the summer. We had absolutely no money—actually $8.40—so any existing theatre was ruled out, because we couldn't afford it. A former carnival man whom I happened to know had a tent; a man that I was buying gasoline from had a vacant lot; we scrounged the dump yards and found enough scraps to put together a stage, and we produced old-fashioned melodramas.[18]

Then some neighbors of the theatre declared the operation a public nuisance, and the group was forced to report regularly to City Council meetings in order to maintain its license. No regional theatre had less auspicious beginnings than the Mummers. In Mack Scism, an engineering graduate of the University of Oklahoma, the Mummers had a leader with professional ambitions but only amateur credentials. His interest in the theatre came late, when after studying engineering he happened to take a position as a teacher of speech at a high school in Oklahoma City. His personality, like Nina Vance's, was a regional one but much more colloquial in its expression. His spirit remained an amateur one. Again, Margo Jones herself had a hand in the beginnings of the Mummers, coming to Oklahoma City in the first season to help promote the new theatre. Scism remembers her as "one of the great teachers that I have known in my life."[19] Yet even more regularly helpful were Nina and Zelda, upon whose theatres he deliberately and admiringly patterned his own.

After the first successful summer season in 1949, the Mummers moved downtown and introduced arena staging to Oklahoma City with productions of *Louder, Please!* and *Summer and Smoke.* In 1950, the group presented Moss Hart's *Light Up the Sky, Rope's End, Blithe Spirit, Joan of Lorraine, You Touched Me,* and *Two Blind Mice,* mostly the light innocuous fare of community theatres. While they soon found a deserted warehouse for oil field equipment and converted it into a theatre they could call their own, the Mummers remained for the next seventeen years an amateur community theatre—complete with a committee to read and select plays (which is heresy in professional theatres led by authoritarian directors). By 1958, the annual income of the theatre was $40,000, used to pay six staff people: Scism, a scene and lighting designer, an office manager, a teaching assistant (for the children's theatre attached to the theatre), and two part-time helpers. The cost of mounting a non-musical play was usually under $1,000. Five years later, there had been considerable growth: there were 2,400 subscribers rather than the lonesome twelve in the first season; the budget had risen to more than $100,000; and the plays presented were somewhat more adventurous—for example, *The Chalk Garden, Dark of the Moon,* Anouilh's *Antigone,* and *Cat on a Hot Tin Roof.*

In this period, the Mummers were treading a fine line between being a proud community theatre and aspiring to more. In 1963, Scism boasted that the Mummers had given five hundred people in Oklahoma City an opportunity to work in the theatre, many for the first time; as he later pointed out, "I would say that none of us were trained to run the theatre or to be in the theatre at all. . . . Our stage manager was a crack executive secretary who didn't know anything about stage managing, and now you won't find a better stage manager. . . . It is foolish to pay money to job in from New York, if there is someone locally who can handle it just as well."[20] And yet, "We were never geared primarily for participation. Just because you volunteered six hundred hours that didn't mean that you got a part."[21] The amateur status of the Mummers saved the theatre from the severe financial traumas that plagued professional theatres outside New York, and in fact on an amateur basis the theatre never lost money and sometimes made a little. Overall, the Mummers appeared to be in a very healthy situation.

Apparently the Ford Foundation thought so, too. As early as 1959, Ford awarded Scism a $10,000 grant for travel and study in Europe, the United States, and Canada, enabling him to see firsthand nearly a hundred theatres. Then, in 1962, citing Scism's "abilities as a producer,"[22] Ford bestowed on the Mummers not only more than a million dollars but also an awesome challenge: to reshape itself from amateur to fully professional status. Why the Mummers? Apparently *because* it was an amateur theatre. According to the Ford Foundation and Mack Scism himself, Ford plowed money into the Mummers Theatre out of a desire to test the idea of turning an amateur theatre into a professional one, something which had never been done successfully in America (although it has been done a number of times since then). The Mummers must have seemed a logical choice for this experiment, and I suspect that the theatre's location on the vast prairies of America also appealed to Ford's sense of cultural justice; if this gargantuan feat could be accomplished in a spot so remote and isolated as Oklahoma City, then it could happen anywhere in this country. Ford's largesse to the Mummers Theatre was partly an investment in Mack Scism and partly a radical attempt at elementary decentralization.

It is a sad commentary on American values that the Ford money to effect the transformation was money with which to build a huge new theatre. The first grant, $1,250,000 in 1962, was second only to the Alley's in that series. It was also similarly structured, with $500,000 for a decade's support of the company when in the new theatre, and $750,-000 for construction, if matched by local sources. In oil-rich Oklahoma, the match was made within one month. A second grant in 1966 was a combination of new money ($535,000) and the release of the general support funds to help complete the building in the wake of rampant inflation. (The construction of a new Mummers Theatre had been delayed by more than five years of wrangling over a site within the city's urban renewal complex.) Looking back now, it is clear that it would have been more logical to give the Mummers money to professionalize themselves, to improve their impoverished production standards, and then—when the community had supported the theatre's evolution into a professional unit—to award money with which to build a new home. However, that is hindsight; at the time of the first major grant, a more dynamic and visible route was necessary for so grandiose and public an experiment.

From its start, the Ford support of the Mummers Theatre prompted hard feelings and even resentment in regional theatre circles, particularly among leaders of fully professional companies suffering large deficits and getting no major help from Ford. Often the Mummers

Theatre was dismissed by others as a theatre steeped in amateurism, and Mack Scism was viewed as an intellectual lightweight playing with a toy in the desert. There was therefore considerable astonishment when Scism, with his architect John Johansen and stage designer David Hays, produced a huge new theatre building which showed considerable freshness and verve in its conception. Perhaps the Ford Foundation had been right all along.

Yes, if architecture were the only standard. The larger challenge was to effect the transformation from amateur to professional status, and that challenge was one which the Mummers had to meet themselves, from within themselves. They started to professionalize the acting company in 1967, allowing three years of transition before opening the new building. And yet, even as the theatre was under construction, Scism was wondering how the challenge would be met: "Will the community which has become accustomed to the idea of a successful amateur theatre accept the same organization as professional? That is the test that we are undertaking now."[23]

The new Mummers Theatre opened in the fall of 1970 with *A Man for All Seasons*, featuring Edward Mulhare. The building was a striking success as an architectural and theatrical instrument, although it was considered an unsightly horror by some in Oklahoma City (one rich man offered to pay the many thousands of dollars it would cost to plant trees to hide the new theatre from public view). The transformation from amateur status was not a success, however. By going professional, the Mummers had overreached their community. As reported by Arthur Ballet, "The new, professional company which opened the theatre consisted of a staff composed of only a few natives. . . . That meant that a lot of local actors (the Original Mummers, so to speak) and theatre buffs were alienated. They had once *been* theatre in Oklahoma City, and with the shift to professionalism they were relegated to fund-raising, dutiful attendance, and 'general support' functions. Their response seems to have been, 'Thanks a lot, but no thanks.' "[24] The Mummers had changed too late—at a time, as we shall see, when the rules had changed. The other early theatres which enjoyed big infusions of outside support (for instance, the Alley) had already become professional when that support came their way; they could handle it. The Mummers simply had too far to leap, and they collapsed in the attempt. By the spring of 1972, the marvelous new building stood empty in Oklahoma City—with no trees to hide it but an armed guard to protect it from vandalism.

Several weeks after the doors were closed, the Mummers shared American Institute of Architects honors with the Alley as being among the most original and successful new structures in recent years. This was small consolation for Mack Scism, who had given his adult life to the theatre. He and his Mummers were the victims of their own experiment—an experiment in willing into being what should have been allowed to evolve.

Of the four acorn theatres begun during the 1950s, the Milwaukee Repertory Theater is the only one still in operation. It was started in 1954 by local talents as the Fred Miller Theater (named after its primary benefactor), but from the beginning it was a professional theatre, housing stock productions. It was managed by Mary John, who has described its start: "On returning to my home city, I felt the absence of professional theatrical activity in my own life would be unendurable, and that the growing decline in visits of professional touring companies to Milwaukee was an unnecessary impoverishment of the city's cultural life. I found myself talking about this to a number of like-minded people, and we decided to do something."[25] More than three thousand Milwaukee citizens contributed $115,000 to found the theatre. Again, Margo Jones from Dallas played a key advisory role. Mrs. John and her colleagues deliberately chose to limit the number of seats (to 350) in their former movie-house theatre because "Margo Jones advised us that an undersupply of tickets creates a strong demand for them."[26]

In the beginning, the Fred Miller Theater was designed to be a profit-making operation. It made money, and in fact some of that profit served as a subsidy for a School of Performing Arts conducted in conjunction with the theatre. In the early years, the theatre offered an extensive bill of fare, often with well-known actors: Julie Haydon in *Shadow and Substance*; Sylvia Sidney in *Angel Street*; Eva Le Gallienne in *The Corn Is Green*; Ethel Waters in her Broadway success *Member of the Wedding*; and Geraldine Page in *Summer and Smoke*, which had brought her off-Broadway prominence. It appeared to be a comfortable, efficient, and predictable organization.

That was from the outside only, however. Within, the Fred Miller

Theater was a hotbed of strife and friction, with the professional staff at odds with community leaders who took an uncommonly active role in day-to-day affairs. The situation soon became intolerable, and the problem was complicated by a strange clause in the Miller's bylaws which allowed any member of the Milwaukee press to attend and report on the theatre's board meetings. When Mary John and the local leaders clashed, the dirty linen ended up being aired in the local newspapers, and Mrs. John was ousted from her job. The end of the Fred Miller Theater looked imminent. However, there soon arrived on the scene one Edward Mangum—Zelda Fichandler's professor and original partner in Washington—who took up the reins. He stayed only a short time as the managing director, but during that period he first introduced New York director Ray Boyle to Milwaukee as the guest director of *The Rainmaker*. Boyle, who had worked previously at both the Barter Theatre and the Cleveland Play House, replaced Mangum, and by 1959 the theatre was playing to 95 percent of capacity, with an annual budget of $170,000. Star performers were being paid $1,000 per week and the other actors $100. Boyle himself, in being rehired for the 1959–60 season, was given a $50-per-week raise to $250 (a fact reported in a press release from the theatre, apparently to deflect the press's interest in reporting the internal workings at the Miller).[27]

Like those who had preceded him, Boyle ran the Miller as a standard stock theatre. When he left in 1960, the opportunity arose to make something more of the theatre. This was at a time when the cultural mood of the country was changing and when the growth of theatres like the Alley and Arena Stage was gaining publicity in other cities, among them Milwaukee. The board of directors decided to put Milwaukee onto the new bandwagon and turn their theatre into a professional resident operation—nonprofit, with emphasis on more serious plays, and of course presenting a challenge to their own ability to raise money to support it.

Almost immediately, the new organization enjoyed a great boon: the arrival, in residence, of the newly formed Association of Producing Artists (APA), headed by Ellis Rabb. The APA spent the fall of 1961 in Milwaukee, and, judging from the usual excellence of its work, it must have afforded for Milwaukee a high-level introduction to the values of repertory and ensemble performance.

When the APA left Milwaukee, one of its founding members, Jack

McQuiggan, stayed behind as the·new producer of the Milwaukee Repertory Theater, formed out of the pieces of the former Fred Miller Theater. McQuiggan organized an efficient operation with himself as the sole leader (except for one season when Paul Shyre served as the artistic director). By 1966, the Milwaukee Repertory Theater was on a reasonably even keel. Yet in the same year, the theatre's leadership changed again. McQuiggan was hired away by another regional theatre, the Trinity Square Repertory Company in Providence (whose artistic director Adrian Hall had come to Milwaukee to guest-direct a play for McQuiggan). To replace the producer, the Milwaukee board hired one of its own members, former chairman Charles McCallum, who had co-founded the theatre with Mary John and who had also served briefly as McQuiggan's business manager.

Mild and pleasant, McCallum had little theatrical flair of his own, but when he started he had the great good sense to engage as artistic director Tunc Yalman, a Turk trained at the Yale School of Drama. Yalman took over the leadership of the company in the 1966–67 season, and he set out to create a true ensemble of actors, young and dedicated to staying together long enough to develop a specific style. The combination of McCallum and Yalman turned out to be good for the Milwaukee Repertory Theater. Under their joint management, attendance at the theatre increased by more than 500 percent. They secured funding from the Rockefeller Foundation for a series of new plays called Theatre for Tomorrow, which they presented at odd hours for special audiences. Under the sponsorship of the extension division of the University of Wisconsin, the company spent its summers in residence in Spring Green, the site of Frank Lloyd Wright's home and school, Taliesen. The theatre even managed to coax Alfred Lunt and Lynn Fontanne out of their retirement in rural Wisconsin to see the Repertory Theater's production of their Broadway success *Design for Living* (they said they liked it).

In 1969, the Repertory Theater moved into a new arts center in the center of Milwaukee (although as a johnny-come-lately it was relegated to the bowels of the building). That same year, Yalman introduced the concept of rotating repertory (alternating performances of different plays within weekly periods) and found that the plays attracted 95 percent of capacity and nearly 20,000 subscribers.

In 1971, Tunc Yalman was succeeded as the artistic director by

Nagle Jackson, a frequent director for the American Conservatory Theatre in San Francisco and a guest director at the Mummers and other regional theatres. Charles McCallum retained his position. What was interesting in the change was the orderliness of it in a theatre which was once rife with controversy. Yalman had announced a year ahead that he would leave at the end of the 1970–71 season, five years after taking the helm. His reasons were straightforward: he felt it was time for the theatre to have a new artistic viewpoint and time for him to move on to other assignments. He then helped in finding his replacement. As we shall see, such orderly calm is rare in changes of leadership at regional theatres. That it could be so in Milwaukee is a tribute to the levelheaded competence of the Repertory Theater. After some stormy early days, the theatre has settled down. It is one of the quietest of all regional theatres, and its community, respecting and appreciating that, has responded by supporting it heartily. Among acorn theatres, the Milwaukee Repertory Theater today would be a good model.

Two other acorn theatres were started in 1957, and both have since met their deaths. In both cases, the theatres perished when the artistic leader left and was not replaced.

The Charles Playhouse was the first regional theatre in New England. It opened in 1957 in a loft above a fish market at the bottom of Beacon Hill. Its founders were Boston lawyer Frank Sugrue and Michael Murray. Sugrue served as the managing director, and Murray, who was from Washington and knew the work of Arena Stage, was the artistic director. Like the Fred Miller in Milwaukee, the Charles started as a stock company with no pretense of being a resident company on a permanent basis. When I was a college student in Boston in the early days of the Charles, one could go to the bottom of Beacon Hill, climb the stairs to the loft, and see classics modestly but competently staged.

Boston being the old-line city that it is, the Charles Playhouse found its early life particularly rough, competing for support with the venerable Boston Symphony Orchestra and various museums. However, like the other acorn theatres, the Charles had leaders who would not give up, and the theatre eked out its existence. In 1958, Sugrue and Murray decided that their loft theatre was not suitable either artistically or economically for the kind of theatre they wanted to have, and so they moved their operation to a former nightclub (originally a church) on

45

a back street behind the major theatres of downtown Boston. They began to budget their productions to break even at 40 percent of capacity, which meant that the theatre could keep going even if it sold no more than half of the tickets for each play.[28] Even on such a realistic (even pessimistic) budget, the Charles Playhouse continued to find it difficult to make its way in Boston.

Once again, it was the Ford Foundation which provided a major change of direction for an acorn theatre. The foundation provided money for the directors of the Charles Playhouse to visit the major acorns in Washington, Houston, and San Francisco (The Actor's Workshop). This trip opened the directors' eyes to the possibilities they had been missing by avoiding the idea of a permanent resident company. Whereas they had always opted for the ease of casting their productions one at a time, they now decided that the company approach of Arena Stage, the Alley, and The Actor's Workshop was the wave of the future, and the Charles Playhouse turned from a stock approach to a company philosophy. After that, the Charles Playhouse proceeded to build a regular audience of nearly 10,000 subscribers, and Establishment help became more available.

Then, in 1968, there came a blowup at the Charles Playhouse. Blaming "exhaustion of creative resources that results from the constant petty maneuvering for survival,"[29] Michael Murray resigned his post as the artistic director, and Frank Sugrue was left in sole control. He reverted to the former stock system, disbanding the resident company and returning to a policy of casting each production from scratch and entrusting it to a guest director. And yet Sugrue, working with artistic adviser and director Louis Criss, was taking a surprisingly adventurous approach to programming—perhaps in an attempt to compensate for the loss of artistic director Murray. For the 1969–70 season, for instance, the plays included *The Iceman Cometh*, *The Indian Wants the Bronx* (guest-directed by Michael Murray), Feydeau's *A Flea in Her Ear*, Brecht's *In the Jungle of Cities*, Edward Bond's *Narrow Road to the Deep North*, and Anouilh's *Antigone*. Except for the Feydeau, these plays constituted a somewhat heavier series than Murray himself had ever planned. In fact, it was probably too one-sided, with no plays on the bill to attract large enough audiences to support the season economically. There was a severe disaffection of the audience; by 1970, there were only 5,600 subscribers, down almost 50 percent from a high of 11,000 in 1966.[30] Things were very shaky at the Charles.

Nevertheless, the 1970–71 season promised to be even more special in its appeal. For that season, only Tennessee Williams's *The Rose Tattoo* could be considered a box-office attraction, and a mild one at that. The other plays announced were a new piece, *In Three Zones*, by Wilford Leach; Pirandello's *Naked*; the macabre English comedy *Loot*; and Ionesco's *Exit the King*. Only *In Three Zones* got onto the Charles stage, however; the theatre was abruptly closed on November 1, 1970, with a $200,000 debt hanging over it. There was some talk of raising that sum from the Boston community in order to reopen the Charles, but no further announcements were made on that matter. Frank Sugrue used the Charles Playhouse to house an independent commercial production of *Jacques Brel Is Alive and Well and Living in Paris*, later moving it to the Hotel Somerset and producing the musical *Dames at Sea* to go with it. Other producers sometimes used the theatre—and the Charles name—for independent productions, but the institution was gone.

The Front Street Theatre of Memphis was the most colorful acorn theatre of the 1950s, and its color was derived from the personality of its leader, George Touliatos, a fiery Greek. Touliatos started producing in Memphis in 1954 with an amateur group called Theatre 12. Housing for this venture was in the basement of the King Cotton Hotel—in a former swimming pool, with the plays in the deep end and the audience in the shallow. In 1956, Touliatos left to take his MFA degree at the University of Iowa; during his absence no plays were produced by Theatre 12. Then, in the spring of 1957, he announced from Iowa, through the Memphis press, that a new group called the Front Street Theatre was being organized and that four plays would be presented during that summer.

The first season of the Front Street Theatre was also mounted in the King Cotton Hotel, but this time in the ballroom. There were four plays: *The Tender Trap, Mrs. McThing, Private Lives,* and *A Streetcar Named Desire,* the last with young Carrie Nye, a Memphis native, as Blanche DuBois. The budget for all four plays was a mere $7,200, and at the end of the summer there was a $4,000 surplus. However, despite the apparent success of the venture, the management of the

47

King Cotton Hotel decided that their ballroom was too important a space to be committed to a new theatre without stars, so the Front Street Theatre was sent back downstairs to the swimming pool. In a sense, the Front Street Theatre was never again out of deep water.[31]

In 1959, however, the theatre did get out of the swimming pool and into its own home, an old movie house with 375 seats. At that point, too, its first three Equity actors were hired—at $70 a week for rehearsals and $135 a week for performances. While not particularly high salaries for the period, they were twice what the other, non-Equity actors at the Front Street were earning. The plays included *Cat on a Hot Tin Roof, Othello, The Mousetrap, Fallen Angels, Don Juan in Hell*, and three musicals—*Guys and Dolls, Call Me Madam*, and *The Boy Friend*.

This dizzy range of plays, from Shakespearean classics to potboiler musicals, was typical of the Front Street Theatre. The fourth season, for instance, went from the solid classicism of *Henry IV, Part 1* and the then avant-garde *Waiting for Godot* to the obviousness of *The Solid Gold Cadillac* and the pandering of *Babes in Arms*. By the sixth season (1962–63), the programming at the Front Street seemed almost schizophrenic in its attempt to please everybody: *Oklahoma, The Student Prince, Where's Charley?, The Fourposter, Two for the Seesaw, I Am a Camera, Gypsy, Peter Pan, Come Blow Your Horn, The Fantasticks, The Caretaker, Period of Adjustment, Bye Bye Birdie, Gigi*, and *South Pacific*. From the beginning, the theatre had to depend on a steady sampling of Broadway musicals to keep its head above water, and this seeming sellout to commercial values relegated the Front Street Theatre to a low rung on the regional theatre ladder. Actually, the dependence on musicals and commercial comedies was necessary, given the nature of the Memphis community; there, the uphill battle to gain audience acceptance of classical theatre, let alone deficits for it, was even harder than in many cities where audiences seem naturally inclined toward more sophisticated and more cosmopolitan tastes in theatre.

Besides, George Touliatos relished the challenge of trying to make Memphis want the Front Street Theatre; it appealed to his panache. While the Front Street Theatre had the requisite board of directors and an army of lady volunteers raising money and selling tickets, Touliatos was always a lone leader and a much more obviously autocratic one than Zelda Fichandler in Washington or even Nina Vance in Houston.

It is no wonder that his favorite role, among many he played in Front Street productions, was the absolute monarch in *The King and I.* George Touliatos bulldozed the Front Street Theatre through its constant financial crises without major help from national foundations or expansive local givers. Because of his fierce charm, he was able to disregard the facts that were dragging the theatre down and to concentrate instead on juggling crises so that none would trip up the theatre. Still, other people noticed that there was something seriously wrong; as early as the third season, one person close to the situation described the Front Street as "a merry-go-round in quicksand."[32] The several times I visited the Front Street Theatre, it seemed to be an organization walking a high-tension wire.

In the end, however, such voltage could not be sustained. Finally, in 1967, George Touliatos was worn out, frankly sick of the Sisyphean struggle to sustain a theatre which still had not been able to carve out for itself a lasting place in the Memphis community. I would not say that Touliatos gave up; rather, I suspect that he paused, looked at what he had wrought, found it incredible, and bolted. He left Memphis and spent a year teaching at Stephens College in Missouri. The Front Street Theatre, carrying an accumulated deficit of $200,000, proceeded under the direction of general manager Harvey Landa, who did not enjoy the panache of Touliatos. After one faltering season in the movie-house theatre, a vague relationship was worked out with Memphis State University to house the company on its campus, and Professor Keith Kennedy became the artistic director of the company. The university was careful not to become embroiled in the Front Street's financial problems: "Both Front Street and MSU emphasize that future Front Street productions will be budgeted to break even, and that no university funds will be used to reduce the deficit accumulated by the theatre over 11 years of operation."[33] The directors announced a season only slightly more ambitious than former Front Street seasons: *Showboat, The Time of Your Life, Romeo and Juliet, Knacker's ABC, A Moon for the Misbegotten, A Flea in Her Ear,* and *Stop the World—I Want to Get Off.* Still, only 1,600 season tickets were sold, and the season never got beyond *Showboat.* The Front Street Theatre disappeared.

George Touliatos returned to Memphis, delving into myriad projects more attuned to his personality than nonprofit theatre. He is an interesting figure in the history of the regional theatre, because his abandonment of what he created was one of the first backfirings of the acorn approach and because he then applied his energies to other and totally unrelated pursuits. Unlike Mack Scism, who has said that he would like to go back to Oklahoma City and to make a theatre work there, George Touliatos gives no indication that he regrets leaving or that he misses the Front Street Theatre. It is sad to note that Memphis does not seem to miss it, either.

All six early acorn theatres I have described so far survived at least ten years of torturous growth, their leaders balancing their sense of personal mission with the social and political strategies necessary to exist in cities not really ready for their artistic and financial demands. Some still survive, and two—the Alley and Arena Stage—have grown from small acorns into mighty oak trees. Yet of the original six, three theatres have perished, making a 50 percent mortality rate (actually, the rate is much higher if we realize that there must have been many other shorter-lived unsuccessful attempts during the 1950s which were never recorded). Why did so many theatres fail, and what distinguished those that did not? The reasons are many, of course. Some have pointed out that the three theatres which have survived are all the creations of women—but at the risk of being labeled a male chauvinist, I doubt that this is the primary reason for their success. It seems to me more likely that the major reason for survival or death was the nature of the *compromises* made by the theatres: those which survived made creative compromises which strengthened them; those which perished made the wrong compromises. Also, generally, all of the compromises were related to the *institutionalism* of the theatres. For example, Nina Vance and Zelda Fichandler, who both started their theatres in order to direct plays, moved through the years from directing to producing as their main function. They assigned the immediate onstage artistic responsibility to others in order to concentrate on the broader view and on the overall leadership of a growing institution. At first this emphasis grew out of the fact that no one else was willing to manage the organization, but as the organization grew into an institution, management became the more creative responsibility. Also, by orienting their own perspective to management, Nina and Zelda got involved with outside forces such as the Ford Foundation and so received infusions of major financial help; that assistance came at a time when their theatres, having achieved professional status, were strong enough as institutions to absorb and capitalize on it. The change in their own roles from director to producer may have felt personally like a negative compromise, necessary to keep going, but actually it was a creative compromise because it strengthened their theatres as institutions.

The third early acorn theatre which has survived is the Milwaukee Repertory Theater, and the same principle of creative compromise applies to it. Unlike the Alley and Arena Stage, the Milwaukee Repertory Theater has never had at its helm a strong personality who had to choose between onstage work as a director and desk work as the leader of an institution. This lack, even now, may limit the artistic potential of the theatre and may keep it from becoming an oak tree, but the parallel emphasis on things administrative is what gives the Milwaukee Repertory Theater its particular strength. That, too, is a creative compromise.

All three theatres which have perished—the Mummers, the Charles, and the Front Street Theatre—compromised in the wrong way; they compromised on their management. Because of their weakness in this area, the three never really became viable institutions able to survive artistic and financial crises. There was no strong institutional base at the Charles Playhouse and the Front Street Theatre to absorb the departure of artistic directors whose competence or flair had compensated for administrative weaknesses. The case of the Mummers is somewhat different in that it was the Ford Foundation's involvement which masked the theatre's institutional insecurity. Ford was bestowing from outside a new identity which happened to be out of proportion to the original organization, its leadership, and its community. When that new identity and these other pieces did not mesh, there was no institution to be an adhesive force.

The fact that they finally perished does not mean that these three early theatres should never have existed. In all new endeavors, there are those among the first who cannot survive because of circumstances or their own idiosyncrasies (or even inadequacies) or perhaps because they are ahead of their time in their communities. Still, there were many years of work, hundreds of productions, and many new talents found and nurtured by these theatres and others like them which have gone unsung. To have started and tried in the 1950s and to have lasted through all the changes of all the rules in the 1960s is a major accomplishment, and tribute is due those who willed their survival as long as they could.

Right or wrong, creative or misguided, compromise without surrender was a way of life for the early acorn theatres living in poverty and amidst public apathy. In San Francisco, however, there was another acorn theatre which equated compromise with surrender and so rejected it. Because it refused to compromise—and lived and died from that refusal—The Actor's Workshop deserves a special place among acorn theatres.

I think of The Actor's Workshop as "Beethoven by the Bay." I had a Latin teacher once who pointed out what was, for him, the difference between two kinds of artists, Mozart and Beethoven. Mozart, he said, is always fine—exact and well honed, the epitome of competence, and above all dependable. Beethoven, on the other hand, is far from that— sometimes sublime and sometimes ridiculous. His point was that in the arts exactitude and precision, while admirable in themselves, may fall short of sublimity—and that if one tries to be sublime, one runs the risk of ending up ridiculous. Most regional theatres soon advanced to the point where they were like theatrical Mozarts, doing their jobs well and at a predictable level of competence. They were always serviceable, never ludicrous, usually interesting, and rarely splendid. Only The Actor's Workshop was like Beethoven—often ridiculous and occasionally sublime. What is more important is that the Workshop, while the most decentralized of theatres geographically, was the only one which assumed that it would become a central ideological force, and this gave it special distinction.

An official biography of the Workshop outlined its inception: "Begun in 1952 without stars, fanfare, real estate, or capital, The Actor's Workshop is an act of imagination by two professors at San Francisco State College, Jules Irving and Herbert Blau, native New Yorkers who are convinced that the destiny of the American theatre lies as far off-Broadway as possible, in permanent companies dedicated to ensemble playing."[34] This explanation of the genesis was a particularly anti-Broadway one, emphasizing the feelings that stood behind all early regional theatres. Actually, the genesis of the Workshop was far less philosophical. Jules Irving had had some experience in the theatre in New York, including work as a juvenile actor in Broadway productions. Herbert Blau had started out (like Mack Scism) to be an engineer before turning to the literary life. The men became well acquainted in the late 1940s while seeking their advanced degrees at Stanford University, and both were married to young actresses. Both joined the faculty of San Francisco State College, Irving in the drama department and Blau as a professor of English. The forming of The Actor's Workshop was as much as anything a way found by the men to keep their actress wives busy in the otherwise theatrically barren city of San Francisco. The Workshop was meant to be "a healthy coming together of sorts, mainly of relatively experienced actors who were tired of playing in little theatres or with college groups, there being no alternative in San Francisco."[35]

Although its founders came from the educational theatre world and were very cerebral, the Workshop at the start had no particular social, intellectual, aesthetic, or academic commitment: "We asked no existential question; we were recouping no cultural losses, toppling no icons, breaking no classifications, rewriting no history, assuaging no ontological guilt, shattering no systems. . . . We said very little about the world outside. . . . Like our politicians, our group was cautious, politic, and already committed to being uncommitted."[36] In fact, in recording the history of the Workshop in his book *The Impossible Theater*, Herbert Blau makes much of the fact that the Workshop was born at the height of the McCarthy anti-intellectual era and reflected that era's fear of commitment.

The Workshop started in a loft behind a judo academy, where the thud of bodies hitting the floor provided strange accompaniment for performances. It is significant that the name of the group was in the singular—The Actor's Workshop; it was intended to be a place where each individual could pursue his craft. While a small group of intellectuals was invited to showings of the first work, Irving and Blau were more interested in conducting a studio that would provide a congenial atmosphere for experimentation, not only with esoteric drama but also with their own untested and unknown talents. At the beginning, the Workshop lacked even the tentative social purposes of an Alley Theatre or an Arena Stage. It was a strictly private and personal venture, with no special broader philosophy: "If there wasn't ideology behind us there was inordinate self-consciousness, including anxiety now over the absence of ideology."[37]

Regional Theatre: The Revolutionary Stage

Yet those in the Workshop naturally sought more and more to extend themselves and to get attention. When the *San Francisco Chronicle* critic Luther Nichols asked at the end of the first year to see their production of Lorca's *Blood Wedding*, they let him come—and he praised it, causing a swelling of public interest in the group. They were following the path of all early acorn theatres: "I blush to add that as soon as we recognized our illicit appeal, we encouraged it. Our mailing list increased, and more actors appeared."[38] In 1954, they moved to a former Ford Motor Company warehouse, creating a small theatre with a platform stage and 180 seats and opening it with *Lysistrata*. Three other productions—*The Crucible, Camino Real,* and *Death of a Salesman*, with Jules Irving acting in all three—attracted considerably more attention and larger audiences. Still, these did not bring with them increased stability; the situation was very tenuous. Blau describes it as "like Sisyphus rolling his stone. . . . It became a matter of pride—we would not go under!"[39]

In 1955, Irving and Blau moved the Workshop again, this time to a 650-seat theatre on the second floor of the Marines' Memorial, a YMCA-like servicemen's club in downtown San Francisco. The Workshop was becoming better known and, in Blau's words, a "public nuisance" as well. In 1955, the Workshop signed with Equity the first off-Broadway contract ever issued to a group outside New York. While the signing gave the Workshop professional status, it did not provide good incomes for the few Equity actors in the large group. Even as late as 1959, the five Equity actors in the Workshop were receiving only $20 per performance (and nothing for rehearsing), and only two of them were on a yearly contract—one at $55 a week, one at $110. The salaries of all Workshop actors, whether Equity or not, came to a total of only $230 per week. Yet with characteristic vigor, within a year (and with their first large grant from the Ford Foundation), Irving and Blau were taking venturesome strides. In 1960 the Workshop started rotating its repertory (making it the first regional theatre to try an experiment that was radical for its time) and doubled the number of performances it gave each week. The number of productions also increased. In addition to the facilities at the Marines' Theater, Irving and Blau opened a small basement theatre down the street, the Encore, for production of particularly esoteric works. Blau's production of Beckett's *Endgame* opened the Encore. In fact, Blau's work on the Beckett canon became a key element in the Workshop's programming. In 1957, he staged *Waiting for Godot*, which became a Workshop standard (with Jules Irving sometimes playing the role of Lucky). It was this production which the group took to perform one evening at San Quentin penitentiary outside San Francisco—because it was the only play in the company's repertoire which met the prison's rule of no women on the site. The company was concerned that the play's complex intellectualism would not reach the inmates, but the men, knowing the pain of waiting, responded enthusiastically. Out of that occasion came the San Quentin Drama Workshop, in which inmates performed under the direction of Actor's Workshop leaders.

By 1963, when I joined the group, the Workshop's budget had risen to $330,000 per year, and the group was well known and respected among the theatrical elite. Still, while it had moved downtown and had technically "gone public," it had not joined the mainstream of San Francisco life. Its approach to its work was more than non-Establishment—it was *anti*-Establishment. Like Arena Stage, the Workshop had started as a private profit-making venture (with the sale of 1,000 shares at $10 each); and, also like Arena Stage, it had found that its financial straits forced it to change to a nonprofit status in order to raise money. But, even more than at Arena Stage, the internal constituency of the Workshop was composed of powerless people. Irving and Blau attracted others like themselves—poet James Schevill, novelist Mark Harris, and literary troublemakers Kenneth Rexroth and Lawrence Ferlinghetti. The board of directors of The Actor's Workshop was very much in agreement with the anti-Establishment ideas being developed by Irving and Blau but was unable to raise enough money to sustain the organization. And so, while the Workshop did move downtown, did later represent the United States at the Brussels World's Fair and San Francisco at the Seattle World's Fair, did present its production of *Waiting for Godot* in New York, did receive grants from the Ford Foundation, and did win accolades in the national and world press, it never found wide acceptance and solace in its home city. In fact, through its thirteen-year life in San Francisco, the Workshop had a hate affair with the city.

I am convinced that some of the blame for this antagonism rests with San Francisco—a city in love with itself, just interesting enough to be pretentious. The programmed chic of San Francisco could not accommodate The Actor's Workshop, which was always shabbily housed, radically opinionated, and sometimes "holier than thou" in its anti-Establishment pronouncements. Of course, the cleavage between San Francisco and the Workshop was a two-way street. Had the theatre leaders been willing to compromise by flattering the city's power structure, the city might have responded favorably and might have provided a niche for the institution. But compromise was not possible for Jules Irving and Herbert Blau; they were concerned only with theatre, and they saw no value in diverting their energies into the social and political extracurricular activities that could have shored up their operation.

If one wanted, one could see a kind of suicide wish in their approach. Blau in particular reveled in writing newspaper articles and program notes that bluntly alienated, even insulted, the popular attitudes of the city. There was active promotion of the theatre in its later years but never in a popular vein; as the Workshop's director of public relations, I had the smallest publicity budget in the country for a theatre its size. There were subscribers who could help to make the theatre's future secure, but they never exceeded 5,200, a meager number compared to the subscription lists of theatres in other cities of the same size (Arena Stage could boast subscription rolls nearly three times as large at the time). Particularly in Blau one sensed a strong if subconscious fear that if many people seemed to agree with the Workshop by subscribing to its plays, then there would be a lessening not only of production quality but also of the very eliteness and exclusivity of the organization. Following a visit in 1961, Nan Martin wrote perceptively of this elitist tendency: "For people like Herbert Blau . . . any successful theatre venture is, by the very fact of its success, highly suspect and in some way a compromise with 'the enemy.' "[40]

Of the two leaders, Blau was the more virulent in his distaste for tradition and accommodation. Irving, more a promoter and much more pragmatic, was better able to ride the bumps and take advantage of crisis for the benefit of the institution. (His willingness to do so may have had a good deal to do with the fact that, unlike Blau, he gave up his teaching position at San Francisco State College and was dependent on the theatre for his only income.) Still, both men made the same and united choices: to be experimental, to embrace blatantly unpopular ideas, to stretch beyond their immediate obvious capabilities, and

56

to speak out against rigidities of form and formality. Through these choices, they preserved the freedom to be themselves, but at the same time they forfeited the acceptance and stability that a more socially reasonable approach could have assured. Their choices were conscious, deliberate, and belligerently uncompromising.

These characteristics were reflected in their repertoire. They had started with fairly traditional plays like *Hedda Gabler* and *Playboy of the Western World* (as well as lesser works such as *I Am a Camera* and *The Girl on the Via Flaminia*, which used the tawdriness and even the fire escape of the original loft). But this was at the start, when there was no overarching philosophy ruling their choice of plays and the manner of mounting them. Later, when a Workshop philosophy did develop, they turned to avant-garde and negativistic work—*Endgame*, *Waiting for Godot*, a barbaric *King Lear*, and American premieres of *Mother Courage* and *The Birthday Party*. The negativism comes through in Jules Irving's comment, "I don't want to be doing *Mary, Mary* when the bomb drops"[41]—not if, but *when*.

In addition, the Workshop presented more premieres of new American plays than did any other regional theatre of its time, concentrating on the works of friends Mark Harris and James Schevill, and several cerebral, rambling plays by Blau himself. Surely there was constant though affectionate friction in the Workshop offices, as Blau sought more new and exotic plays and Irving sought more works geared to building audiences and sustaining an always flagging institution. One typical season, in the planning of which both men had their say, was the last full season presented under their leadership: *Taming of the Shrew*, Pinter's *The Caretaker*, Brecht's *The Caucasian Chalk Circle*, Conrad Bromberg's *The Defense of Taipei* (a world premiere), Frisch's *The Firebugs*, *Night of the Iguana*, and Aristophanes' *The Birds*. *Shrew* was mounted chiefly to attract student audiences, and *Iguana* was as close as the Workshop ever came to "commercial" fare (even then, there was considerable chagrin around the theatre at having "given in" to popular theatre).

These plays were offered in the 1963–64 season, during my stint at the Workshop, and two of them in particular illustrate the theatre's perilous balance between the sublime and the ridiculous. *The Caucasian Chalk Circle* was sublime, and *The Birds* was ridiculous.

To understand the problem of *The Birds*, one must understand

Herbert Blau, who directed it. Despite the later roasting New York gave him, I still maintain that Blau is one of the most brilliant men in the modern American theatre as well as a man with natural but somewhat unexpected human warmth. (One pleasant memory of Workshop days is the sight of Herbert Blau setting off with his son Jonathan for an unintellectual San Francisco Giants baseball game.) Blau's problem both in San Francisco and later in New York was that his brilliance stayed inside his mind and rarely got expressed in stage terms. To hear Blau analyze a play is to relish the range of a man's mind; to see the physicalization of his ideas is to despair that he did not stop at the perfect thought. *The Birds* exemplified this problem.

Blau had a precise and very original idea for *The Birds*: to treat it as what we came to call a "classical-lyrical-vaudeville-jazz extravaganza." He adapted the ancient comedy to contemporary, even topical terms, turning Athens into San Francisco and making the play itself a comic invective against civic smugness and decay (another example of his belligerent negativism toward the city). He commissioned a new jazz score from a disciple of Dave Brubeck. He included modern dance. He ordered bird costumes fashioned from thousands of felt feathers in vibrant colors. He sent members of the cast to beaches and parks in the city to study the movements of birds and develop their own individual birdlike walks, stances, and attitudes. In short, he reconceived *The Birds* as a pastiche of Aristophanes, Olson and Johnson, Norman Mailer, and Florenz Ziegfeld.

The one thing Blau did not do was to realize that he had, in fact, conceived one of the wildest and most original musical comedies ever. If he had realized that—if he had been able to *admit* it—then he might have been able to give to the society he cared for a work at once relevant, incisive, and gloriously refreshing. Had he been able to discipline his idea, then the piece so brilliantly conceived in his private mind might have been brilliantly realized in public performance. As it turned out, I suspect that Blau did not really care whether the show worked or not on the stage; his interest in *The Birds* had been climaxed and satisfied by his conceiving it. The production ended up a hodgepodge, a ridiculous event.

The sublimity never achieved in *The Birds* was everywhere apparent, however, in the Workshop's San Francisco production of *The Caucasian Chalk Circle*, far and away the most enthralling experience

58

I have had in regional theatregoing. The play was staged by Carl Weber, who had worked with Brecht at the Berliner Ensemble. He was not so much a director as a field marshal. The Workshop actors, accustomed to a more intuitive "method" approach to character, were irritated and even frightened by Weber's literal approach: "Three steps northvest, zen a 37-degree turn and a vun and vun-half inch smile, pleece." Yet despite the tension and absolutism of rehearsals, the actors kept trudging for Weber while the rest of us knelt on the lobby floor cutting up fake Oriental rugs to make costumes. We all stayed up until five o'clock in the morning for two successive days before the opening, and still we could not master the technical intricacies of the production in time to have a complete run-through of the play. *The Caucasian Chalk Circle* opened to the public one night late in 1963, without ever having been performed in its continuous entirety; it received a standing ovation that rocked the roof of the Marines' Theater and launched a capacity run of many weeks. People who had never heard of Brecht, much less the Workshop, stormed the doors of that shabby theatre. It was an extraordinary expression of talent, devotion, and adrenalin—the kind of event that makes one want to give one's life to the art of the theatre.

The Caucasian Chalk Circle was a high point for The Actor's Workshop because in that production the peculiar, estranged, but vehement strengths of the company were all working at fever pitch. The nobility and the belligerence of the Workshop were pulling together. There was the courage to throw caution to the winds and spend money out of proportion to the budget but in proportion to the grand conception of the production. *The Caucasian Chalk Circle* was one of the major production statements of what The Actor's Workshop was.

The production also showed another and important internal aspect of the Workshop: its group spirit. Irving and Blau, like other acorn leaders, were absolute masters of their institution, and yet in the Workshop there was a communal spirit akin to that of the Group Theatre. The company was a coming together of families; not only the Irvings and the Blaus but also another half-dozen husband-and-wife teams worked together regularly. This group spirit showed up on occasions like those two nights when everyone worked until five in the morning; in spite of their Equity union rights, no actor ever asked for overtime pay. (When I was at Arena Stage, I prepared checks for actors to pay them the extra dollars due for each hour they had stayed beyond rehearsal requirements. I never even heard of such a check the next year at The Actor's Workshop.)

There were other, somewhat legendary examples of this loyalty: young Alan Mandell visiting from Canada and happening to see *The Crucible*, then staying on as the Workshop general manager at no pay, living in his office backstage in the warehouse theatre; husbands and wives both working full-time and splitting one salary between them; and, most colorfully, the dedication of Robert Symonds, who came traveling through San Francisco from his native Texas and stayed on to become a leading actor and director with the company. For five years, Symonds regularly rehearsed all day, performed in the evening, and then worked till dawn in the San Francisco produce market, unloading vegetables to support his wife and three children. When in 1960 the Workshop shared in the Ford Foundation grants for the employment of $200-per-week actors, the theatre could finally repay that commitment. Jules Irving, looking back, pays affectionate tribute to Symonds: "I remember very vividly coming back . . . landing at the San Francisco airport, knowing that we had this grant, and that three of our own actors were going to be on it. And I made a beeline for the Curtain Call [a bar where the actors gathered to unwind after performances], and I called Bob Symonds off in a corner, and I said, 'Bob, we've gotten a grant, and you can leave the produce market. I can now afford to pay you $200 a week.' And tears welled up in Bob's eyes, and he said, 'Thank God, 'cause I couldn't have lasted one more month.' "42

The communal spirit of the Workshop must have impressed the Ford Foundation, which supported the Workshop despite the fact that its leaders were less predictable and tractable than those of other theatres. Nan Martin, traveling on behalf of the foundation in 1961, understood how they were different: "You cannot equate business success with the artistic value of a production. I'm not saying that this is the total viewpoint of the Actor's Workshop, but it's certainly one of the sturdy legs of their attitude toward what they want to do in the theatre. . . . It is the kind of feeling that makes it difficult for a great many people to understand what the Actor's Workshop is trying to do. The goals of the Actor's Workshop will never be as financially supportable as the goals of Washington's Arena Theatre and the Alley Theatre in Houston. But they don't set out to be and they cannot be."43 The Work-

60

shop shared in the Ford largesse of 1962, but its grant ($197,000) was much less than those for other theatres of similar size and scope. I suppose that Ford hesitated to pour mammoth sums into the Workshop because the theatre had never secured the support of San Francisco's community leaders and so had less hope of eventually making itself a permanent fixture in the city. Perhaps Ford doubted the Workshop's *institutional* potential.

The other acorn theatres, moving gradually toward institutionalism, survived the original apathy of their communities and grew fairly steadily. The Actor's Workshop, unlike them, never worked realistically or consistently at breaking down community apathy and even distrust. In 1963, speaking for the community, *San Francisco Examiner* critic Stanley Eichelbaum was warning Irving and Blau that a "broader-based audience is imperative for self-sufficiency."[44] Speaking for himself and his theatre, Blau was saying, "I must confess to distrusting audiences more than I love them."[45] Neither side was in any mood to compromise.

In cultural circles, we tend to assume that the institution is always right in such a situation and that the community is always wrong. There is real danger in such an assumption. I remember discovering at one point in the Workshop offices that the general mailing list used to promote productions of the theatre had shrunk from 20,000 names to under 16,000. Further investigation revealed that rather than go to the bother of changing addresses when people moved, members of the dedicated Workshop staff through the years had simply thrown the old address plates away. San Francisco may have been unsupportive, but the story of the Workshop is not a simple story of perfect people being cruelly rejected by their philistine community.

Jules Irving and Herbert Blau were like other early regional theatre leaders in saying to Broadway, "We banish you!" They differed from them in that they said the same thing to their own city as well—all the time that they were living and working there. We shall return later for the outcome of this banishment and San Francisco's return of the favor. We leave The Actor's Workshop for now at the end of 1964, at the height of its egoism and the depth of its institutional weakness—disenchanted, bitter, and brilliantly negative—an acorn straining to be more.

5 Oak Trees: The Guthrie Theater and What Came After

"Give us a theatre and your support, said Guthrie and Rea, and we will give you great classical drama, excitingly performed, and make your state the home of the greatest repertory theatre in the United States."

Morison and Fliehr, In Search of an Audience

"The Guthrie . . . broke the pattern . . . because it started at the top."

Theodore Hoffman, Show

The advent of the Kennedy administration in 1961 introduced a new tone to American cultural life. After the apple-pie nonintellectualism of the Eisenhower years, there was at last a new young awareness in Washington. Robert Frost was invited to read a poem at the inauguration; Pablo Casals was not only a familiar name but an honored guest in the White House. Kennedy himself wrote, "To further the appreciation of culture among all the people, to increase respect for the creative individual, to widen participation by all the processes and fulfillments of art—this is one of the fascinating challenges of these days."[1] The President and his fashionable First Lady seemed to be inviting America to consider itself civilized. Because this striking couple liked them, the arts were chic.

It was an era of relative calm and extraordinary affluence and a time when everyone seemed to be getting educated. Foreign films were making big profits in metropolitan cities. Lincoln Center, the first of many cultural centers, was being built. The performing arts were attracting $400,000,000 in admissions each year, and more money was being spent on concert admissions alone than on tickets to professional baseball games. Books were a billion-dollar industry, and the paperback market in particular was going wild. (Just after World War II, paperbacks were by definition "dirty" books; we used to sneak down to the corner newsstand to leaf through them. But by the early 1960s, many paperbacks were literary classics and no longer relegated to the dens and playrooms of America; they had surfaced in livingrooms and on bookshelves built of boards and bricks.) In short, the cultural climate seemed to be changing, and something new called a "cultural explosion" was assumed to be taking place. Among its bibles were Alvin Toffler's *The Culture Consumers*, published in 1964, and the Rockefeller Brothers Fund panel report *The Performing Arts: Problems and Prospects*, issued in 1965.

While the Toffler and Rockefeller books appeared to prove the existence of a "cultural explosion," another more weighty tome, the Twentieth Century Fund's *The Performing Arts: The Economic Dilemma*, in 1966 almost immediately put the term to rest. This book pointed out that the "cultural explosion" had already proved to be largely a myth; the natural increase in population and per capita income had given the appearance in the early 1960s of increased interest in the arts, but the *percentage* of people interested in the arts had not grown significantly. However, the public was not generally aware of the analysis of Professors William Baumol and William Bowen, the authors of the book, and it was far more cheering to hear the figures on concert admissions versus baseball attendance. There was much impressive talk about culture, and there was a virtual explosion of foundation grants and community programs and speeches, all of which looked and sounded like a "cultural explosion." During the first half of the 1960s, it did not matter that the "cultural explosion" did not exist; the American people assumed that it did and acted upon that assumption.

The new atmosphere in America, officially sympathetic to culture, allowed the early ad hoc strivings of the first regional theatres to take on new significance. Coming at a time when the best of the theatres were beginning to see and assume a clearer tomorrow, the supposed explosion encouraged them to change from mere organizations into institutions. This subtle but essential change was greatly encouraged by the arrival on the scene in 1957 of the Ford Foundation, which began to apply its resources formally to cultural programs. While other foundations were soon involved in similar endeavors (including the

Rockefeller Foundation starting in 1963), Ford led the way. Its entry into the regional theatre field in the late 1950s was the first major turning point of the revolution because it provided the first hint of legitimacy and the primary building blocks of institutionalism.

Ford's activity in the beginning was very modest and very personal. In 1957, W. McNeil Lowry, a former reporter and teacher then in charge of a very small piece of the Ford pie—a division called Humanities and the Arts—went out across the country to see what was happening culturally. In theatre, he saw it all: Nina Vance in Houston, Zelda Fichandler in Washington, Jules Irving and Herbert Blau in San Francisco, Mack Scism in Oklahoma City, George Touliatos in Memphis, John Reich at the Goodman Theatre in Chicago, numerous university theatre programs, and some community theatres. Out of his explorations came a group of small grants to young directors, to be used however they chose to increase their own awareness or their theatres' development. The first grants to regional theatres were partially designed, I believe, to be tests; through them I think Lowry was trying to identify those people who reacted well to the Ford challenge. The uses of the small grants revealed the goals of their recipients, and it is interesting to note that the directors in the original group who have received regular support from Ford ever since are those who used their first grants in ways considered proper at that time. For instance, Nina Vance and Zelda Fichandler used their money for travel and study to increase their awareness; they did right. Mack Scism used his money to travel in Europe and around America, talking to theatre people like Nina and Zelda whom he had not met before; he did right. These three leaders were among those whose theatres were most heavily supported by Ford after that.

After the test grants had identified possibilities in theatres throughout the country, Ford called together some two dozen leaders of professional, university, and community theatres to discuss common problems. Surprisingly, this conclave was the first time that Nina Vance, Zelda Fichandler, Jules Irving, and other leaders got to know each other at all well. At last the isolation of these people throughout the 1950s was being broken down; each person saw that others were suffering too and that no theatre was alone in its poverty and its tenuous hold on its community. This meeting, with its sense of unity and common peril, helped to turn the early regional theatre strivings into a *movement* in

64

America. The new fraternal spirit, combined with the assumption of a cultural explosion and the interest of the Ford Foundation (which was increased after 1960, when Lowry's program became a major division of the foundation with more money at its disposal), made regional theatre look like the wave of the future. I was just finishing college at that point (1960) and believed with many others that to work in professional theatre outside New York was not only a noble but also a natural thing to do. People "in the know" and with the good of the theatre at heart were going to work in regional situations. Centrifugal force was the new force in the American theatre.

All the theatres called together by the Ford Foundation in the late 1950s were acorns—there was no other kind. Yet it was natural that the movement started by the small unknown theatres would soon aid in the development of theatres sanctioned by the power structure of communities, large and famous from their inception—theatres which were, in short, "oak trees," planted fully grown.

There were two major differences between the acorn theatres and the oak tree theatres—one an institutional difference, the other a personal one. Institutionally, the difference was in scope. The early acorn theatres were started by anonymous people seeking places in which to work and to define their own untested talents. Their anonymity forced them to start small, to work with no money and no power and with people as unknown as themselves. The oak tree theatres, coming at the time of the new cultural climate, could bring civic power to bear upon their purpose; they could be not only embraced by the Establishment but willed into being by it.

The personal difference between the acorn theatres and the oak tree theatres lay in the relationship between the two kinds of leaders and the central theatre of Broadway. The acorn leaders had banished Broadway without having fully experienced it; theirs was an abstract, philosophical rejection of the central theatre. The creators of the first oak tree theatres were people saying "no" to Broadway after many years of experience there; their rejection of the central theatre was specific and personal. For the first time, there were people banishing something they knew firsthand.

The first and prototypical oak tree was the Minnesota Theatre Company—better known now as The Guthrie Theater—which burst upon the American theatre world with its gala opening in May of 1963. The story of the creation of this theatre has been fully told from Tyrone Guthrie's point of view in his book *A New Theatre*, which describes in detail why and how the Guthrie was born. It came to be primarily because of the boredom with Broadway felt by three men: Sir Tyrone Guthrie, Oliver Rea, and Peter Zeisler. Guthrie was world-famous—a former director of both the Old Vic and Sadler's Wells in London; the artistic genius of the Stratford Shakespearean Festival in Canada; a director of commercial successes in London, New York, and around the world; and the author of books about the theatre and himself. Rea, though not so famous, was highly respected as a Broadway producer, with *Member of the Wedding* and Judith Anderson's *Medea* to his credit. Zeisler was the least known of the three because his kind of work was the least visible—the organization and administration of all back-stage elements—but through the years he had developed into one of the shrewdest and toughest production managers in the commercial theatre.

The personalities of the three men could not have been more disparate. Guthrie was the English knight, all molten-golden-noted and pronouncement-prone. A highly theatrical figure himself and nearly six and a half feet tall, he was the dominant personality in public and private and the easiest to promote. Zeisler, in contrast, was shorter, rough-edged and a scrapper, as tough as a union organizer. Rea was the most subtle, a natural aristocrat, smooth, detached, a good fund-raiser. One cannot imagine these three men choosing to spend an evening together, but they did decide to create a theatre together, which is a completely different thing. Together, they had the ability to accomplish great feats. In Guthrie's own words, "The sum of our three experiences and skills was more than three times the value of each singly."[2]

The Guthrie-Rea-Zeisler project began in March of 1959 over breakfast at New York's Plaza Hotel, an elite potted-palms setting in vivid contrast to the inception of any previous regional theatre. In the beginning, their project had little if anything to do with the concept and virtues of decentralization, and it was curiously lacking in urgent commitment. According to Guthrie, "All of us felt considerable dissatisfaction with the theatrical set-up as we found it in New York, and for very similar reasons. But dissatisfaction is a negative state of mind. About the positive steps which we should take we were neither clear nor unanimous."[3]

First they toyed with the idea of establishing a "mid-Atlantic" company, producing plays in both London (where it would be cheaper) and New York (where it could be more profitable), but this idea was abandoned partly because it seemed too vague and partly because Rea and Zeisler, as Americans, would have found it difficult to obtain work permits in London. Finally and somewhat glibly, the trio developed what Guthrie in his book calls "A Plan": "Our programme would be classical; only those plays would be chosen which had seemed, to discriminating people for several generations, to have serious merit; which had, in fact, withstood the test of time. . . . about one play in four should be an American play of potential classic status; this to be offered to any city which felt deprived of live theatre and would take us under its wing."[4] They were aiming for the ultimate classical repertory theatre, with heavy emphasis on Continental playwrights. Indeed, although Guthrie maintained that all three partners wanted "to start a professional theatre where it would be filling a need" and were "bitten by the missionary bug," the fact was that their particular mission was very much based in colonialism. While Guthrie insisted that he and his associates did not want it to appear that once again Britain was "trying to instruct the colonists,"[5] the truth was that Guthrie was indeed trying to do so; he just did not want it to look that way.

The three men were particularly dispassionate in looking for a city in which to set down their theatre. They wanted a place "large enough to support a theatre, and small enough to enable us to be a big frog."[6] As central personalities, they found it hard to imagine where such a place could be: "It was also clear that, with the exception of five or six cities which were used for the 'tryouts' of Broadway productions, and with the exception of Chicago, every other city in the United States was grossly undersupplied. It was not, however, clear whether all these cities regarded this as a deprivation; whether, in fact, they were not entirely content to remain in a theatrical Sahara, entirely content with what they had—movies, TV, amateurs working with high aspirations and low budgets, and rather grubby little shows in dark night-clubs."[7] Nevertheless, Guthrie—with his partners beside (or below) him—came down from Olympus one day in September, 1959, to consider possibilities. They started by taking Brooks Atkinson, at that time the drama critic of the *New York Times,* to lunch at Dinty Moore's (another setting full of Broadway habitués). Atkinson, accommodating as always and responding to the Plan, arranged a *Times* article in which the reporter wondered whether any cities would take up the challenge put forth:

Concerned over the centralization of the legitimate theatre in New York and the general lack of opportunities for burgeoning professional actors, three prominent show people have taken steps to remedy these conditions.

The group, composed of Oliver Rea, producer, Tyrone Guthrie, director, and Peter Zeisler, production manager, plans to establish a permanent company outside the limits of Broadway.

In his office yesterday, Mr. Rea . . . enthusiastically provided some of the details. He and his associates hope to present at least ten classics or outstanding works in a city "where there is an interest in the theatre and not in touring companies.

". . . Some of the plays contemplated for production are 'Hamlet,' 'Don Carlos,' 'Volpone,' 'The Alchemist,' 'St. Joan,' 'Mourning Becomes Electra,' 'Orestes,' 'Skin of Our Teeth,' and plays by Tennessee Williams and Eugene O'Neill.

"We are prepared to form a company of professional actors who will, in our estimation, be able to act these plays in a lively and intelligent way. We believe that such a company can be fully successful and useful only if its work can be closely identified with the name of the city where it plays."

Too many cities, Mr. Rea said, are being relegated to a more and more provincial status where their "inhabitants have very little corporate opportunity to originate their own cultural ideas."

. . . Mr. Rea estimated that it would take two years to get his project going. But, after conducting a one-man survey, he came away convinced that the project would gain the necessary support.

"Many people in many cities," he said, "are ready to welcome any reasonable possibility of making their own city more articulate and more lively in its cultural aspects."[8]

Seven cities responded to the story in the *Times*; during the fall of 1959 Guthrie and Rea visited all of them, looking for interest in elaborating and supporting their idea of a theatre (Zeisler could not travel with them because he was then busy stage-managing *The Sound of Music* on Broadway).

Significantly, of the seven cities canvassed by Guthrie and Rea, five—Boston, San Francisco, Chicago, Cleveland, and Milwaukee—already had functioning professional theatre institutions. In fact, in Cleveland the two men conferred with the board of directors of the Play House itself. However, most people within the topmost power structure of the other four cities were not involved in the local theatres and so could easily consider a competitive new theatre under famous leadership. In the fall of 1959, no acorn theatre could possibly have looked like a reasonable alternative to one led by the world-renowned Sir Tyrone Guthrie. Nor was there any reason at that time for Guthrie and Rea to feel any qualms about locating their theatre where less secure theatres with prior claims were trying to stay alive. Their idea was simply in a different league. Describing his visit to San Francisco, Guthrie recalled an encounter with two local theatre groups, one of which was probably The Actor's Workshop: "We visited two semi-professional groups operating semi-permanently in semi-theatres. They too were polite, but obviously interested in consolidating their own position rather than in the somewhat different project with which we were concerned."[9] For such celebrities coming out of New York to investigate the "provinces," the existence of other theatres was irrelevant and competition inconceivable. For Guthrie himself, the attempt to create a full professional theatre somewhere outside New York at the turn of the 1960s had no precedent to be acknowledged. It was not in his nature to follow anybody—not from six and a half feet up. He considered the cities "suitors"—as if they were vying for his idea, pushing over each other to get to him. Actually, in only three cities—Milwaukee, Detroit, and Minneapolis—was there any substantial interest; and only in Detroit was there any formal assurance from the beginning of the major funding necessary for the project. Still, despite Detroit's assurance, the three men preferred Minneapolis for several reasons. First, of the three cities, Minneapolis was farthest from New York and so least in its social, economic, and psychological grip; the remoteness of Minnesota underlined the commitment of the trio in leaving the center. Second, Minneapolis was an up-and-coming city without much touted culture and therefore was a dynamic little pond in which the theatre could be a very big frog. Third and essentially, it was the city where the power structure seemed most energetic. The mood of Minneapolis caught the trio's fancy. I imagine one reason for this is that Minneapolis is one of few cities of its size in this country which, at least on the surface, give the visitor the impression that the citizens there consider life possible. This cannot be so readily said of any of the other six cities surveyed by Guthrie and Rea; furthermore, the impression must have been a heady experience for them, coming as they did from New York, where everything seems possible except life itself.

And so the Guthrie-Rea-Zeisler idea, in the spring of 1960, came to rest in Minneapolis. The nature of the Twin Cities power structure which summoned the trio is particularly noteworthy because that is what helped assure the success of the venture. The invitation did not come from a typical group of men in their fifties and sixties, at the peak of their powers. It came instead from the sons of such men—from what Guthrie called a "generation of Heirs Apparent." The triumvirate—and particularly Rea, the suave, socially adept manager—very consciously sought out not the city's patriarchs but their scions. They went not to old John Cowles, who owned the *Minneapolis Star* and *Tribune*, but to young John, Jr. Young Cowles, like other Juniors who would inherit power, was looking for an appropriate *pro bono publico* project which could be his civic achievement, and he took on the theatre idea and above all the responsibility for raising the necessary money. This concentration on Heirs Apparent was a master stroke because it assured the participation of not only the current power structure (their parents) but also the future one (themselves). It also allowed the theatre professionals coming into an unfamiliar situation to deal with their contemporaries rather than with older and presumably more rigid men.

The trio from New York shrewdly made another key stipulation at the start: the bulk of the money had to be committed before they would take up residence in the city. This put the onus on the local powers instead of on themselves, a much more realistic arrangement for a theatre which was intended to be a locally supported public institution. The local powers delivered—more than $2,250,000 to build a new theatre to Guthrie's specifications. The largest gift was from the Walker Foundation, which gave not only a parcel of land for the theatre building but also $500,000 toward construction. The smallest gift was the much-touted $6.37 from a Sunday school class in Mankato, Minnesota, eighty miles southwest of Minneapolis. The gift of the Sunday school class has become legendary; its arrival is pictured in a commemorative motion picture, *Miracle in Minnesota*, filmed during the first season in 1963. Somehow, while completely true, the story of the Mankato Sunday school class gift does not ring as true as it might in a smaller, more acorn context. One senses that someone in the Guthrie planning office saw the return address on the envelope, heard the change jingling, and quickly called the *Minneapolis Star* and *Tribune* to send reporters and photographers down to see the envelope being opened—or that the whole incident was later restaged for the press and cameras. This is all very natural and very good public relations; but it is also a far cry from Zelda Fichandler in a beer factory, Michael Murray above a fish market, or Jules Irving and Herbert Blau behind a judo academy. The regional theatre was learning in Minneapolis how to entice the "right money" out of the "right people," including Sunday school classes.

The creation of the theatre was not a cynical phenomenon, however. It was in fact the broadest and most public manifestation of regional theatre to date. One of the first of many right decisions was to give the institution the formal name of Minnesota Theatre Company, stressing a statewide rather than a local identity. This choice had several reasons behind it. Given the intense, bitter, and often mutually defeating rivalry between the Twin Cities of Minneapolis and St. Paul, the founders did not want to favor one over the other in the name. Also, it was clear that the Twin Cities, by themselves, could not provide a large enough audience to sustain a major theatre; statewide support was needed. The broad name was part of a deliberate and structured attempt to be indigenous on a vast regional scale. An even more fitting name might have been the Upper Midwest Theatre Company, for from the start the theatre was designed to serve not only all of Minnesota but Iowa, Wisconsin, and North and South Dakota as well. This five-state area was considered the "market area" of the theatre, the largest of any regional theatre in America. It was a logical plan, for the Twin Cities serve as a commercial, financial, social, educational, and cultural headquarters for a far-flung population throughout the five states. One department store, Dayton's in Minneapolis, attracts shoppers on a once or twice yearly trip from hundreds of miles away. The theatre (which used the Dayton's charge account list to solicit its audience) was structured to attract a similarly wide constituency.

Another master stroke in the inception of The Guthrie Theater was its superb volunteer organization, the "Stagehands." Founded in 1962, one year before the opening of the theatre, this group of 1,400 women was charged with the responsibility of selling season subscriptions for the inaugural season. Chapters were established in out-of-the-way towns far from the Twin Cities. The women took on the personal challenge of convincing their friends of the continuing value of the Guthrie. They were excellent goodwill ambassadors for the theatre, and their efforts provided more than 21,000 subscribers and an overall attendance of more than 193,000 in the first season of the theatre—a new high in

71

regional theatre patronage at that time. As a grass-roots effort, the "Stagehands" were without precedent and later became a model for many other women's volunteer organizations working for other regional theatres and cultural organizations.

The Guthrie Theater opened with Guthrie's modern-dress production of *Hamlet*; the first season also included *The Miser*, *The Three Sisters*, and *Death of a Salesman* (the last was Guthrie's choice of an American play with "potential classic status"). More than forty actors were in the company, which for the first time in the history of regional theatre featured "name" actors—Hume Cronyn, Jessica Tandy, George Grizzard, and Rita Gam. Their presence in Minneapolis represented a radical departure in the regional theatre world. Whereas the use of stars was considered suspect and even unfair in the early years of the movement, the opening of the Guthrie with stars a few years later was looked upon with favor. Cronyn, Tandy, Grizzard, and Gam—led by Sir Tyrone Guthrie—were viewed not as stars but as the best American actors, joining in the inaugural season of the great new American repertory theatre. Besides, Hume Cronyn was a superb Miser, and when you are that good, your stardom is excusable.

The decision to include Cronyn and Tandy was particularly wise because this husband-wife team is a warmly human pair of actors, and their presence at the top of the Guthrie company in 1963 (and again in 1965) provided leadership which was rare and prized. And yet their presence tended to create some imbalance in the company; it was hard for other actors to adjust to star superiority and for the stars to adjust to company equality. For instance, in 1965 I visited The Guthrie Theater with director Alan Schneider, and we had drinks after a performance with Hume Cronyn and Jessica Tandy. In his civil but firm way, Cronyn was complaining about the Guthrie policy of listing all actors' names alphabetically and so equally. Listening to his protestations, I sensed that it is much more agreeable to be an alphabetical company actor when your last name is Abbott than when it is Young.

The first season of The Guthrie Theater was a total success in critical acceptance, in attendance, and financially. The theater showed a small surplus, as it did again in 1964. By 1965, when I first saw the company at work, they were deeply established in their civic and regional situation. From the start, the company was strong and solid (if also somewhat stolid). The actors had good voices, they moved well, and they were above all serviceable. In particular, they were a *Guthrie* company—uniformly competent, with no actor strong enough to compete with the overwhelming figure of Guthrie himself. The biggest star—and no one dared to object to this—was Sir Tyrone.

The second season, in 1964—with Grizzard but without Cronyn and Tandy—featured *St. Joan, Henry V, Volpone,* and *The Glass Menagerie.* In 1965, Grizzard left and Cronyn and Tandy returned; the plays were *Richard III, The Way of the World, The Cherry Orchard,* a return engagement of *The Miser,* and *The Caucasian Chalk Circle* (the first European play not an obvious or long-standing classic). In this year, the theatre's budget exceeded a million dollars for the first time, and its first deficit ($82,000) was sustained.

At the end of the 1965 season, his seed-planting done, Guthrie resigned as the full-time artistic director. His influence, like his name on the building, remained. He was succeeded by his associate, actor-director Douglas Campbell, who shared his mentor's imposing manner but not his largesse of talent or his ability to command and lead. Oliver Rea also left, and by 1966 Peter Zeisler, who had started as the technician of the team, was managing the theatre on his own. The deficit kept growing; nevertheless, Zeisler kept expanding, even adding a second short season in nearby St. Paul. The budget climbed to a new high of $1,200,000 in 1967. Campbell left at the end of that season; Zeisler hired two co-directors to work under him: Edward Payson Call, who had started as a Guthrie stage manager and had directed the brilliant *Caucasian Chalk Circle* in 1965, and Mel Shapiro from Arena Stage.

The new threesome, and particularly Zeisler, had to face the fact that the bloom was off. The first season at the Guthrie had been so glamorous and the phenomenon so new and compelling that there was no possibility of following it with anything as impressive. Subscriptions had dropped by 10 percent in the second season, and by the middle of the 1960s they had leveled off at between 12,000 and 15,000. People who had come in the first year from near and far just to see the new theatre felt no need to return. Having started at the top, the only direction in which The Guthrie Theater could go was down. To counteract flagging public interest, Zeisler turned more and more to contemporary work—*The Visit, Thieves' Carnival,* and Brecht's *Arturo Ui,* for example. The original adherence to time-tested classics was put aside in favor of more modern and more modish work. Guthrie returned in

73

1967 to stage a mammoth production of *The Oresteia,* here called *The House of Atreus.* The grandiose theatricality of this one production temporarily rescued The Guthrie Theater, critically and spiritually. Still, the nagging question remained: Was The Guthrie Theater superimposed on its community?

All of the acorn theatres may have been tentative and insecure, but at least they were indigenous—carved, even hacked, out of their communities. The leaders of The Guthrie Theater, the first oak tree, had to deal with the fear that they had willed their theatre in Minneapolis without regard to natural growth—and that when this superimposition caught up with them, they could perish. They had all the luxuries of top rank, but none of the benefits of slow testing and acceptance. The rest of us working in the regional theatre in the middle of the 1960s were quick to point out this dilemma in Minneapolis. For instance, while working at the acorn Actor's Workshop in early 1965, I went to Minneapolis for several days to study the advanced promotion methods of The Guthrie Theater. I remember joking that the first thing I would see upon my arrival would be the gully in the ground marking the spot where the Guthrie had been dropped from the sky. (It wasn't there, but I wrote home explaining that it had probably been filled in one dark night by an office boy.) We in the acorn theatres wanted to believe that the Guthrie had been dropped out of the sky. I think we resented the fact that this new theatre was suddenly "granddaddy," and that our theatres, after years of struggle, were suddenly only its offspring. We had always assumed that oak trees came from acorns growing up, not that they could be planted fully grown. We were bitter about those sharpshooters in Minneapolis taking shortcuts, doing market research, getting a $337,000 Ford grant even before their opening night and then being able to get the *New York Times* to cover that opening night. We thought that it had been too easy for Guthrie, Rea, and Zeisler—and deep down, I think, we half hoped that their theatre would turn out to be a cultural Edsel.

Yet while we resented the glamour of The Guthrie Theater and scorned its lack of indigenous beginnings, we still yearned to bask in its majesty. Throughout the middle 1960s, we all flocked to Minneapolis to study the brilliant management and production techniques of the Guthrie. The congenial staff there was virtually overrun by dozens of other theatre leaders coming to learn how things could be done when all conceivable resources were at one's disposal. "Granddaddy" was the new lodestone and measure for regional theatre. It drew us like a magnet, not only because it appeared to be the best but also because it corroborated all that we had been doing. The fact that three people who had succeeded in the Broadway idiom had rejected that idiom in favor of our revolution was a major psychological boost for all of us. In the ideological conflict between the central and regional theatres, we had taken a giant step forward; the great Guthrie was on our side. What did it matter that the giant himself did not seem to notice our army? We considered him our most powerful tactical weapon. Throughout the country, theatres adopted a new definition of themselves: "regional professional theatre, like the Guthrie in Minneapolis."

The emergence of The Guthrie Theater was the second major turning point of the regional theatre revolution because it further legitimatized the movement and gave it national weight. It gave hope to all regional theatres that they too could become known on a national level, that the *Times* might soon cover their opening nights, and that actors like Hume Cronyn and Jessica Tandy might soon set aside a season for them. The opening of the Guthrie was a turning point because it brought national attention to the movement. Soon, formal notice was being paid. In February, 1965, for example, the Esso Repertory series began on National Educational Television. Produced by David Susskind, the series consisted of thirteen one-hour dramatic programs featuring theatres of the period (ironically, the Guthrie was not part of the group). During the same period, *Show* magazine featured a sympathetic analysis of the regional theatre scene by Theodore Hoffman, the Boswell of the movement. More potently, *Time* magazine, often an insular New York voice, reported on the regional theatre. In a feature article entitled "The Rise of Rep," *Time* paid the movement a backhanded compliment: "America has thus been made safe for citizens who live and breathe theatre. The Lincoln Tunnel is no longer a rainspout leading from the hanging gardens to the desert. And the most curious footnote to all this is that Broadway shows are having difficulty finding understudies. On the mere rumor of such an opening, six candidates would once have appeared like genii. But now *Luther*, for example, is playing without a substitute Luther because almost every serious actor who can walk or crawl has gone off to a rep company."[10]

Important as the enhanced legitimacy and new attention were, another more important possibility opened up with the emergence of The Guthrie Theater: the possibility that from the regional theatre might come a National Theatre for America. Before the Guthrie, there had been scant justification for such an idea. The Guthrie was the first regional theatre that looked as if it could conceivably develop into the realization of this long-cherished dream, and the fact that it was in Minneapolis, a thousand miles from New York, lent credence to the theory that a National Theatre might evolve from the regional revolution. Perhaps the Guthrie itself would eventually be the one to so develop; but it was also possible that it had simply opened the way for some other theatre. Who could say which one? The struggle for national supremacy had started, and that was the essence of this second major turning point.

In the wake of The Guthrie Theater came a quick succession of other oak tree theatres. First was the Seattle Repertory Theatre, opening in the fall of 1963—and very much the creation of that community's power structure.

Seattle has an energy and a get-up-and-go attitude similar to that of Minneapolis. Fortunately, the 1962 Seattle World's Fair had provided for the city a complete civic center, in which stood a conventional 800-seat proscenium theatre. The city fathers groped for a new purpose for the building; hearing about the incipient Guthrie Theater and other regional theatres, they soon determined to create their own in Seattle. They approached Stuart Vaughan, fresh from his highly praised work with Joseph Papp's New York Shakespeare Festival and the original Phoenix Theatre off-Broadway; he accepted the job and immediately set out to form a classical repertory company. Vaughan has described his Seattle experience in *A Possible Theatre*. His reasons for accepting the Seattle challenge were standard logic for the regional theatre of that time:

A city outside of New York seemed a better place for the establishment of an acting company for several reasons. The geographical distance, in itself, dramatized the decision the actor was asked to make. By the act of moving, he was making a certain commitment. Being out of New York meant being away from the commercial attractions of television, films, and plays. The acting company could not be a showcase, because it was physically distant from the marketplace. . . . The theatre would be the major theatre of the city, and as such recipient of such attention and concern as that particular place could muster for theatre. . . . All this meant that the new theatre would find its identity more rapidly. Our own style of production and way of working could be more effectively evolved away from the distractions of New York.[11]

The new repertory theatre opened with Vaughan's production of *King Lear*, paired with Frisch's *The Firebugs*, directed by André Gregory, Vaughan's young associate director. Nine thousand subscribers rallied to the inaugural season, and the future looked very good.

Like the Guthrie, the Seattle Repertory Theatre under Vaughan performed its plays in rotating repertory, offering as many as five different plays during a single week. Vaughan's choice of plays was predictably classical. Except for Robert Ardrey's *Shadow of Heroes*, a play about the Hungarian uprising, all of the plays in the first Seattle season were familiar works: *Julius Caesar, The Importance of Being Earnest, Twelfth Night, Hamlet,* and *The Cherry Orchard* were typical choices. Aside from the Ardrey and Frisch plays, Brecht's *Galileo* was Vaughan's least traditional offering.

Vaughan was a director as autocratic as Guthrie but without his theatrical flair. The company he gathered in Seattle was a formal grouping, and it was particularly colored by Vaughan's appearance in many leading roles (including Brutus in *Julius Caesar* and Jack in *Earnest*). Not only an actor and a director but also his own producer, Vaughan, of all regional theatre leaders, was probably the only one who could be considered an ideological descendant of Henry Irving, the nineteenth century English actor-manager.

Two years after the inaugural production, there was a locking of horns between Vaughan's assumed autocracy and what he considered the philistinism of the Seattle Repertory board of directors. Board president Bagley Wright fired Vaughan one day late in 1965—and reports ran wild that Vaughan reciprocated by punching Wright in the nose. Vaughan dwells upon the incident in his book, much to the board's detriment. I suppose that the problem arose from the fact that Vaughan had gone to Seattle expecting to run his theatre with the kind of absolute control enjoyed by the leaders of acorn theatres, but instead found himself up against the proprietary attitudes of the power structure which had founded the theatre and had hired him. Vaughan's experience in Seattle illustrates a major difference between acorn and oak tree theatres—namely, that in the former the artist chooses and rules his employers, whereas in the latter the employers choose and rule.

77

Regional Theatre: The Revolutionary Stage

The employers chose Allen Fletcher as a replacement for Vaughan. Fletcher, whose experience had been concentrated in Shakespeare festivals in Stratford, Connecticut, and San Diego, was equally formal but nevertheless the opposite of Vaughan in temperament. Fletcher was gentle and accommodating, soft-spoken and retiring; all assumed that his relations with the board of employers would be much smoother than his predecessor's. For a while, they were; under Fletcher's leadership, the Seattle Repertory Theatre began to modernize its repertoire. It also began a series of experimental productions in a small second theatre, the Off Center. Attendance during Fletcher's first full season, 1966–67, reached more than 175,000—more than double the first season's. Early in 1968, his contract was renewed for another two years. In 1969, he ended the practice of rotating the repertory, long desired by almost all regional theatres in order to maintain their companies' artistic freshness but a severe drain on any theatre's financial resources. The action was typical of his reasonable and conservative approach. In the same year, the company journeyed to Bergen, Norway (Seattle's sister city), to perform *Who's Afraid of Virginia Woolf?* and a new play by resident playwright Jon Swan. In addition to the international tour, the company also instituted a commendable practice of taking classics (*The Imaginary Invalid, She Stoops to Conquer,* and others) on tour through the parks of the city and throughout the state of Washington during the summer months. Fletcher's artistic leadership was complemented by the propriety and efficiency of the management of Donald Foster, a well-placed local gentleman, and the Seattle Repertory Theatre was regarded in the late 1960s as one of the most forthright of American regional theatres.

Then Bagley Wright struck again. Midway through the 1969–70 season, Fletcher's fourth at the helm, Wright ousted him: "At the regular monthly meeting of the Seattle Repertory Theatre's Board of Trustees this afternoon, President Bagley Wright announced that Allen Fletcher's contract would not be renewed."[12] An appalled acting company, some of whom had been through this trauma with both artistic directors, revolted against the theatre and aired its dirty linen in public.

The dismissal of Fletcher made it appear that something was rotten in Seattle. Given Vaughan's autocratic approach, it was not difficult for outsiders to place at least part of the blame for his ouster on himself. The same could not be said of the mild Allen Fletcher. Now Vaughan's charges of philistinism seemed well justified. The villain of the piece seemed to be Bagley Wright, the president of the board who apparently had enough power simply to announce that Fletcher was fired. Wright's hold over the theatre seemed confirmed by another announcement in 1971—with the theatre seeking to raise $200,000, Wright had offered to match the first $100,000 raised, dollar for dollar. In effect, the president was halving the goal by giving half of it himself. Presumably he was able to exert extraordinary influence because he was paying the institution's piper.

Wright's influence in both financial and artistic affairs seemed to prove that oak tree theatres could become toys in the hands of the local power structures that create them. Therefore, there was some surprise when Wright celebrated the achievement of the funding goal by removing himself from the presidency of the board. The way was open now for the theatre to be more under the control of its professionals.

Meanwhile (and one of Wright's last actions), a new artistic director had been chosen for the company: Duncan Ross, director of the professional training program in theatre at the University of Washington and formerly associated with Michel St. Denis at the National Theatre School of Canada and the Old Vic in England. Ross, ably complemented by manager Peter Donnelly, set out to make the Seattle Repertory Theatre more popular. Their first season, 1970–71, featured Arthur Kopit's *Indians, The Miser, A Flea in Her Ear, Hay Fever, The Price*, and *Richard II*; more than half of the performances were completely sold out. Of these, in turn, more than half were of *Richard II*, which sold out because Ross had secured Richard Chamberlain to play the melancholy monarch. Chamberlain was praised locally and nationally for his portrayal, and the production staged by Ross was later offered in Los Angeles and at the Kennedy Center in Washington, D. C. In Seattle, the Chamberlain production put the Seattle Repertory Theatre into black ink for the first time, showing how much the presence of an obvious star can do to help the reputation and the box office of nonprofit theatres. It is likely that Duncan Ross will continue the policy of engaging name actors. In the 1972–73 season, for instance, David McCallum was scheduled to play Richard III, and Rita Gam joined the company to play Marguerite in *Camino Real*. Subscribers took up nearly 90 percent of available seats, and the company was playing to consistently full houses.

Regional Theatre: The Revolutionary Stage

It appears now that the Seattle Repertory Theatre has weathered its early storms. It ran the risk of being the first oak tree theatre to become the pawn of its lay leadership. That it did not proves that men like Bagley Wright should not be rashly judged—just as they should not rashly judge men like Stuart Vaughan and Allen Fletcher.

Stuart Vaughan was involved in still another oak tree theatre, the Repertory Theatre New Orleans. Upon leaving Seattle, he was rescued by Roger Stevens, then the chairman of the new National Endowment for the Arts, who installed him in New Orleans. Stevens at that time (1966) was providing federal funding for three "laboratory" theatres designed to produce classics for high school students in prescribed areas. New Orleans was one of three locations for the project, along with Providence and Los Angeles. The Repertory Theatre New Orleans opened in the fall of 1966, one year after Vaughan's dismissal from Seattle. It was a theatre that had not been created by the local power structure, let alone by the individual leader, but by federal decree. Together, National Endowment funds and Office of Education funds provided more than a half-million dollars per year for three seasons. Under the arrangement, the Repertory Theatre was able to create productions for students, paid for by the government, and then to show them to adults at no additional production cost to the theatre. It seemed an ideal situation.

It was—except for the city of New Orleans, which appears to be below sea level not only physically but psychologically as well. There is a group of young and vital theatre enthusiasts there, but they appear held down by their elders, their ambitions disregarded and even suppressed. New Orleans seems a city without hope, the urban opposite of Minneapolis and Seattle. Repertory Theatre New Orleans could not overcome the lassitude of its city; despite a population of more than a million, the city could not provide audiences for more than three adult performances per week during the three years of federal support. The citizens may have been grateful for the opportunity afforded their children by the theatre, but they could not have cared less for themselves. Their apathy was complicated by the popularity in the city of Le Petit Théâtre de Vieux Carré, one of America's richest community theatres and an organization hostile to the Repertory Theatre from the beginning.

80

Another factor, of course, was Vaughan himself. His experience in the far reaches of the West had not tempered his arrogance. Luxuriously subsidized by the federal government, he saw little need to relate to the community around him. His theatre, secured from the outside, did not bother to develop itself for the time when Uncle Sam would no longer be paying the bills. By the time the government funding came to an end in the spring of 1969, the Repertory Theatre New Orleans had not really tried to make itself an integral and necessary part of the local scene. The few civic leaders who had noticed the theatre still resented the fact that the federal government had imposed such a nuisance upon them. It was as if Vaughan and his cohorts were simply getting in the way of Mardi Gras. Vaughan left New Orleans and returned to New York.

Early in 1970, the new board of directors of the theatre hired actress June Havoc, who had appeared in Vaughan's production of *The Rivals* in New Orleans, to reorganize the theatre. Given her reputation, she was able to galvanize additional support. The group found an old temple and converted it into a new facility for the theatre, and Julie Harris came to New Orleans to appear in the Repertory Theatre's production of *The Women*. Nevertheless, these changes did not significantly alter the community's apathetic attitude toward the theatre, and at the end of the 1970–71 season Miss Havoc departed. The board of directors tried to interest director Jacques Cartier in coming to New Orleans; but when the board could not raise enough money to meet his budget needs, he did not come. After limping through part of the 1971–72 season with guest directors, the board finally called a halt and closed the theatre. By then, of course, it was all very far removed from the original, federally funded project. There needed to be no embarrassment in Washington.

Some had wondered whether The Guthrie Theater had been superimposed on Minneapolis, but in comparison the Repertory Theatre had been ground into New Orleans. Apparently it is next to impossible to plant a full-grown oak tree below sea level.

It is natural that sprawling Los Angeles would discover culture with a vengeance—then try to centralize it in a city with no downtown. The Los Angeles Music Center is the home of the Center Theatre Group, which is actually two theatrical producing organizations. The larger of the two theatres is the Ahmanson, a gigantic auditorium for touring commercial productions, also used as a tryout spot for Broadway-bound shows. The Ahmanson has no character of its own and no continuity of artistic policy, but it is big business. It opened in 1967 with the American premiere of Eugene O'Neill's *More Stately Mansions*, starring Ingrid Bergman; next came a tryout of Robert Goulet and David Wayne in *The Happy Time*, and finally a visiting engagement by the Royal Shakespeare Company from England, in *As You Like It* and *Taming of the Shrew*. Later productions have included Greer Garson in Shaw's *Captain Brassbound's Conversion*, Jack Lemmon in *Idiot's Delight*, and Maggie Smith in *Design for Living*. The Ahmanson is Hollywood's idea of live theatre.

The other component of the Center Theatre Group is its regional theatre, the Mark Taper Forum, a 750-seat semicircular auditorium originally designed to be a lecture hall in the cultural center. The Mark Taper operation grew out of an earlier theatre in the Los Angeles area, the Theatre Group at UCLA. It had begun in the late 1950s when actor Robert Ryan proposed to Dean Abbott Kaplan a production of *Tiger at the Gates* on a miraculously low budget of $10,000; this seemed a suitable figure to Kaplan, who plunged in. Soon he engaged as artistic director John Houseman, who had co-directed the Mercury Theatre of the 1930s with Orson Welles and who had served as the artistic director of the American Shakespeare Festival and as the producer of the films *Julius Caesar* and *Lust for Life*. Recognizing that a classical theatre could not compete economically with movies and television for talent, the Theatre Group engaged actors for single productions and limited runs, thus providing the opportunity for them to work briefly "live," as so many actors performing only electronically yearn to do. The Theatre Group continued steadily for seven years, producing plays with known actors but no star billing and paying minimum Equity salaries. The most popular play in the period was *King Lear*, featuring Morris Carnovsky, which played to 99 percent of capacity on the UCLA campus in 1964. For that production, young Gordon Davidson, who had worked with Houseman at the American Shakespeare Festival, joined him as the assistant director and stayed on to replace him. Under Davidson's leadership, the Group took on a decidedly more adventurous look. Its production of *The Deputy* toured the country, and its production of the Lillian Hellman and Leonard

Bernstein operetta *Candide* helped to reestablish that work's prestige after an overblown and heavy-handed original Broadway production staged by Tyrone Guthrie.

In 1966, Davidson was invited to move his theatre to the new Music Center in Los Angeles. Although somewhat leery of the travertine propriety of the new situation, Davidson accepted the challenge. Continuing the non-star policy in a star-mad city, he opened the Mark Taper Forum in 1967 with John Whiting's *The Devils*, a bruising, erotic play about witchcraft in medieval France. It was a compelling debut but also a harrowing one. The Los Angeles County Board of Supervisors, representing the government which owns the land on which the Center sits and not a group noted for its gentle liberalism, was up in arms over what it considered a licentious production. The whole Mark Taper experiment seemed in doubt.

Fortunately, however, Davidson stood his ground. Also, he had the support of the grande dame of Los Angeles culture, Mrs. Norman ("Buffy") Chandler, wife of the owner of the *Los Angeles Times* and the woman who had raised the money to build the Music Center. Mrs. Chandler went to bat for Davidson but in her own way: she promised the Board of Supervisors that if they desisted, she would guarantee that in the future an internal Standards Committee would judge the propriety of all Mark Taper (and other Music Center) offerings. If this looked like censorship, at least Mrs. Chandler was keeping it in the family, and she won for Davidson a stay of expulsion. Actually, Mrs. Chandler's solution has turned out to be not censorship but what Davidson calls a "shrewd and wise notion of self-policing"; anyway, the Standards Committee hardly ever meets. Davidson has been able to view the entire incident philosophically: "The reality, pressures, and responsibilities of living and working in a publicly owned facility (Los Angeles County) are enormous. Political sensitivity to the righteous wrath of taxpayer pressure is immediate and disconcerting, but freedom of artistic expression is essential to any creative endeavor and ultimately the answer to our theatre's work lies in the community's realization that we cannot be all things to all people."[13]

Having survived the initial awkward incident, Gordon Davidson has made his Mark Taper Forum a very lively and *au courant* theatre of high quality. Over 25,000 Angelenos subscribe to the seasons of plays, which range from classics like *Uncle Vanya*, directed by Harold Clurman, and *The Miser*, starring Hume Cronyn and directed by Douglas Campbell (a transplant from the Guthrie success), to new plays like *In the Matter of J. Robert Oppenheimer* and *The Trial of the Catonsville Nine*, both of which Davidson later restaged to acclaim in New York.

The production of new plays is what gives the Mark Taper Forum its special flavor, and Davidson has said that new work is the "thrust and force" of his theatre. The crucible for this new work has been a series called New Theatre for Now, supported so far by a half-million dollars from the Rockefeller Foundation. Because the theatre is in the movie and television capital of the country, it can attract a large group of writers eager to experiment as they cannot by day at their office typewriters or in story conferences. In the first two years of New Theatre for Now, twenty-six playwrights were represented; and over the years, it has produced new plays by Paul Zindel, Jules Feiffer, John Guare, Megan Terry, Jean-Claude van Itallie, Lanford Wilson, and other innovative writers. In fact, *The Trial of the Catonsville Nine* started in the New Theatre for Now and later moved to the main stage of the Mark Taper Forum. The work of Davidson and director Edward Parone in the new play series won the Margo Jones Award for the Mark Taper Forum in 1970.

Gordon Davidson can afford to concentrate on new plays at the Mark Taper Forum partly because he is next door to the Ahmanson Theatre in the Music Center. Because the Ahmanson is offering more conventional fare and so is satisfying a public need, Davidson is free to experiment and to attract new audiences. One weekend in Los Angeles during the first year of the Mark Taper Forum provided for me a striking experience in audience-watching, showing how varied fare can attract varied patronage. On Saturday night, I saw *More Stately Mansions* at the Ahmanson, among many rat's-nest hairdos, beaded gowns, and sling-back shoes. On Sunday, I saw Durrenmatt's *The Marriage of Mr. Mississippi* in a major production at the Mark Taper Forum, among a healthy smattering of pageboy hairdos, madras dresses, and sensible shoes. On Monday, I saw three short new plays in the New Theatre for Now program at the Taper, in the midst of a grab bag of straight hair, pants, and sandals. There was not much overlapping of audiences, but there was clearly an extensive spread.

In keeping with the variety in his audiences, there is variety in Gordon Davidson's mind. He is constantly experimenting with new concepts and techniques, some of them admirably simple and modest for so gargantuan and extravagant a city. Recently he leased the basement of the Pilgrimage Theatre near the Hollywood Bowl, where he mounts experimental plays with no pay for the actors and no admission charge for the audiences. Another program sends actors out into area schools to read and discuss poetry with students. In a somewhat more formal vein, he has instituted an Improvisational Theatre Project which, like Arena Stage's Living Stage, takes performances out directly into the communities of Los Angeles. Of all oak tree theatres now operating, the Mark Taper Forum probably stands the best chance of expanding its own purposes and horizons. This is partly because of its location in fast-moving Los Angeles, which more and more assumes its supremacy among American cities and which Davidson calls "the one other city in the United States [outside New York] where one can have a substantial company doing a certain body of work,"[14] but it is mostly because of Gordon Davidson, who is smart, ambitious, and talented—a man going far. (He will appear again at a later point in this account.)

In October of 1968, a new theatre opened which was to become a parody of the oak tree genre: the Atlanta Repertory Theatre.

The Atlanta Memorial Cultural Center, built at a cost of more than $13,000,000 (modest by current standards) was a memorial to the victims of an Air France crash in 1962 which claimed the lives of many prominent Atlantans visiting Paris on an art tour. Heavily financed by Coca-Cola money, the Center was designed to be proof of Atlanta's growing importance as the economic, educational, social, and cultural focus of the Southeast. The Atlanta Symphony, under the baton of Robert Shaw (of Chorale fame), moved into the Center. To accommodate opera, ballet, and drama, the Center fathers created an umbrella organization called the Atlanta Municipal Theatre. The AMT was to present all three forms, plus plays for children, in its 868-seat auditorium. The name of the Atlanta Municipal Theatre was an old one; there had long been an amateur group in the city using the name. An entrepreneur, Christopher Manos, was hired to manage the new Municipal Theatre operation when it moved into the Center. For the Atlanta Repertory Theatre, Michael Howard, a director and acting teacher from New York, was hired to be the artistic director.

Howard had a grandiose idea: to open the Center theatre with the repertory, opera, and ballet companies all appearing at once on the same stage in a gigantic debut. He chose for the occasion John Dryden's masque *King Arthur*, never before performed in this country (or at least never before noticed). Howard's idea was certainly large enough for the opening of a major cultural center, but it cost half a million dollars in itself and was a fiasco. Also, the promoters of the theatre, opera, and ballet companies had all foolishly sold subscriptions to all three companies' seasons without compensating for the fact that *King Arthur* was the first production of all three. Atlantans who had subscribed to all three art forms ended up with three times as many tickets as they needed for the first production!

The most serious problem, however, was that the Atlanta Cultural Center quickly found itself impaled on the curse of nearly all cultural centers: it had spent all its money on bricks and mortar and had put aside no money to support the work of its constituents. In the face of a disastrous debut, the Atlanta Repertory Theatre had no back-up reserves. Within weeks of its gala opening, the Repertory Theatre was being strangled by its own poverty and lack of competent planning. Christopher Manos removed himself from the scene. The Repertory Theatre limped along for several more months. June Havoc came to Atlanta to stage a new production of her Broadway play *Marathon 33* for the theatre. Still, by the beginning of 1969, the Atlanta Repertory Theatre was a shambles. It closed.

In the middle of the spring, however, the Atlanta Arts Alliance, the parent organization of the cultural center, regrouped its forces for another try. The Municipal Theatre dropped the idea of an opera company but managed to salvage the ballet and repertory components. Michael Howard was retained as the artistic director of the latter; he mounted four productions in the spring—*You Can't Take It with You*, *Twelfth Night*, *The Little Foxes*, and *Major Barbara*. For the 1969–70 season, the Alliance gamely decided to continue. David Bishop was engaged to manage the repertory organization, and its name was changed to the Alliance Theatre. Michael Howard planned a standard season of plays, including *The Threepenny Opera*, *Much Ado about Nothing*, *Charley's Aunt*, and *The Devil's Disciple*—all very safe plays. Nevertheless, the season brought a loss of a quarter of a million dollars, and Howard left at its end (and joined the faculty of the Yale School of Drama). Starting in 1970–71, the Alliance seasons were cut from twenty-eight weeks to seventeen, with each play running two weeks instead of four. With such short runs, the theatre was destined to be more a stock company than a repertory theatre.

Because Atlanta really *is* a fast-moving and fast-growing city, it should be a good setting for professional theatre, and the otherwise barren Southeast needs such a resource. It is still too early to know whether the Alliance Theatre will serve the function, but the beginning has been hardly auspicious or encouraging.

With the possible exception of Gordon Davidson's Mark Taper Forum, no oak tree theatre following the Guthrie came near to challenging its eminent position in the field; the Guthrie was still "granddaddy," although it was a patriarch with growing pains of its own. The other oak tree theatres had even more shaky early years, and their problems flowed from their origins. They had been willed into being by community leaders rather than being forged by individual artists; while this meant that they were more readily supported financially, it also meant that for them an individual identity was more elusive. They were official, formal, institutional—and much less personal.

The regional theatre had revised the scenario and had introduced some stars into the cast. It had broadened its scope, and it had become much more visible. It had gained an insight into what a National Theatre might look like and be. As a result, the revolution was turning in a new direction. The detour had begun.

6 Saplings: Small Theatres of the 1960s

"The 'acorn' theory is still with us. . . . Its ideologues
want everyone to go through the agonies of their own
slow growth and fail to recognize that the process invites
speed-up, variation, and large scale application."

Theodore Hoffman, The Drama Review

With the legitimatizing of the regional theatre form by the entry of
philanthropy and the opening of the Guthrie, and with the presumed
cultural explosion to justify the need for theatres and to make communities feel guilty if they did not have them, there was a near rash of
new regional theatres during the 1960s. Because of the change in the
climate, communities were more receptive to attempts to start theatres
(though not necessarily more willing to support them financially once
they had begun), and there came to be a new breed of theatre leaders
who, while young, were surprisingly adept at putting together the necessary pieces. Unlike the leaders of the early acorn theatres, these new
leaders usually recognized and appreciated the need to involve members of the community's power structure and did so as much as possible
from the beginning. They were far more sophisticated in their use of
advertising techniques to gain an audience, particularly an audience
of subscribers, and they were far more aware of the potential of national
attention to benefit their theatres at home. In short, because the acorns
had paved the way and had defined the rules and because the Guthrie
and other oak trees had brought attention to the situation, the new

leaders were able to skip over the first tentative steps and start their theatres in a stage of middle development. To complete the image, I shall call these new theatres of the 1960s "saplings"—little oak trees.

Like the differences between the acorn theatres and the oak tree theatres, the distinctions between the saplings and the other two kinds of theatres were both institutional and personal. Institutionally, the new saplings stood between the other two kinds; they were started by people as unknown and untested as those who began the acorns, but their anonymity no longer required them to start at the very bottom, and they could rally to their purpose more civic power—sometimes as much as the oak tree theatres enjoyed. The creation of a sapling theatre was accomplished far more facilely than that of the tenuous acorn and sometimes as dispassionately as that of the oak tree. The new theatres were usually started by people coming in from the outside, sometimes after studying many communities from afar and "choosing" one as the Guthrie trio had "chosen" Minneapolis. Indeed, if the new breed of leaders had been older and better known men, they would have created oak tree theatres; had they been lucky enough to be English knights, they too would have answered the call of colonialism. Except in size, the new sapling theatres were institutionally more like oak trees than like acorns.

On the personal level, the new saplings were more like acorns in the anonymity of their leaders, but the similarity stops at that. The creators of the early acorns were people in their twenties during the 1950s. They remembered World War II vividly, and some had fought in it; they remembered the hardships of the Great Depression; and they were living in an era of prosperity, calm, and faith in institutions. Indeed, the acorn leaders were of a time when everyone accepted the rules and tried to follow them to get ahead. The creators of the sapling theatres were people in their twenties during the 1960s. Although they remembered no world war and no depression and had known only affluence, they were living—particularly after November 22, 1963—in an era of despair, violence, and lack of faith in institutions, a time when the rules were breaking down and the way to get ahead seemed to be to break the few left and make new private rules for oneself. There appeared to be no reason to suffer the rigors which, for earlier leaders, were their only chance. The lesser capacity for commitment in the new generation of leaders bred a recalcitrance in them which threatened many a sapling theatre in its first years. More significantly, this restive-ness was fanned by a new and different attitude toward the central theatre of Broadway, an attitude which reflected the mobility and impermanence of the 1960s. The acorn leaders had banished Broad-way abstractly, philosophically, without ever having experienced it. The oak tree leaders, particularly the Guthrie trio, had banished Broadway specifically and personally after having mastered it. The leaders of the new saplings, however, were not yet ready to banish any-thing. They were keeping their options open, and they were leaving Broadway among those options. The end-over-end life of the 1960s seemed to demand and merit that.

The Long Wharf Theatre in New Haven, Connecticut, is perhaps the most complete example of the sapling approach. It was started in 1965 by two young Yale graduates—Jon Jory, son of actor Victor Jory and an alumnus of the Yale School of Drama, and Harlan Kleiman, a Brooklynite who had gained a Yale degree in both business adminis-tration and drama. Of the two, Kleiman was the more bluntly aggres-sive, and his whirlwind creation of the Long Wharf Theatre established him as the boy wonder of the regional theatre in the mid-1960s. Klei-man's methods, outlined in Julius Novick's book *Beyond Broadway*, were slick and willful: "One of Kleiman's maxims is 'Always use people to get other people.' 'Almost all the money . . . was raised by putting this one in contact with that one, pulling strings, learning where the pockets of gelt are.' They tried to find people whose energies exceeded their commitments, and commit them to work for the theatre; they tried to get in touch with the widest possible variety of social, political, economic, and ethnic groups."[1]

The Kleiman approach worked, and the Long Wharf Theatre opened in the summer of 1965 in a cinder-block produce market on the wrong side of the tracks. In New Haven, the wrong side of the tracks can be the kiss of death; but the Long Wharf was an instant success, with more than 8,000 subscribers in its 440 seats. The four-play summer season, cannily chosen for a balance of art and commercial appeal, featured *The Crucible, The Hostage, Little Mary Sunshine,* and a pair of short plays, *The Private Ear* and *The Public Eye.* Attend-ance during the summer season was nearly 100 percent of capacity, and the 1965–66 season immediately following played to 85 percent of capacity.

However, hanging over the Long Wharf from its inception was the possibility that it, too, was superimposed and that this would catch up with it. This happened, and even sooner than might have been expected. In 1966, critic and teacher Robert Brustein came to the Yale School of Drama as dean, and he set about the difficult task of waking up the school. One of his means was a professional repertory company in residence at the school, about a mile from the Long Wharf. And the Yale School of Drama, asleep or awake, is on the right side of the tracks in New Haven. Soon, the Long Wharf and Brustein's Yale Repertory Theatre were on a seesaw in seeking audiences and attention in a city surfeited with theatre (the Shubert Theatre in New Haven had long been known as "the birthplace of the nation's greatest hits" because of the large number of plays it housed on their way to Broadway). In competing with Yale, the Long Wharf had no major financial resources on its side, and the theatre was in constant economic crisis. During the 1966–67 season, when attendance at the Long Wharf dropped to about two-thirds of capacity, the leaders were forced to mount a "Save the Theatre" drive to raise the $90,000 needed to forestall bankruptcy. In the middle of this crisis, there surfaced in the New Haven press an announcement that Yale was interested in absorbing the Long Wharf. Working quickly, the Long Wharf leaders stirred up enough public dismay and support to convince the board of directors to turn down the university's offer. Money was raised and the crisis passed, but it took its toll on individuals. Disaffected, Jon Jory left the Long Wharf— "because of a policy disagreement with the corporation"[2]—and pursued a peripatetic career as a guest director in other regional theatres. At the end of the 1966–67 season, Kleiman also departed. It was natural that Kleiman would leave; his large ambitions could not be satisfied in the small New Haven situation. Moving to New York, he began to produce in the commercial (off-Broadway) theatre.

The Long Wharf board of directors needed to replace the theatre directors, and particularly artistic director Jory, quickly, but the financial weakness of the theatre did not allow it to secure a prestigious new artistic director. Therefore, the board chose someone "in-house"—Arvin Brown, who had been Jory's assistant and who had directed Long Wharf productions of *The Three Sisters*, *Misalliance*, and *Long Day's*

91

Journey into Night (the last featuring Mildred Dunnock). Ironically, the choice by default ended up saving the Long Wharf, for in Arvin Brown the theatre had a truly rare find. Brown's credentials were impeccable. He had attended both Stanford and Yale and had worked on a Fulbright with the Bristol Old Vic in England. He was quiet, meticulous, and highly talented. In a telephone interview when appointed, he said, "I have a strong concept of what our theatre's role is in the community. I think it lies in the continuing development of a small acting company whose abilities will be constantly challenged and expanded."[3]

The Long Wharf's location less than a hundred miles from New York helped Brown in building a company of top-rate actors who did not need to divorce themselves from the central theatre in order to work in New Haven; it also helped him to attract better known actors for occasional work—not only Mildred Dunnock but also Morris Carnovsky, Teresa Wright, and Stacy Keach, who first played his highly acclaimed Hamlet on the Long Wharf stage under Brown's direction. The strategic location was also helpful in bringing attention to the numerous premieres on which Brown concentrated much of his creative energy. In 1968, he staged the American premiere of Thomas Murphy's play *A Whistle in the Dark* at the Long Wharf, and a year later he repeated his success with the same play off-Broadway. In 1970, he garnered new acclaim for his theatre and himself with the American premiere of Gorky's *Country People* in New Haven, and in 1971 he staged the premiere of Robert Anderson's *Solitaire Double Solitaire*. This last production and *You Can't Take It with You* were offered by the Long Wharf at the Edinburgh Festival in 1971; when the company returned to America, the Kaufman-Hart play opened the Long Wharf's 1971–72 season, and the Anderson play went to Broadway with Brown again directing. The 1972–73 season boasted two American premieres of English plays: David Storey's *The Changing Room* and *Forget-Me-Not Lane* by Peter Nichols, author of *Joe Egg*. Five years after Brown's appointment, one could look back on the Long Wharf's progress and note that the development he had called for had been the theatre's primary thrust. Brown knew what he did best; he knew what the theatre and New Haven could and would support; and he had the ability to realize his concept. What was originally the wrong side of the tracks has become the place to be, theatrically, in New Haven; New Haveners cross the tracks to keep in touch with Arvin Brown's work. His theatre is one of the few sapling theatres in which one person has made almost all the difference.

Forty miles north of New Haven, the Hartford Stage Company is another theatre created by an outsider (though with neither the flair nor the chutzpah that characterized the Long Wharf). The Hartford Stage Company was the brainchild of Jacques Cartier, a Californian. After graduating from the Yale School of Drama and while teaching at Smith College, Cartier systematically studied a half-dozen American cities as possible sites for a professional regional theatre. Demographically, Hartford looked as good as any other city, and so he set out to create his theatre there. He raised more than $100,000 privately (a healthy portion of it coming from the insurance magnates for which Hartford is famous). He found an abandoned supermarket in downtown Hartford, had it converted to a 225-seat theatre with a thrust stage, and opened in the spring of 1964. The repertoire was very traditional: *Othello, The Country Wife, The Importance of Being Earnest,* and other classics. Because the company included fellow Yale alumnus Paul Weidner, a director who favored more stylized plays, the repertoire was also heavy in works like Goldoni's *Servant of Two Masters* and the Molière canon.

From the start, the most severe problem of the Hartford Stage Company was the smallness of its theatre—those 225 seats. Soon the theatre was selling virtually all of them, largely on its growing subscription rolls; but the small number of seats meant that it was doomed to constant deficits, at times approaching one-third of the season's budget. In 1968, this squeeze as much as anything else led to Cartier's departure to other, unspecified pursuits. He was replaced by Weidner, who broadened his own range to accommodate a more eclectic repertoire and who, with the help of manager William Stewart, was able to continue to build the institution despite its too-small auditorium. By the 1971–72 season (which included the theatre's most popular play, *Long Day's Journey into Night*), the theatre had to turn away up to 10,000 patrons who could not get seats. The total attendance had increased from 32,000 in 1964 to 56,000 and clearly would have been much greater if the theatre had been able to accommodate all who wanted to attend. Obviously, the time had come for a larger facility. The Stage Company named controversial Philadelphia architect Robert Venturi to design a new theatre, and it set out to raise $2,000,000. At that price, the new theatre would have to be bare-boned and simple, but it would have 350 seats at the start and the potential to be expanded to 500 at a later date when further growth required it. The new facility is scheduled to be ready late in 1974. The company will enter the new theatre in a significantly more healthy financial position, having erased its debts in 1972 with the help of a major Ford Foundation grant.

Under both Jacques Cartier and Paul Weidner, the Hartford Stage Company has maintained a steady, low profile. It is there, it is growing, and it is serving the community; the community is supporting it in return. As Paul Weidner says, "The fact that we have existed for nine years and haven't gone under has surprised a lot of people in Hartford."[4] And perhaps a lot of people in the theatre itself.

In Springfield, Massachusetts, Stage/West is the youngest regional theatre in New England. It opened in 1967 on the grounds of the Eastern States Exposition, the largest fair in New England; it is housed in an exhibition hall there, with 400 seats purchased from the old Metropolitan Opera House in New York. (Each September, the company must dismantle its theatre and other equipment to make way for troops of young boys and girls who use Stage/West's building as a dormitory while exhibiting their wares at the Exposition.) Like the Long Wharf and the Hartford Stage Company, Stage/West was created by an outsider working with local forces—in this case Stephen Hays, who received his training at the Cleveland Play House. Hays, however, is perhaps the mildest of sapling theatre creators who came in from outside, and his approach to managing and sustaining Stage/West has been gentle.

In the first season, Stage/West also had an artistic director, a Guthrie-sized giant named James Cromwell. He was apparently too large (and too progressive) for Springfield, which, while the same size as New Haven and Hartford, is a city without any major industry like insurance, any famous educational institution like Yale, or any clearly identifiable urban point of view. Discouraged by the narrowness of the city, Cromwell left after only one season, and Hays, as the producing director, continued briefly by himself before being joined by John Ulmer as the artistic director.

Even with early budgets as low as $150,000 a year, Stage/West has

94

faced regular financial peril, and yet there have never been obvious crises being blabbered around town. This is probably because the quiet leadership of the theatre complements the modesty of the town. Whereas a personality like Harlan Kleiman's promoted expectations difficult to fulfill, Hays's quieter personality has allowed him to anticipate problems. Stage/West is a theatre with a very low threshold, and, knowing its place, it may outlast many other more ambitious companies. It is a good example of a theatre and its community matching each other.

Although it began in 1963, Center Stage in Baltimore was consciously modeled on Arena Stage in Washington—even to the point of starting as a profit-making corporation because Arena Stage had, although the Washington theatre had long since turned nonprofit. (Arena Stage's executive director Thomas Fichandler regularly traveled back and forth between Washington and Baltimore, advising the Center Stage beginners.) It was housed first in a former gymnasium, then in a former cafeteria with 350 seats.

Like other sapling theatres, Center Stage had its early tribulations in leadership. The original leader, Edward J. Golden, was soon replaced by William Bushnell, who had been trained at the American Shakespeare Festival. The artistic director was Douglas Seale, a diminutive Englishman known for his productions of the Shakespeare history plays and a veteran of Shakespearean festivals in Connecticut and in Canada and England. Under Bushnell and Seale, the theatre moved along at a fairly even but hardly striking pace. Then in the fall of 1966, Bushnell suddenly left to take a similar position with another regional theatre, the American Conservatory Theatre in San Francisco. To replace him, Center Stage hired Peter Culman, an alumnus of both Williams College and the Barter Theatre. There really was not room in so small a situation for two strong personalities, and within a year of Culman's arrival, Seale left Baltimore. Culman, in charge by himself, instituted a policy of bringing in creative talents for individual productions and not maintaining any continuity of personnel. While this policy tended to make a consistent artistic viewpoint impossible, it did allow Culman to screen various artists and decide with whom he wanted to work regularly. Finally he chose an artistic director: John Stix, a man with considerable Broadway and off-Broadway experience not only in staging plays but also in coaching actors and a mainstay of the Actors' Studio. As described by Culman in 1971, the changes in the structure of the Center Stage company had been pendulumlike: "Five years ago we had a company with very few guest actors; we then went to the point where we brought in practically nothing but guest actors; and we now have nothing but a resident company with one or two guest actors. . . . Given John's commuting between here and New York, we have evolved a very successful situation wherein we get the best of both worlds; that is, we are able to continue to develop and nourish a company down here, and we are in a position to not only bring in guest actors, but also guest directors and designers who can draw upon the talents of the company."[5]

Culman and Stix have complemented each other better than Culman and Seale did, and their alliance appears to be a healthy arrangement for Center Stage. In recent years, touring has become a major aspect of the theatre's program; the Maryland State Arts Council and a local bank have helped to pay for the theatre to take productions throughout the state. In 1972, the theatre offered the first professional all-black production of *Death of a Salesman*, and two Center Stage productions, *Slow Dance on the Killing Ground* and the musical *Park*, were transferred from Baltimore to the New York stage in 1970. The theatre also survived some official public outrage occasioned by its mounting of *The Trial of the Catonsville Nine*, a liberal play in which the subject was too close for comfort (Catonsville is a suburb of Baltimore).

Again like other sapling theatres, Center Stage has suffered economically from its own rapid development. As explained by the president of the theatre's board, "One of the Theatre's somewhat paradoxical problems in the past was that it grew too rapidly."[6] In its first five years, its audience increased fourfold, its budget tenfold, and its income gap nearly fortyfold! The severity of the financial situation reached its peak in mid-1969, when serious consideration was given to closing the theatre because of a large accumulated deficit. However, the community leaders involved in the theatre held fast, and the staff trimmed $100,000 from the 1969–70 budget, even achieving a small surplus at the end of that season. By 1972, the theatre was much closer to being on an even keel. Like the Hartford Stage Company, it was helped to solvency by a major Ford Foundation grant.

96

Again like the Hartford Stage Company, Center Stage is one of the quieter sapling theatres. It maintains a low profile nationally, but it commands steady respect and loyalty locally. It has lasted long enough to have become an assured institution in Baltimore; like all regional theatres, perhaps its greatest achievement has been its own survival.

Of the new theatres which came into being during the 1960s, two on the East Coast were outside the sapling genre and were more like late-coming acorns. They were the Washington Theatre Club and the Theatre Company of Boston, and both of them were mavericks.

The Washington Theatre Club was started in 1960 by a husband-wife team, John and Hazel Wentworth, who not only produced plays but also conducted a theatre school on the Club premises. Actually, "Club" is a misnomer that was necessary because District zoning laws prohibited a theatre in the residential neighborhood of northwest Washington where the group found quarters in a former coach house and stable. In its early days, the Club moved back and forth among amateur, semiprofessional, and fully professional standings, depending on the project of the moment; it was the strongest of several groups in orbit around the larger Arena Stage.

In 1966, the Club became permanently professional with the introduction of a new director, Davey Marlin-Jones, who had had experience in summer stock and with the Equity Library Theatre in New York. While continuing the acting school with Mrs. Wentworth, Marlin-Jones also set out, in his new position, to find a point of view for the Club's producing branch. Naturally, any approach had to take into account the reputation, influence, and audience of the larger and richer Arena Stage across town. As Marlin-Jones himself later pointed out: "They have created an appetite for the theatre. Secondly, because of the size of Arena there are things they can automatically do better than anybody and things that are prohibitive because of their size. That automatically opened up opportunities for us."[7] In short, by the middle of the 1960s Arena Stage had become so large that it could not always act with the dispatch or with the freedom it had enjoyed in earlier, poorer days. That left a gap which the Washington Theatre Club could move in to fill. Marlin-Jones began to concentrate on the production of new plays and on the resurrection of plays which had been admired but which had failed to find an audience in New York (as

Arena Stage had done in its early years). The few seats—145 in the coach house theatre—limited the potential income of the Club, and so Marlin-Jones was obliged to find plays using few actors and making only modest demands in physical production. This restriction actually helped in encouraging a specific point of view and a cohesive acting style within the company.

Marlin-Jones did find the right plays for his situation: resurrections of plays like *My Sweet Charlie* and productions of new plays like Lanford Wilson's *The Gingham Dog* (which later went to Broadway). Soon, the Club was receiving up to a thousand scripts a year from new playwrights and from agents wanting to see old plays resurrected. When asked how the Club was contributing to the American theatre in general, Marlin-Jones pointed out that "The biggest thing we've done is to launch 75 writers in the Washington area [who] were never heard of."[8] By 1969, his reputation for finding and propelling new work was so well established that he received the Margo Jones Award—three years before it came to Zelda Fichandler across town.

Also by 1969, the Club had outgrown its cramped coach house quarters. A newly activated board of directors committed the Club's resources to a $100,000 renovation of a former church into a 360-seat theatre, nearly three times as large as the coach house (which was maintained as a place for more experimental work). In its new theatre, the Club became involved in all kinds of ancillary activities—chamber music and jazz, special productions of new plays for children, public readings of new scripts, and even an art gallery—all of which broadened the institution but also made it larger and possibly more unwieldy. It was in 1969, too, that the Club received a quarter of a million dollars from the Ford Foundation. By the time that Davey Marlin-Jones left his post in 1972 (and was succeeded by New York director Stephen Aaron), the Washington Theatre Club had become official; it was in no one else's orbit any longer.* In fact, it has moved so fast that some other group will have to fill the maverick role in Washington now.

The evolution of the Theatre Company of Boston from maverick to official status has been less clear and steady than that of the Washing-

---

* The greatly increased program of the Club has created economic woes, too; at this writing, the Club is facing a severe financial crisis, aggravated by the dearth of local sources of support that has also plagued Arena Stage.

ton Theatre Club, and part of the reason may well be that the Charles Playhouse was less of a fortress to storm than was Arena Stage. However, it may be due even more to the fact that the Theatre Company has been less interested in official status and acceptance and more satisfied with its maverick status in and of itself. In this sense, the Theatre Company of Boston is a descendant of The Actor's Workshop.

Of all the new theatres of the 1960s, the Theatre Company had beginnings most like those of the acorn theatres, particularly in its inability to attract civic power to its cause (or its disinterest in doing so). It was the brainchild of David Wheeler, a Harvard graduate and professor at Boston University; its first home in 1963 was a 95-seat room in the dismal Hotel Bostonian. In that year, the Theatre Company presented the first of what became many American premieres—Ann Jellicoe's English comedy *The Knack* (which later became a Mike Nichols New York success and a film). In 1964, John Arden's *Live Like Pigs* was premiered and subsequently had a four-month run off-Broadway. These early attempts earned for the Theatre Company a reputation for adventurousness. In 1965, the group moved to slightly larger quarters in the Hotel Touraine, its second fleabag downtown hotel. Among the actors in the group was Dustin Hoffman, then relatively unknown, who played (among other roles) Nicholas in Chekhov's *A Country Scandal* and Ben in Pinter's *The Dumbwaiter*.

The emphasis on new plays continued; while these works attracted only tiny audiences, the Theatre Company proceeded doggedly. Modest recognition came in 1966 with a $14,000 grant from the Rockefeller Foundation for a Festival of New American Plays. Between 1967 and 1969, the group offered the first American showings of Arden's *Left-Handed Liberty*, Jean-Paul Sartre's *The Devil and the Good Lord*, Robert Lowell's *Phaedra*, and a double bill of Pinter's *The Dwarfs* and *The Local Stigmatic* by Heathcote Williams (which also moved to an off-Broadway run). The Rockefeller Foundation renewed its grant for new plays, and the University of Rhode Island gave the group a contract to be artists in residence on its campus in the summers of 1966 and 1967. In 1967, the Theatre Company finally moved to a space it could call its own, an old 400-seat movie theatre in Back Bay. It was home, but the group could not afford to heat it and so for two seasons had to close down during the midwinter months.

As a maverick operation in conservative Boston, the Theatre Company hung by a slender thread; it had an even harder time making ends meet than did the Charles Playhouse with its more familiar repertoire and more comfortable location. But the Company, like The Actor's Workshop before it, was more determinedly tenacious than the Charles and more its own master. Like Jules Irving and Herbert Blau in San Francisco, David Wheeler drew around him literary figures including Harvard's Geoffrey Bush and William Alfred (author of *Hogan's Goat*) and novelist John Hawkes, who had served an apprenticeship as a playwright with The Actor's Workshop in 1964. Again like Irving and Blau, Wheeler involved those people who would support his own efforts, and this meant (just as it had at the Workshop) that his board of directors was committed to his work but unable to raise the necessary funds to support the effort. The Theatre Company never developed a power base in Boston, partly because of its outré approach but mostly because Wheeler, like Irving and Blau, was more interested in pursuing his own work than in achieving permanence for his theatre.

In 1968, when Michael Murray left the Charles, there were rumblings in Boston about a possible merger of the two theatres, but a structure could not be fashioned, and the pairing did not go through. The Charles collapsed, and the Theatre Company went underground. Its two managers, Frank Cassidy and Sara O'Connor, left for other work, and David Wheeler continued to carry the company on his own. It surfaced briefly in 1971 for one play at Harvard's Loeb Drama Center. Wheeler then left for a stint as associate director at The Guthrie Theater, but by 1972 he was back in Boston, producing—this time *The Basic Training of Pavlo Hummel*, featuring Al Pacino, fresh from his triumph in the film *The Godfather*. Once more, like Irving and Blau before him, David Wheeler seemed to thrive on adversity. This in itself made his Theatre Company more interesting than the sedate Charles Playhouse it complemented, counteracted, and outlasted.

Most sapling theatres of the 1960s, perhaps *because* they were based on the involvement of civic powers, quickly became institutions which reflected more the attitudes of a community than the ideas of a single individual; indeed, this is what has made them basically conservative. Of course there have been variations in this pattern—for instance, David Wheeler's Theatre Company of Boston (which was hardly a sapling, anyway). In general, however, theatres too frequently came to be controlled technically, financially, and (what is more regrettable) psychologically by the community forces which were talked into creating them. There has been less force of individual personality evident in the development of the sapling theatres than in the earlier acorns.

One exception to this rule was Cincinnati's Playhouse in the Park under the direction of Brooks Jones, who through his force of personality turned an ordinary institution into an exciting one. Jones was an anomaly in the regional theatre: he was the only new-generation leader from an upper-class background, an heir to the Jones and Laughlin steel fortune. He graduated from Princeton, where he worked at the university's McCarter Theatre. (After college and before taking over the Playhouse in the Park, he was a folksinger and guitarist in nightclubs.) Aside from Oliver Rea, he was the only regional theatre leader, to my knowledge, who did not need to work to live. While such a background is no virtue in itself and does not make a man talented, it did give to Jones a grace in the operation of his theatre which was a very potent force. It allowed him to approach his work with humor and dash, which are often lacking in other people who sometimes cannot afford them. Jones also had the advantage of coming to the Cincinnati theatre after it had started; he did not need to ask the local power structure to help him create something new, and so he was not obligated to return any favors. Coming in 1962, he was actually the third producer; the theatre had opened in 1960 in a century-old shelter house at the top of Eden Park in Cincinnati, a building transformed with $40,000 provided by a hundred local supporters.

Because of the location in the park and the modesty of the shelter house theatre, the Playhouse was one of the most friendly and casual of regional theatres, and this complemented Brooks Jones's personality. Over the years, he presented a repertoire that was eclectic and not particularly noteworthy—several American premieres of European plays, the works of Samuel Beckett followed by American farces, and almost every season *The Fantasticks*. For Jones, the spread of the repertoire was its point; coming out of Princeton through nightclubs, he liked both literature and show business. The range of talent in his company, too, varied from exciting to ordinary. In addition, the theatre always needed money and always carried large debts. (So far as I know, Jones never blacked out any debts with his own money, which was right, since such a move could have jeopardized the community's proprietary interest in the institution.) In other words, the Playhouse in the Park suffered the same problems faced by all regional theatres and had no special answers for them. Yet alone among the new young theatre leaders of the 1960s, Brooks Jones did not appear mired in his theatre's problems. Indeed, through the force of his own personality, he was able to skip along the surface of them. (He reportedly once told the Ford Foundation that he didn't want their money—and of course they obliged by not giving him any.) He was not a particularly gifted director, and he was a rather cavalier manager; but he was a *leader*, which meant that his mind was in charge, not the community's attitudes. This is what made the Playhouse in the Park one of the most enjoyable regional theatres in the country, a place it was fun to visit.

Aside from the atmosphere of the place, Brooks Jones's primary achievement while in Cincinnati was the designing of a new theatre for the Playhouse, which opened in 1968. With architect Hugh Hardy, he conceived a building which is one of the most refreshing theatres in North America because it has a sense of humor about itself. In the lobby, for instance, the ceiling is carpeted; and one wall is devoted to "graffiti" tiles signed by everyone who gave $25 or more to the building fund (including Tallulah Bankhead). The plaza outside the new theatre is illuminated by a random pattern of airport landing lights, and from that plaza the audience can look through large plate glass windows into the workrooms where scenery and costumes are made. Explaining the spare, informal approach taken in designing the theatre, architect Hardy reflected the spirit of the place: "The people themselves *are* the adornment for the theatre."[9] Significantly, the spare, informal approach also allowed the Playhouse to build its new theatre for no more than one million dollars, an extraordinarily low figure for the form and the period. Given his grace and force of personality, Brooks Jones could afford to build a new theatre for only a million dollars. He did not need a personal monument.

The problem with force of personality is twofold. First, the personality may be more interesting than the theatre around it, and second, it may foster a cult of personality. This, indeed, is what happened in Cincinnati. Within two years of the opening of the new theatre, Brooks Jones left his Playhouse, ostensibly to make films. The real reasons were no doubt more personal, and Arthur Ballet suggests one that makes sense: "The feeling in Cincinnati is that Jones used up his energy creating and moving into the new building. I suspect it would be closer to the truth that Jones had explored as much of the scene as he wanted to . . ."[10] As it turned out, Brooks Jones, being who and what he was, did not really *need* the Playhouse in the Park. His own personality was his primary creation, not the theatre; in the end, I think, the theatre got in the way of his personality, so he left.

To replace Jones, the board of the Playhouse in the Park hired Word Baker, an off-Broadway director who had staged several productions in Cincinnati. He proceeded along traditional regional theatre lines, offering the usual plays and a smattering of small musicals. The audience continued to come, and the community still supported the theatre. The carpet stayed on the ceiling and the graffiti on the walls. But the force of personality was gone. In 1972, Baker was dismissed, supposedly because he would not commit himself to Cincinnati and would not accept greater involvement in decisions by the board. Perhaps the board had grown accustomed to Brooks Jones's charisma and missed it in Baker, who could not charm or overwhelm the situation. He was replaced by Harold Scott, the first black director to be put in charge of a regional theatre. It is too soon to know what Scott's approach will be—but whatever it may be, Brooks Jones remains a hard act to follow in Cincinnati.

Three more new theatres first saw the light of day in the middle years of the 1960s. In 1964, Richard Block, a graduate of Carnegie Tech (the cradle of many regional theatre talents), went back to his home town of Louisville and started a small theatre. Block was only twenty-six at the time. Meanwhile, another man, Ewel Cornett, had founded a similar theatre in the same city. Unable to survive separately in so sparse an environment, the two soon combined, and Block emerged the leader of the new organization, the Actors Theatre of Louisville. He was lucky to find an abandoned railroad station on the banks of the Ohio River; it was scheduled for eventual demolition, but meanwhile it would serve as an uncommonly comfortable and picturesque theatre with a good deal of ambiance. There he produced plays less notable for their production values (which were low) than for their daring in a community like Louisville: *Slow Dance on the Killing Ground*, *Endgame*, and N. F. Simpson's English comedy *The Cresta*

103

Run were bold choices for a community as conservative as Louisville.

Block's company and stage work were simply not up to his sometimes ambitious repertoire. Director Pirie MacDonald, writing about his various experiences as a roving director in regional theatre, summed up the weaknesses of the Louisville group: "My worst experience was arriving at a small regional theatre several years ago in time to see the opening performance of the production preceding mine. I was to put the exact same actors into rehearsal the next day in a slender piece of English absurdist wit, *The Cresta Run*. Having seen that opening night, I made my big mistake: I didn't leave town. True, the actors had not won their Equity cards at a firehouse raffle. They were "pros" who, through specific casting to fit their individual qualities, could be effective. But as a group they were simply not up to meeting the demands of one challenging play after another."[11] No doubt Block would have hired better actors if he could have, but like many theatre directors he was caught in the bind of being able to hire, for financial reasons, only relatively inexperienced actors who could not command large salaries. Given this limitation, he was forced to work on a treadmill of mediocrity.

Either Block became discouraged or else he became too completely identified with that treadmill, for he left Louisville in 1969. (He announced that he would make films and travel in Europe; eventually he ended up operating an art gallery in New York.) In part, his departure was occasioned by disaffection with that uphill, never-ending struggle against the poverty and slow acceptance that have always threatened small regional theatres. However, I suspect that another part of the reason was probably dissatisfaction with Block on the part of the lay leaders of the Actors Theatre. Block did not have a large image either in Louisville or beyond it in the world of theatre; perhaps the board of directors of the Actors Theatre, faced with his demand for a "sabbatical," decided that with the board's five years of experience it now could reach higher and so granted him a permanent leave.

As it turned out, the board was shrewd. It hired as Block's successor Jon Jory, co-founder of the Long Wharf and then guest director at many theatres (and, ironically, one whom Block had called in the year before to help him educate his board of directors to the realities of non-profit theatre operation). Jory was much more of a showman than the somber Block, and he felt more at home with comedy and lighter entertainment; classics were rare in his first seasons, which were leavened by such old-time crowd-pleasers as *Tobacco Road, Charley's Aunt, Our Town,* and even *Angel Street.* Much more of a huckster, too, Jory plunged into original ancillary activities—for instance, the mounting of industrial shows for local corporations during the theatre's "dark" months. He also titillated the community with kooky promotion ideas like the distribution of bumper stickers boasting, "Actors Theatre does Shakespeare in the nude," and "Actors Theatre does Shaw in Yiddish." Louisville loved the lighthearted approach.

Under Jory's fast-paced direction, the Actors Theatre grew rapidly (a phenomenon I shall describe later on). Jory, who had not been right for New Haven, was exactly right for Louisville. The Actors Theatre was fortunate to last long enough to get its second, stronger wind.

Theatre Atlanta, in the capital city of Georgia, was another example of a community theatre that was turned into a professional regional one. There had been active theatre on a community level in Atlanta since the Civil War; the name Theatre Atlanta came out of a merger between the local Theatre Guild, the Atlanta Community Theatre, and the Playmakers in 1957. In 1965, the group hired a professional director, Jay Broad, who had directed a praised production of Calderón's *Life Is a Dream* off-Broadway and who had been one of the key figures in the start of Theatre St. Paul (a short-lived sapling theatre that started in the wake of the Guthrie during the 1960s). Coming from several years as the managing director of the Civic Playhouse in Fort Wayne, Indiana, Broad was a bridge between community and professional theatre. Disavowing a total and potentially unsettling sudden change to fully professional status, he hired a company of half a dozen Equity actors from New York and other regional theatres and half a dozen local amateur actors whom he made Equity by signing union contracts with them.

However, even before Broad's arrival, Theatre Atlanta had been planning a major leap forward. The tragic air crash that led to the building of the Atlanta Memorial Cultural Center had also benefited the theatre. Mrs. Frania Lee, a daughter of Texas billionaire H. L. Hunt, was paying for the construction of a gleaming new theatre to house Theatre Atlanta as a memorial to her daughter, who had been killed in the crash. The theatre building, like several others of its period, was modeled after the Guthrie, with a thrust stage similar to the Minneapolis one.

Broad opened the new 765-seat theatre in 1966 with *The Royal Hunt of the Sun*, and followed with an eclectic and crowded repertoire including *Waltz of the Toreadors, After the Fall, Member of the Wedding*, and *Macbird* (the last of which enjoyed a run of twenty-seven weeks and seemed to prove an interest in political satire among Atlantans). His production of *Caesar and Cleopatra* attracted national attention when it occasioned the unexpected (and no doubt controversial) sudden appearance of black actress Diana Sands, who substituted as the kitten of the Nile when the white actress originally cast for the role was injured just before opening night. During the 1967–68 season, Theatre Atlanta played to more than 85,000 patrons.

Part of Broad's eclectic approach was to do controversial, politically oriented plays like *Macbird*; when another original play failed to materialize for the 1968–69 season, he hastily concocted a substitute bill—*Red, White, and Maddox*. A political satire in revue form, the new show was deliberately aimed at Georgia's ax-toting governor; it was an adaptation of *The Riddle of Lester Maddox*, an unauthorized biography by *Atlanta Constitution* columnist Bruce Galphin. While a great success at the box office, *Red, White, and Maddox* was an albatross for Broad and Theatre Atlanta. Mrs. Lee, who technically owned the theatre she had donated, found the production offensive to her clearly rightist sensibilities; after long court fights, she finally succeeded in evicting the Theatre Atlanta company. Her action, of course, was met with righteous indignation from the theatre's leaders, although, as Broad later conceded, "In all fairness to her . . . we were not too prompt in our rent payments."[12]

Later in the 1968–69 season, *Red, White, and Maddox* was brought intact to Broadway by producer Edward Padula, but at home in Atlanta the theatre was dead. An attempt to revive the company in the 1969–70 season collapsed after one production—ironically, it was another production concocted by Broad. By 1970, of course, the other Atlanta theatre, which had been stillborn at the Atlanta Cultural Center, had restructured itself into the Alliance Theatre, and there was not yet room even in fast-growing Atlanta for two large and expensive theatres.

With the demise of Theatre Atlanta, director Broad turned his attention to playwriting and met with some success (his play *A Conflict of*

Interest was premiered at Arena Stage in 1972). He became known more as the man who had perpetrated *Red, White, and Maddox* than as a man who had professionalized a community theatre.

In Buffalo, the fate of still another community theatre which turned professional has been better. The Studio Theatre was a long-standing amateur group in Buffalo, with not only an ongoing production program but a school of theatre as well. However, seeing the wave of professional regional theatres emerging in other cities, the leaders of the Studio decided to turn in that direction, and in 1965 they engaged entrepreneur Neal DuBrock to handle the transition. Unlike Broad in Atlanta, who co-opted the amateur talents by unionizing them, DuBrock organized a fully professional theatre and counted on the continuing school to satisfy the touchy amateur urges. Converting a downtown nightclub into an attractive 500-seat theatre with a thrust stage, DuBrock opened the doors of the professional Studio Arena Theatre in the fall of 1965 with José Quintero's production of *A Moon for the Misbegotten*, featuring Colleen Dewhurst and James Daly. Miss Dewhurst returned to Buffalo the next year to play Regina in *The Little Foxes*, and George Grizzard opened the 1966–67 season as Cyrano de Bergerac. In general, however, in its first two seasons as a professional theatre, the Studio Arena Theatre used a resident company and resident directors. This vacillation between visiting stars and unknown resident actors must have confused the theatre's audience, which did not rally to productions that lacked name actors.

By the 1967–68 season, the Studio Arena Theatre had started to move away from the resident company idea and more and more toward the stock approach also evidenced by the Charles Playhouse under Frank Sugrue and Center Stage under Peter Culman. DuBrock proved to be a manager of considerable acumen—and also a friend of playwright Edward Albee. In the 1967–68 season, he obtained first production rights to Albee's short plays *Box* and *Quotations from Chairman Mao Tse-Tung*, which were presented in Buffalo before their New York engagement and were directed by Albee's usual director, Alan Schneider. The premiere, and the talents involved in it, brought a new local and indeed national recognition to the Studio Arena Theatre. DuBrock was onto something too good to miss. After this, he turned to the stock approach, allowing him to book Schneider again and to engage actors whose names would ring bells in Buffalo. The repertoire also changed, and *You're a Good Man, Charlie Brown, Come Blow Your Horn,* and *A Funny Thing Happened on the Way to the Forum* became typical of the Studio Arena schedule. The classics became the exception rather than the rule, even after director Warren Enters joined DuBrock as a permanent associate. Later, the theatre featured premieres of Lanford Wilson's *Lemon Sky* and a new rock opera, *The Survival of St. Joan*—both of which DuBrock subsequently co-produced in New York. Celeste Holm appeared in 1972 in a musical version of *I Remember Mama,* and the theatre co-produced *Hair* in Buffalo and raised the eyebrows of county government leaders, who threatened to cancel the theatre's appropriation for such naughtiness. In general, however, the theatre was accommodating public taste. Faced with a gray and plodding city of no particular charm, DuBrock opted for plays and personnel that would sell and so sustain his naturally expensive operation. Purists may complain, but there is no doubt that DuBrock and his theatre are giving Buffalo what it wants, if not what the purists think it may need. The purists, after all, can easily (and not too expensively) fly down to New York for more exotic fare.

The Studio Arena Theatre is an example of a "manager's theatre," similar to the Charles Playhouse and Center Stage in the late 1960s. The manager's theatre is one in which there was never an artistic director or from which the artistic director departed, leaving the managing or executive director in complete charge. It is perhaps natural that this should happen, given the fact that the manager of a regional theatre is apt to be better understood by the board of directors than is the more elusive and often more rebellious artistic director. What makes a "manager's theatre" viable is its proximity to New York. Being near the supply of theatre artists, the manager can engage actors and directors for short periods of time without permanently interrupting their commitment to New York, which still provides the most lucrative work. In most cases, the manager does not even require that productions be rehearsed in his theatre. By rehearsing in New York and then flying to the manager's city for the run of the play, actors can work in a regional theatre without losing more than four or five weeks of living and working in New York, which remains their focus.

Obviously, in a manager's theatre there is no sense of ensemble company work over any period of time and no continuity except through the manager himself, a situation which only increases his power. Lacking an ensemble and faced with the added expense of hiring better known actors and directors for single productions, the manager justifies his stock approach simply and directly—by hiring on an ad hoc basis, he can engage better actors and directors. After all, is it not likely that Colleen Dewhurst will offer a better Regina than Mary Smith, no matter how loyal Mary may be and how willing to commit herself to a whole season in, say, Buffalo?

In Buffalo, of course, the Studio Arena Theatre has not remained exclusively a manager's theatre. An artistic director was hired to work alongside the manager. But the artistic director was one able to function in the central New York scene and able to bring his associates out with him to work in the theatre for brief periods. The manager remains the key figure, and the theatre's proximity to New York allows him to play the field. A manager's theatre may be regional in location, but its gaze is always on the central city, looking to see who is free to come out next and work a month for it.

In acquiring an Equity company in 1969, the 44-year-old Goodman Theatre in Chicago joined the new professional regional theatre wave of the 1960s. The architect of the change to professional status was John Reich, the Austrian who had long been included in the inner group of regional theatre leaders first identified by the Ford Foundation's W. McNeil Lowry in 1957. Since the 1950s, Reich had headed what was essentially a training center for actors, designers, and other theatre hopefuls under the aegis of the prestigious Art Institute of Chicago. Out of the Goodman have come many notable talents, including Geraldine Page and other actors who have figured prominently in the Broadway and off-Broadway theatres.

The fact that Chicago had no professional theatre beyond the Goodman had long been an embarrassment. In fact, even Mayor Daley had formed a committee to study the need for a regional theatre during the middle of the 1960s (a committee for which Oliver Rea of The Guthrie Theater served as a consultant). But because it was far down on the list of Daley priorities, a full-fledged regional theatre never got under way in Chicago. Finally, Reich stepped in to fill the gap. He engaged two English Douglases—Campbell, late of the Guthrie, and Seale, late of Center Stage; together they set out to redress Chicago's lack by signifi-

109

cantly altering the Goodman Theatre. In making the change to a fully professional company, Reich sacrificed the close relationship that professional guest actors and students had had in the earlier days, at least when working on stage together, but he gained the quality he had sought and, most notably, a much more imaginative repertory because he no longer needed to program plays that would serve students' needs without revealing their inadequacies. With the fully professional company, the Goodman could mount more interesting fare—for example, Hochhuth's *Soldiers, The Man in the Glass Booth,* Anouilh's *Poor Bitos,* and a new play, *Assassination, 1865*—all this while the formal schooling continued much less visibly under the guidance of revered acting teacher Charles McGaw. The change to professional production had been Reich's long-sought dream; with that accomplished, he retired in 1972. Kenneth Myers, a former manager of Broadway productions, replaced him.

The Goodman Theatre has a large regular audience, and its position in the community is strengthened by its relationship to the venerable Art Institute. Whether the Goodman can qualify as a major regional theatre in big Chicago will depend, ultimately, on how major a theatre a "second city" thinks it needs.

Many of the theatres of the 1960s were created in cities along the eastern seaboard and notably in old-line cities of historical and social weight—Boston, Baltimore, Washington, and the smaller cities of Hartford and New Haven. With their cultural tradition, these cities should have been among the first to boast regional theatres (and Boston and Washington did have two early acorn theatres), but most of them were followers, coming after the initial thrust of the regional theatre revolution had been made in the Midwest, Southwest, and Far West. Because one of the key points of the revolution was decentralization, its emphasis was on the far-away; the old-line cities nearer Broadway came late into the game. Among them, Philadelphia and Providence both took up the gauntlet in the middle years of the 1960s, and their theatres are two of the most interesting of the sapling theatre period.

In Philadelphia, the Theatre of the Living Arts was established by two local women, apparently as a forum for their own talents, but even before the theatre opened it had left them behind. The board of directors, who represented primarily a "new rich" element of Philadelphia society rather than its highest level, appointed André Gregory as the artistic director. He was the bright son of a Russian-born real-estate magnate and had gained early regional theatre experience with The Actor's Workshop and as the associate director in Stuart Vaughan's first season at the Seattle Repertory Theatre. Gregory opened the theatre in January of 1965 with Brecht's *Galileo*. His company included some of the best actors in the regional theatre at that time.

Gregory himself has one of the keenest—though most faddish—minds ever applied to a regional theatre, and his short tenancy at the Theatre of the Living Arts was riddled with attention-getting controversy. His choice of plays was hardly tame (*Endgame, Poor Bitos, The Last Analysis*), and his production techniques were oriented toward shocking and even appalling an audience. *Poor Bitos* had a bare breast long before nudity was even considered possible, let alone popular, in the theatre. The climax of Gregory's tenancy and his undoing was his world premiere production of Rochelle Owens's *Beclch*, a tribal ritual about primitive life cum sexuality in Africa. Nudity and gigantic false phalli were everywhere, and while the production was genuinely exciting, the play was a bore. The board of directors of the Theatre of the Living Arts was not bored, however; the members were incensed, and within weeks Gregory was out of his post and his manager David Lunney with him. Mutually incriminating stories ran wild in the Philadelphia newspapers, with Gregory and his board accusing each other of misrepresentation, tactlessness, and worse. After Gregory left and had regained his composure, he looked back on the situation with more perspective: "The real causes of my dismissal were artistic policy, money, and communications problems, in that order. The Board and I were both working to create a theatre in Philadelphia. The difficulty was that we were trying to create two different kinds of theatre."[13]

Why Gregory was fired from his post does not need lengthy attention (and the story is already well told by Julius Novick in his survey, *Beyond Broadway*). The important fact is that in Gregory the board of the Theatre of the Living Arts had chosen one of the few potentially major talents to be involved in the creation of a sapling theatre. From the beginning Gregory had assumed that he had the requisite talent to affect things beyond his immediate situation; his talent was too large and too vaulting to be absorbed and served by a theatre just born and not ready to support his ambitions.

Shortly before their departure, Gregory and Lunney had hired as public relations director John Bos, who had worked in a similar capacity at both Arena Stage and Center Stage. When the two leaders left, Bos stepped in and picked up the pieces—which was good for the theatre, for he is a crackerjack promoter. Starting with the 1967–68 season, Bos cut back greatly on the theatre's budget and instituted a summer series of classic films to raise money. He dispensed with the idea of one artistic director and instead either booked touring productions from New York or engaged resident and guest directors under himself (thus turning the Living Arts into another manager's theatre). Having shored up the operation, he was ready by the 1969–70 season to engage young Tom Bissinger, a veteran of off-off-Broadway, as artistic director—ready, in other words, to risk his own situation.

However, Bos miscalculated in the important area of repertoire. In his first season, his choice of plays had been interesting but above all what regional theatre people call "solid"—*The Entertainer* by John Osborne, Pinter's *The Caretaker, The Importance of Being Earnest,* Anouilh's *The Rehearsal,* and a new play, *A Scaffold for Marionettes.* It was a season not unlike what André Gregory might have chosen, although Gregory would have mounted the plays more shockingly. It was a good transitional season. But then, in the next season, Bos included in the repertoire only one classic (*Six Characters in Search of an Author*), along with unfamiliar plays like Sam Shepard's *La Turista* and John Guare's *Muzeeka.* For 1969–70, the Bissinger season, Bos announced a series that included a classic so rare that it might as well have been a new play (*The Recruiting Officer*) and new plays like *Gargoyle Cartoons, Harry, Noon, and Night,* Rosalyn Drexler's *The Line of Least Existence,* and something called *Patchett and Tarses Stage a Spontaneous Demonstration.* Perhaps Bos was trying to compensate for the lack of an artistic director working as his equal. Like Frank Sugrue after Michael Murray's departure from the Charles Playhouse, he was choosing adventurous plays which could establish his own reputation as a producer. This was admirable, but his choices tended to put him out on a limb. It was both too much and not enough for Philadelphia, and the 1969–70 season was the last for the Theatre of the Living Arts, which went bankrupt. Under André Gregory, the theatre had had considerable talent but a mess of an organization. Under John Bos, the organization improved, but the work on stage dissipated and moved away from its potential audience. It was embarrassing for a city of the magnitude and distinction of Philadelphia. Natives of that city maintain that despite its traditions it has an inferiority complex, particularly in its relationship to New York. Perhaps that explains the demise of the Theatre of the Living Arts. Certainly any city that considers itself second-rate will have a hard time sustaining a theatre based on banishing the capital.

In Providence, the Trinity Square Repertory Company had early years as difficult and controversial as those of the Theatre of the Living Arts, but unlike the Philadelphia theatre, Trinity Square has managed to survive. That it has succeeded is mostly attributable to the stamina and drive of Adrian Hall, a lanky Texan who received his early experience with Margo Jones in Dallas. When Hall first came to Providence in 1964, Trinity Square was a community theatre. His leadership has propelled it through the years to a position of high rank among regional theatres.

Hall's career in New York had started in the traditional, almost storybook manner as a janitor for the blind producer Stella Holt at off-Broadway's Greenwich Mews Theatre. Soon, however, he was directing off-Broadway—O'Casey's *Red Roses for Me* and the musical *Riverwind*. With Miss Holt, he spent two months in Hawaii in 1962 on a Ford Foundation grant to investigate the potential for a professional theatre in the new state (they concluded that the idea was not yet feasible). When he left the New York scene and ventured to Providence, Hall found the move from the center a "tearing, searing" experience: "I was attracted not so much to Providence or to the situation as I was to the fact that I had to have a place where, for the next ten years, I could find myself in the theatre."[14] His commitment may have been primarily to his own development, but at least he saw the connection between that development and the theatre as an institution. While his talent was potentially as great as André Gregory's, Hall had the patience that Gregory lacked. His talent was more suited to a theatre outside New York.

Two years after Hall's arrival in Providence, the federal government provided massive funding that enabled Hall to expand the Trinity Square operation and to professionalize it fully. In 1966, as part of a three-city experiment, the new National Endowment for the Arts and

113

the United States Office of Education provided Trinity Square with $535,000 to be used for the presentation of its plays to high school students. Trinity Square called the program "Project Discovery." Starting in the 1966–67 season, which featured *St. Joan, Ah, Wilderness!, A Midsummer Night's Dream,* and *The Three Sisters,* the theatre offered each of its productions to 40,000 high school students from Rhode Island who were bused to Providence to see the plays. As in the case of the Repertory Theatre New Orleans under Stuart Vaughan (another installation of the national program), the federal government was paying for the creation of Trinity Square's productions, which the theatre could then offer to adult audiences without additional production costs to itself. The theatre jumped ahead, not only in budget (which increased nearly sixfold) but also in prestige and acceptance in Rhode Island. Trinity Square was serving youngsters, always a worthwhile purpose and good for a theatre's image. The federal funding was the most important factor in Trinity Square's emergence; as Hall says, "Project Discovery was our margin."[15]

The federal program lasted through three seasons, as it was designed to do, and then it was phased out. Unfortunately, the federal government, interested more in visible programming than in an institution's internal strengths, had not provided any funds to develop the means to sustain Trinity Square after the federal phase-out. Even more regrettably, the theatre had failed to apply any of the money it was saving on productions to such development. When the federal program ended, Trinity Square (again like the Repertory Theatre New Orleans) found itself not easily ready to go on by itself. It reverted to the precarious state in which it had existed before the federal funding but without any parallel reductions in its budgets. This was made even worse by an administrative curse which hung over Trinity Square—a different manager every year between 1964 and 1969. Adrian Hall was forced to work with a management which was constantly changing and never comparable to his own leadership on the artistic side.

Still, Hall held fast and succeeded in creating a theatre noted for the loyalty of its acting company and the consistent quality of its productions. From the beginning of his tenure, Hall had been interested in the development of new work for the stage, and in 1968 this interest gained new attention with the premiere of *Years of the Locust,* an epic treatment of the imprisonment of Oscar Wilde. The play was particularly innovative in that it was a piece created as Hall rehearsed it; he was functioning not only as a director but also as a collaborator with playwright Norman Holland. Trinity Square was invited to take *Years of the Locust* to the Edinburgh Festival in 1968, making it the first American regional theatre represented there. In Edinburgh, Hall became acquainted with the work of Polish director Jerzy Grotowski, and this was a turning point in his own development as a director and creator of new work. Returning to America, he asked poet Robert Penn Warren to dramatize his *Brother to Dragons*, which was mounted in Providence in the 1968–69 season. A new stage version of *Billy Budd* followed, and then Roland Van Zandt's *Wilson in the Promised Land*, James Schevill's *Lovecraft's Follies*, and *Son of Man and the Family*, a rock musical play about the Charles Manson incident—all co-created by Hall and a playwright. Hall had found and refined a new form of theatre that could be his, one that gave his theatre a distinctive viewpoint in the growing field of new plays. In 1971, Hall received the Margo Jones Award for his work on new literature for the stage.

For the Trinity Square Repertory Company, the question of where to present all of Hall's imaginative work was a continuing problem. The first home of the theatre was a former church which gave it its name; it was a congenial and intimate space but one far too small to sustain the theatre's total program. During the Project Discovery years, Trinity Square needed a much larger space to accommodate its sizable student audiences, so it contracted with the Rhode Island School of Design to use its large auditorium in downtown Providence. The "Rizdee" auditorium had enough seats, but it was a dull and barnlike space; Trinity Square needed a home all its own. In 1968, the theatre made what Adrian Hall has since called a "bold, silly move"[16]—it purchased the dismantled pieces of the prefabricated ANTA–Washington Square Theatre in New York, where the Repertory Theater of Lincoln Center had been temporarily housed. The pieces were crated and carted to Providence to await reassembling as Trinity Square's new home. The plan seemed a sensible one at first because it could save the theatre perhaps millions of dollars in construction costs. But a proper site could not be found, and Trinity Square eventually abandoned the project. Finally, in 1971, the theatre found a property which could be even better than the ANTA–Washington Square Theatre. The half-century-old Majestic Theatre in downtown Providence came onto the

115

market, and the board of directors purchased the building. It had been, at various times, a legitimate theatre, a vaudeville palace, and a movie theatre. Working with Eugene Lee, a genius who had designed many Trinity Square productions, Hall envisioned a free-form space with 800 seats and gutted the Majestic to create it. It was rechristened the Lederer Theatre in honor of a major donor to the project, and Trinity Square will move into its new home in the 1973–74 season.

To redo the Majestic, Trinity Square needed to raise $850,000, a sum that would have been unthinkable in the early days of the theatre but one that was fairly easily achieved now because of the rapidly growing reputation of the theatre and its artistic director. To the $850,000 goal, the board of directors added another $100,000 to match a 1971 Ford Foundation grant of $356,000, still further proof that Trinity Square had come into its own.

In 1969, Adrian Hall, still forced to wonder whether his theatre was on the right course, admitted that "We'll continue to vamp until the overture begins, I guess."[17] By 1972 the overture had concluded and his show was underway. The reason for this, I believe, is that Adrian Hall's talent has been matched by his devotion to his theatre institution—a willingness to stick with it, to see it through frequent rough going. When asked recently where he would like to be and what he would like to be doing in 1980, Hall replied, "If I'm really able to work and keep working, and if the stimuli keep coming, yes, I'd be very happy to be right here, following the star."[18] That willingness to *commit oneself*—to be not dispassionate, to dive in and go for broke—has been rare among those who created and led the sapling theatres; and those few who are still willing to do so have by far the best theatres in the group.

In joining the ranks of regional theatres, the saplings of the 1960s were coming into a situation in which the thrust toward a National Theatre was gaining ever-greater attention. Still, most saplings in their early years had not reached the artistic level where they could compete in such a race for supremacy. The contest for the National Theatre position was a rather rarefied one, with a very definite (though unwritten) ranking of the contestants. The Guthrie was at the top, although it had not staked out any inviolable claim. Also, by the middle of the 1960s, two acorn theatres—the Alley and especially Arena Stage—were rising to take places near the Guthrie in prestige. Other large theatres moved back and forth in position, particularly as their artistic leadership changed. The situation was fluid, and the race was far from decided. It was a race, informal but intense, simply to be the best. Meanwhile, another group of theatres was more consciously setting out to capture that National Theatre crown.

7 Stabs at a National Theatre

"The dream of all serious theatre people in the United States in the middle of our twentieth century is the establishment of a national theatre."

Margo Jones, Theatre-in-the-Round

The large regional theatres of the 1960s included two special kinds of theatre which, like the Guthrie, seemed to offer the possibility that a National Theatre might develop from them: the festival theatres and the nomadic theatres. The festival theatres were summertime operations outside large cities which featured strictly classical programs; the nomadic theatres operated either year-round or in the winter months, presenting a more eclectic repertoire and serving mostly major urban centers.

The American festival theatres sought to equal the standing of one of the most successful theatrical ventures in North America, the Stratford Shakespearean Festival in Ontario, which because of its superior work and international reputation posed a rigorous challenge to the American regional theatre. The Stratford Shakespearean Festival was started in 1953, in modest physical circumstances but with a grandiose idea behind it. Tom Patterson, a young newspaperman, had the original idea of creating a festival of Shakespeare's plays in his home town, which happened to have the same name as the Bard's birthplace. He enlisted the help and artistic direction of Sir Tyrone Guthrie, who

118

brought English actors Alec Guinness and Irene Worth with him to inaugurate the festival (with *Richard III* and *All's Well That Ends Well*). Lacking any significant funds and forced to overcome considerable apathy in the backwater town of Stratford, Patterson and his cohorts began their operation in a tent beside the Avon River; the only distinctive physical feature of the theatre was a unique thrust stage designed by Guthrie and his favorite designer, Tanya Moiseiwitsch (who introduced a variation of the Stratford design ten years later at the opening of The Guthrie Theater).

The first season in Stratford, spanning six weeks, attracted nearly 70,000 patrons and grossed over $200,000 (Guthrie's original budget had called for costs of $150,000). It was a truly auspicious beginning. The festival was repeated in 1954, again under the artistic direction of Guthrie. The nine-week season that year attracted nearly double the first season's attendance and grosses at the box office. James Mason joined the company and appeared as Angelo in *Measure for Measure* and in the title role of *Oedipus Rex* (which was later filmed by the company with Douglas Campbell in the leading role). Guthrie left the festival after the second season and was succeeded by another Englishman, Michael Langham, who led the company from 1955 through 1967. It was in this period that the festival firmly established itself in Canadian life and as an international institution. Actors like Christopher Plummer (notably as Hamlet, Cyrano, and Antony), Kate Reid, and John Colicos regularly appeared. Some few well-known American actors, such as Jason Robards and Julie Harris, were also seen on the Stratford stage.

Almost immediately after its inaugural season, the festival had outgrown its temporary tent theatre seating 1,500. In 1957, a new and permanent theatre, designed by Toronto architect Robert Fairfield, was opened. The building encloses the original thrust stage, seating 2,258 people wrapped around the stage. In its suitability for classical drama and in spaciousness and efficiency, the Stratford theatre in Ontario is one of the very best settings for repertory theatre on the North American continent. In 1963, the festival acquired the conventional Avon Theatre in downtown Stratford and refurbished it for secondary productions, including Gilbert and Sullivan operettas and more avantgarde Continental plays.

The acting company at Stratford is generally regarded as among the very best groupings of classical actors on the continent, too. The festival has been fortunate in keeping its actors in the company for many years; William Hutt, William Needles, and others stayed with the theatre over the years and became, if not traditional stars, great favorites with summer audiences. The company today is constantly replenished by the addition of young talents from the bilingual National Theatre School of Canada in Montreal, itself one of the finest training grounds for actors on the continent.

While the first stars at Stratford were English and later stars American, the festival's leadership has always stressed the use of mostly Canadian actors. Before the advent of the festival, Canadian actors had very few outlets—principally the Canadian Broadcasting Company and the Crest Theatre in Toronto. The festival at last provided a home for the Canadian actor. In coming to Stratford, Guthrie himself was adamant in his insistence that the company should be primarily Canadian: "The project must be demonstrably a Canadian one, carried out not merely by Canadian initiative, and Canadian finance, but by Canadian actors."[1]

Aside from its excellence in production, this "Canadian initiative" has been the most distinctive element in the Stratford Shakespearean Festival. The theatre got its start partly out of a kind of Canadian inferiority complex vis-à-vis the United States; the initial thrust was chauvinistic: "We'll show those damn Yankees that we have culture up here too." It rapidly became not just a local but a national achievement. This national pride was eloquently voiced at the laying of the cornerstone for the new Festival Theatre in 1957; Vincent Massey, Governor-General of Canada and brother of actor Raymond Massey, said in his speech of dedication, "We are marking a great moment in the story of an enterprise which began as a local effort with unbelievable ambitions. We now see it as a national achievement winning incredible success."

The Stratford Shakespearean Festival and its touring productions have become Canada's most valuable cultural asset and an important vehicle for international goodwill. The festival seasons have expanded to nearly half the year, and they attract well over 350,000 patrons from throughout Canada and the United States and from fifty foreign countries; they bring to the festival nearly $2,000,000 each season in box-office income. The festival employs 70 people year-round, and at the height of each season there are more than 650 people on the payroll. Stratford productions have been seen at the Edinburgh Festival, at the Chichester Festival in England (in a theatre modeled after the one in Ontario), on tour in Canada and the United States, and in New York. In 1967, the company traveled the entire breadth of Canada as part of the country's centennial celebration and then appeared at Expo '67 in Montreal with Christopher Plummer and Zoe Caldwell in *Antony and Cleopatra.* That year also saw the departure of Englishman Michael Langham and the passing of leadership to two Canadian directors, Jean Gascon and John Hirsch (Hirsch later left his post and Gascon continued alone).

Above all, the year 1967 saw the rechristening of the Stratford Festival: it would henceforth be known as the Stratford National Theatre of Canada. What had started in a tent in the boondocks had become a national force. For those working in the regional theatre in America, that was an awesome challenge to match.

In the United States, Shakespeare festivals of modest size developed in many different cities and small towns. In San Diego, the Old Globe Theatre, a replica of the Elizabethan playhouses, operates as a Shakespeare festival in the summer months and as a community theatre during the winter; many directors of the regional theatre got their early classical experience at the Old Globe. In Ashland, Oregon, another festival, again in a replica building, has for many years been a northwestern staple under the guidance of Angus Bowmer. During the 1950s and early 1960s, it provided numerous young actors for The Actor's Workshop in San Francisco. In the East, Shakespeare summer festivals have often been centered on university campuses—in Antioch, Ohio, and on Lake Champlain in Vermont, for example. In addition, many large cities have inaugurated free festivals in the parks for their citizens; the most famous of them, and a model for many others, has been Joseph Papp's New York Shakespeare Festival in Central Park.

Aside from the Papp effort, there is only one theatre festival of major dimensions in America—the American Shakespeare Festival in Stratford, Connecticut, which opened in 1955, two years after the Ontario festival. However, it appears doubtful that the American Shakespeare Festival was patterned after the Canadian one. For one thing, it was already well into its planning stage when the Canadian festival opened.

Secondly, judging from the conventional shape of the Connecticut stage and the theatre around it, no one planning the American venture chose to follow the dynamic staging breakthroughs of the Ontario festival. Also, the reasons for the start of the American Shakespeare Festival were far different from those for the start of the theatre in Canada. The latter was a grass-roots effort, while the former was a summer project of the American theatrical Establishment.

The American Shakespeare Festival Theatre and Academy, as it was formally called, was the brainchild of Lawrence Langner, co-director of the Theatre Guild in New York, who had "cherished the idea of a permanent, professional Shakespeare festival in the United States, 'to give Shakespeare a home in America, to keep his plays alive, and to give an opportunity to younger actors to learn classical acting, which may otherwise become a lost art in America.' "[2] Langner had the help of members of the American cultural and social elite: Roger Stevens, Lincoln Kirstein (patron of the New York City Ballet), and Joseph Verner Reed, a former diplomat and Broadway producer. Actress Katherine Cornell broke the ground for the theatre building. Originally, Langner had hoped that the festival could be located in Westport, Connecticut, where he already had the Country Playhouse for summer theatre tryouts. There was strong sentiment for placing the new theatre in Stratford, Connecticut, however, making a grand total of three Shakespeare festivals in Stratfords around the world (the third, of course, is in Stratford, England, and had been in operation for nearly a hundred years when the American Shakespeare Festival opened). Langner and his friends commissioned a million-dollar building (expensive for its time) in a park setting beside the Housatonic River. It looked like the Elizabethan theatres on the outside, but inside it featured a conventional, Broadway-style proscenium stage which tends to frustrate designers who wish to modify it to resemble the Guthrie's thrust stage.

The American Shakespeare Festival was inaugurated in the summer of 1955 with rotating performances of *Julius Caesar* and *The Tempest*, both staged by the English director Denis Carey. Then a skinny sixteen, I was one of two dozen student apprentices engaged to fill the stage for crowd scenes. Lacking any distinction whatsoever on the stage, I complemented the rest of the company. Raymond Massey played Brutus and Prospero; Jack Palance was Cassius and Caliban; Roddy McDowall was Octavius and Ariel. A young unknown actor from Canada named Christopher Plummer played Mark Antony and Ferdinand in *The Tempest*; he and another unknown, Fritz Weaver, provided the only arresting acting of the season. The productions themselves were scorned by the New York critics, and in general the first season in Connecticut was as disastrous onstage as the first season in Ontario had been extraordinary. Had the American Shakespeare Festival been started in a tent by unknown people, it would have died after that first season. Having been started in a new million-dollar building by Establishment forces, it was allowed another chance. John Houseman was called in, and Jack Landau assisted him. Together they mounted more creditable productions with more appropriate actors: *King John* with John Emery, Mildred Dunnock, and Arnold Moss; *Measure for Measure* with Moss, Nina Foch, and Norman Lloyd; and *Taming of the Shrew* with Miss Foch and Pernell Roberts. The second season was more successful artistically.

Still, the audiences were not as large as the company had hoped. In 1957, this problem was solved by the introduction of major stars, Katharine Hepburn and Alfred Drake. Drake played Iago in *Othello* and Benedick in *Much Ado about Nothing*. Miss Hepburn was Beatrice in *Much Ado* and Portia in *The Merchant of Venice* (in which she was overshadowed by the brilliant Shylock of Morris Carnovsky). Business picked up, and the American Shakespeare Festival became a summer fixture. Katharine Hepburn returned in subsequent seasons, playing Viola in *Twelfth Night* and Cleopatra to Robert Ryan's Antony. Other star performers used over the years included Jessica Tandy and Pat Hingle (in *Troilus and Cressida* and *Macbeth*), Bert Lahr (and later Cyril Ritchard) in *A Midsummer Night's Dream*, and June Havoc in *The Winter's Tale*. Lahr and Miss Havoc played their roles in national tours, as did Miss Hepburn in *Much Ado*. During the late 1950s, first under both Houseman and Landau and then under Landau alone, the festival often turned to "modernizing" Shakespeare by mounting his plays in strange periods: *Much Ado* in nineteenth-century Texas, *Troilus and Cressida* during the Civil War, *As You Like It* in a "modish rural" setting. There was no discernible reason for the changes of period, and the festival was often scorned for these forays, which seemed superimposed on the plays.

The death of Langner in 1962 brought a change in the festival's top leadership. Joseph Verner Reed took the helm; while he left day-to-day management to Berenice Weiler, a former television producer, he took strong hold of the artistic element himself. The Houseman-Landau era was over. Reed engaged Allen Fletcher as the principal director, and Fletcher turned out some creditable work, most notably the very popular *King Lear* featuring Morris Carnovsky in 1963. Joined by Douglas Seale, Fletcher also presented competent productions of the history plays. Recognizing the need for the development of an acting ensemble, the festival under Fletcher embarked on a training program for younger actors. Granted substantial funds by the Ford Foundation (as part of the 1962 largesse), the festival established a winter training institute for its own company. Out of this program came a useful supporting company.

Under Allen Fletcher, the American Shakespeare Festival was on its way to more consistent quality. When he left for Seattle, the festival entered a three-year period, 1966 through 1968, of artistic meandering. Each production carried a different director, and there was no unity of ideas behind the work. The festival was limping through another period of artistic bleakness.

In 1969, Michael Kahn, a New York director with mostly off-Broadway credits, was engaged as the artistic director—the first with that title since the days of Houseman and Landau. His debut was an anti-war *Henry V*, obviously slanted toward protest against the Vietnam conflict. Even though the approach imposed a pacifistic meaning on a martial play, it worked well theatrically; and there was clearly a new urgency and modernity at Stratford, Connecticut—not modernity in the costuming but in the artistic thinking. In subsequent seasons, Kahn followed his initial success with more good work: Moses Gunn in *Othello* and a particularly gripping production of *Mourning Becomes Electra* with Sada Thompson and Jane Alexander. In 1972, Kahn paired *Julius Caesar* and *Antony and Cleopatra*, scheduling them to be seen in sequence, and found new approbation from the critics. The days of embarrassingly bad productions were over, and Kahn was holding fast: "I don't think I'm doing genius work up here, but it's better than it has been. At least we're not getting dumped on. I'm trying to make it into the best regional theater."[3]

Whether work at less than the genius level will be good enough, only time can tell. Certainly the American Shakespeare Festival has become a major regional theatre installation; its audiences each summer nearly equal those of the Ontario festival, although the performances utilize a single theatre only two-thirds as large. It is a very official theatre; its structure, the Establishment look of its board, and the very name "American" give it the air of being sanctioned by the appropriate powers. It is the national home for Shakespeare in America; while that is too limited a focus for a National Theatre, it does assure a permanent place in the upper echelons of American cultural life.

Through the 1940s and 1950s, the American National Theatre and Academy was the custodian of the dream of a National Theatre in the United States. It made periodic generalized statements about the urgent need for a National Theatre and published each statement in *Theatre Arts*, the voice of the theatrical Establishment. In 1945, ANTA executive director Robert Breen and the Barter Theatre's Robert Porterfield collaborated on a National Theatre plan oriented to the identification of new priorities for the postwar era. They asked, "Why hasn't the United States a National Theatre?"—and answered their own question: "Because the basic factors have never been taken into full account in efforts to formulate a national theatre: 1. Our country is too large to have a national theatre represented by one 'shrine' or building, or even ten. Most plans submitted have been patterned after European types. 2. America's traditional spirit of individual enterprise makes it mandatory that individual initiative work out different types of theatre companies to meet the needs in diverse sections of the country."[4]

Breen and Porterfield suggested that the overall purpose of their proposal was "to take the very best of professional theatre to sections that would not ordinarily receive it, at prices which the person of average means can afford." They listed six secondary purposes: "1. To institute a producing company in a locality or territory where the need for theatre is felt and not met. 2. To enable a producing unit to enlarge its sphere of operating by touring, either locally or nationally. 3. To enable an existing company to raise its standards in personnel and play material. 4. To put an existing company in a position to become self-supporting if it needs money to do so. 5. To produce a play which is deemed to be of high calibre and a real contribution, but not likely to receive production under ordinary conditions. 6. To stimulate and assist the assembling of the best in the American theatre to tour foreign countries."[5] In its emphasis upon central support of regional companies, the Breen-Porterfield scheme would have been consistent with the postwar thrust of the earliest regional theatres, but the new generation of leaders starting to create their own theatres did not pick up so general a challenge, for their needs were more literal and more personal. The Breen-Porterfield proposal never went beyond the pages of *Theatre Arts.*

In 1949, New York Senator Irving Ives and Representative Jacob Javits introduced a bill in the United States Congress: "Resolved by the Senate and the House of Representatives of the United States of America in Congress assembled, That the Congress finds that the United States of America, almost alone among the great nations, does not now have a national theater and a national opera and ballet . . . that such arts are effective and vitally important means for the development of the democratic culture of the United States; and that the ANTA has been organized under a charter granted by the United States but that it has not been implemented by the United States; and that the provision of a national theater and a national opera and ballet are in the best interests of the United States and shall be a policy of the United States."[6] Ives and Javits presented no specific plan but instead called upon President Truman to convene an assembly in Washington, out of which would emerge a new organization to develop the national theatre. (They also proposed an appropriation of $250,000 to underwrite the assembly.) Again, the suggestion remained merely that; nothing came of it.

In 1955, ANTA formulated another more complex and high-sounding plan for the establishment of a National Theatre' in the United States. Called the Forty-Theatre Circuit Plan and outlined in an issue of *Theatre Arts* (December, 1955), the scheme was developed by an advisory committee including Broadway producer Richard Aldrich, Warren Caro of the Theatre Guild, John Shubert of the theatre dynasty, and not one leader of a regional theatre of the time. In *Theatre Arts,* the purpose of the plan was boldly stated. "ANTA's primary task is to bring the best plays, interpreted by the best actors, at *minimum cost,* to the entire nation. . . . ANTA feels that its plan is demonstrably practical, that it will benefit the cultural development of our country and have valuable impact upon the education of our youth. ANTA believes this plan is the first step toward the dream of a truly national theatre."[7] Most of the cities considered as locations for the forty theatres called for in the ANTA plan were notably small. Of eighty-four cities listed by ANTA as possibilities, only one, Houston, already had a professional theatre locally managed; only fourteen were cities which were later to develop their own professional regional theatres. Cities as minor as Binghamton in New York, Shreveport in Louisiana, and Fresno in California were more typical of the list.

Significantly, the ANTA plan was not designed to create locally operated theatres but instead a touring circuit of productions mounted in four far-flung "talent centers": New York, Chicago, San Francisco or Los Angeles, and a southwestern city such as Dallas or Houston. Each of the four centers would hire actors and technicians locally. Each would produce ten plays simultaneously, and the resulting forty productions would then be toured. "Following a four-week rehearsal period, the forty productions would be traveled, ten from each production center, to those cities in the circuit nearest to the respective production centers, and would open simultaneously on one night— forty productions in forty theatres in forty cities. . . . Each production would play a total of forty weeks, spread over the forty different places."[8] The plan provided for 1,600 playing weeks during each season. With eight performances per week, and an average of 1,000 patrons per performance, up to 12,800,000 patrons could be accommodated.

In presenting the plan, ANTA did not acknowledge any precedents for it, either in Margo Jones's twenty-theatre proposal or in the appearance of the few adventurous professional regional theatres of the period. In fact, ANTA saw its plan as being the bright new cornerstone of a later, even more desirable grouping of "resident repertory" theatres:

Finally, ANTA's Forty-Theatre Circuit Plan itself would be only the first major step in the establishment of a national theatre. It would not be the end-all, nor would its accomplishment be the final goal. ANTA's Forty-Theatre Circuit would provide theatre on a sound economic basis to a vast portion of our country where professional theatre presently does not exist but, being a touring operation, it would lack two important attributes of a truly national theatre: the integration of the theatre artist into the life of the community and the development of ensemble repertory companies.

However, ANTA's Forty-Theatre Circuit is planned as the keystone on which the two subsequent steps would be built. The physical theatres would

127

be established, the process of audience education would be achieved, a sound economic operation would be demonstrated and, above all, the finances required for running a resident repertory company in the local areas would come directly from the successful operation of the forty-theatre circuit. America can look forward to a healthy, vital, literate national theatre with its attendant educational and cultural values through fulfillment of this plan.[9]

As could be expected from so inbred and centrally provincial an organization, the plan did not even admit the existence of young regional theatres like the Alley, Arena Stage, and The Actor's Workshop, let alone their potential to serve as models. ANTA's Forty-Theatre Circuit Plan, for all its high-flown idealism, was largely a sop thrown by the Broadway establishment to the rest of the country. Also, ANTA did little more about its plan than to announce it in *Theatre Arts* with the "hope and desire that all foundations will interest themselves in this endeavor and make their individual contributions to it."[10] The plan never progressed beyond its announcement in *Theatre Arts* and was never heard of again.*

It is fascinating to ponder what the reaction to the ANTA plan might have been had it come ten years later, in 1965. Then, of course, ANTA would have had to acknowledge precedents and models in the regional theatres; in fact, it would have been eager to do so in an attempt to identify itself with the burgeoning movement of that time. And the regional theatres would have welcomed the acknowledgment. I doubt, however, that they would have rallied to it, because it would have run counter to their collective dream and their individual ambitions. The ANTA plan, after all, proposed that a National Theatre be formed out of many pieces, that it be a composite creation. In 1965, the major regional theatres were in no mood to consider any joint National Theatre efforts; each of them sought to become the *one* National Theatre.

When the 1960s and its "cultural explosion" came along, ANTA was finally able to associate itself with one attempt to establish at least a national touring theatre: the National Repertory Theatre, a youth-

---

* However, when Roger Stevens, an early advocate of the ANTA plan, became chairman of the National Endowment for the Arts in 1965, he suggested a similar plan for a circuit of theatres to be established in shopping centers throughout the country. His plan was scorned by other professionals and did not materialize.

ful enterprise deliberately designed to be nomadic and sponsored by ANTA.

The National Repertory Theatre was an outgrowth of a 1959 tour of Schiller's *Mary Stuart*, which had been successfully produced in New York by the off-Broadway Phoenix Theatre. The production, directed by the ubiquitous Tyrone Guthrie, featured Eva Le Gallienne and Signe Hasso; and it was sent on tour by producers Michael Dewell and Frances Ann Dougherty. This production, contrary to cynical expectations, did exceptionally good business on the road, and this prompted Dewell and Miss Dougherty to form an organization to send other productions of their own mounting on extended tours throughout the country. From the start, the National Repertory Theatre was intended to be a touring company using traditional theatres in various cities, union technicians in those theatres, and a group of actors interested in moving from city to city week by week. Unlike ANTA in its Forty-Theatre Circuit Plan, the leaders of the National Repertory Theatre concentrated on engagements in cities over a million in population. The NRT believed that when they arrived in their regional capitals, the surrounding population would come to them, not that they would be forced to go out around the countryside. Generally, they were right. Attendance grew steadily during the middle years of the 1960s to well over 200,000 in 1967. The organization carefully cemented relationships with more than 4,000 schools in its various cities, which helped greatly to swell attendance.

The repertoire of the National Repertory Theatre was eminently suited to the sensibilities of all America—classics of wide appeal and particularly appropriate for students. Signe Hasso, Eva Le Gallienne, and film personalities Sylvia Sidney and Farley Granger were regular members of the touring company, appearing in *She Stoops to Conquer*, *Hedda Gabler*, *The Rivals*, *The Sea Gull*, *The Trojan Women*, and other classics. In 1967, with the help of a grant from the National Endowment for the Arts, the National Repertory Theatre went to New York and appeared at the ANTA Theatre on Broadway. The plays were O'Neill's *A Touch of the Poet*, Molière's *The Imaginary Invalid*, and Noel Coward's *Tonight at 8:30*, the last directed by actress Nina Foch. Except in the Coward offering, the company was scorned by the New York critics and ignored by New York audiences; the experience was embarrassing. The uninspired productions of the National Reper-

129

tory Theatre proved unable to withstand the rigors of New York exposure and competition.

Yet the NRT was rescued—by the United States Department of the Interior. In Washington, Ford's Theatre, where Lincoln was shot, was being renovated to provide live performances for the first time since 1865. The NRT was invited to become the resident company of Ford's Theatre, and in 1967 it presented *John Brown's Body, The Comedy of Errors,* and *She Stoops to Conquer.* The reprieve was short-lived, however. The NRT became embroiled in a controversy with the president of the sponsoring Ford's Theatre Society over finances. The president insisted that the NRT had promised to break even on its season, whereas the leaders of the NRT maintained that breaking even was impossible and that they had said so from the beginning. The president won the battle, and the National Repertory Theatre disappeared not only from Ford's Theatre but from the American scene.

In its name, the *National* Repertory Theatre, as well as in its broad touring purpose, the NRT had intended to be a nationwide force for good; and it did provide productions for many school students and their parents. Still, the usually low quality of NRT productions was probably a disservice to professional classical theatre because it gave many people a bad first taste. Also, by the time the National Repertory Theatre began to appear in major cities in the 1960s, many cities had their own professional regional theatres offering the classics. Since these theatres were often homegrown and always locally administered, the public's loyalty to them outweighed their interest in the NRT's group of strolling players. In the final analysis, the demise of the National Repertory Theatre can be laid to its own nomadic nature. Wanting to be everything to all America, the NRT never committed itself to a single place and so ended up being nothing to anybody. It died of its own rootlessness.

Unlike the National Repertory Theatre, the Association of Producing Artists (APA) and the American Conservatory Theatre (ACT) did not intend to be nomadic theatres. They were nomadic in their early years because they were unable to find their proper homes and were holding out for a place at the top of the heap.

The APA was founded by actor-director Ellis Rabb in 1960, and its first engagement was in Bermuda. Next, the company took up residence at Princeton University, where it served as the acting company of the McCarter Theatre. Next came a summer tour and a season in the fall of 1961 at the Fred Miller Theater in Milwaukee. Then, after a brief *succès d'estime* at the off-Broadway Folksbiene Playhouse in New York (with George M. Cohan's *The Tavern, The School for Scandal,* and *The Sea Gull*), the APA played the first of many seasons as the resident company of the University of Michigan in Ann Arbor. This arrangement allowed the company to test its productions in a cloistered setting before offering them in more visible situations.

Finally, in 1964, the APA found a permanent berth—in New York. The Phoenix Theatre, founded by Norris Houghton and T. Edward Hambleton in 1953 as a nonprofit theatre offering noncommercial plays, had met with limited public interest. Though its productions were often critically praised and though it had used important directing talents (Tyrone Guthrie and John Houseman) and acting talents (Hume Cronyn, Jessica Tandy, Uta Hagen, and Eli Wallach), the Phoenix Theatre had been unable to fill its Broadway-sized theatre on lower Second Avenue in New York. Seeking a more intimate and controllable environment, the Phoenix moved to a 299-seat off-Broadway theatre. For that location, it soon engaged the APA as its company, and the group became known as the "APA at the Phoenix."

The APA's first productions for the Phoenix were again *The Tavern,* Pirandello's *Right You Are,* Gorky's *The Lower Depths,* and a double bill of Molière's *Scapin* and *The Impromptu at Versailles.* During the next season, the APA came into its own as a New York attraction, particularly with its rightly praised and highly theatrical production of Erwin Piscator's *War and Peace,* from the Tolstoy novel. The presence in major roles of Rosemary Harris, Rabb's wife and a consummate actress, was a vital element in the company's appeal and quality. However, while the company was regularly praised, its place in the city was not assured. The 1964–65 season ended with a deficit of $100,000; with only 299 seats in the theatre, there was no hope of reducing that amount through increased ticket sales. The APA and the Phoenix made plans to move their operation to the Lyceum Theatre on Broadway, a theatre built for the rigors of repertory at the turn of the century and holding 1,000 seats. The plan was indeed courageous, but there were no funds to activate it. To move to the Lyceum, the APA and the Phoenix needed $300,000—far more than the $40,000 on hand.

When a request for the $300,000 was turned down by the Ford Founda-
tion, the plan had to be shelved, and the APA returned to Ann Arbor.
There the company presented its first world premiere, Archibald Mac-
Leish's *Herakles*, featuring Rosemary Harris and directed by Alan
Schneider, and a revival of *You Can't Take It with You*. The Kaufman-
Hart comedy was so successful in Michigan that the APA decided to
take it to New York for a commercial run at the Lyceum, where it
turned into a critical and box-office success (as well as the first of a
spate of Broadway revivals of nostalgic 1930s comedies). The APA had
"arrived"—on terms antithetical to the spirit of the nonprofit and anti-
Broadway regional theatre. Its life and its place in New York had been
saved by a run on a Broadway box office. Most importantly, APA had
held its own in competition with slick Broadway fare.

Buoyed by its commercial success, the APA, again in partnership
with the Phoenix under T. Edward Hambleton, planned a full season
in New York, this time in the Lyceum Theatre on Broadway. Helen
Hayes joined the company for the first Broadway season, which signaled the first time in thirty years that true repertory had been staged
in a Broadway theatre. The new season included *The School for
Scandal*, *You Can't Take It with You*, *War and Peace*, and *We Comrades Three*, the last a staged reading of the works of Walt Whitman.
The APA—now the APA-Phoenix—was gaining a reputation for the
sustained elegance of its work. The summer of 1967 saw the APA in
Montreal at Expo '67, playing alongside the Stratford Festival company from Ontario. The fact that it was the only nonprofit institutional theatre from America to be seen at the Montreal fair lent
credence to the growing reputation of the APA as the best in its field,
and Walter Kerr of the *New York Times* was writing at home that the
group was "the best repertory company we possess." The year 1967 also
brought a $900,000 general support grant from the Ford Foundation.

The 1967–68 season at the Lyceum won new laurels: de Ghelderode's
Pantagleize, staged by Rabb and John Houseman; Ionesco's *Exit the
King*; Eva Le Gallienne's staging of *The Cherry Orchard*, with Uta
Hagen, and another resurrection-revival, George Kelly's *The Show-Off*,
with Helen Hayes. Each of the four productions was superlatively
mounted, and in each case the APA trusted the plays it selected and
presented them on their own terms. Unlike the American Shakespeare
Festival and even The Guthrie Theater in its weaker moments, the

APA believed in their literature and played it "straight." No Civil War Shakespeare for them.

The 1967–68 theatre season was one of glory for the APA-Phoenix. The alliance had forged a civilized alternative to the commercial activities that characterized Broadway. Nevertheless, it was still relegated to a secondary place by the New York theatre community, which did not recognize the validity of repertory on Broadway. Typical of this standoff was the refusal by the League of New York Theatres (Broadway's controlling body) to consider the 1967–68 APA productions for the Tony Awards, which are Broadway's Oscars. Infuriated by this refusal (and its implied rejection of the company), Rabb and Hambleton fired off a protest to the League:

> We are profoundly shocked at your decision to exclude the APA-Phoenix productions from eligibility for this year's Tony Award nominations. Having received four nominations last season and considering that we are currently performing "Pantagleize," "The Show-Off," "Exit the King," and "The Cherry Orchard," which represent one-third of the eligible dramatic productions now running on Broadway, the action of the League is grossly unfair to our company including its actors, directors and designers and discriminates harshly against an organization which is artistically and economically an important part of the Broadway community.[11]

The protest by Rabb and Hambleton was justified because the action of the League was unfair so long as the APA-Phoenix was performing in a Broadway theatre. By refusing to consider the company, the League seemed to be protecting its own commercial interests from being embarrassed by a repertory company whose productions might win more awards than commercial productions.

As it turned out, however, the commercial theatre need not have worried. The APA-Phoenix was in decline very soon, in part through the loss of Rosemary Harris. Divorcing Rabb, Miss Harris had left the company in 1967. Her departure took from the APA its only truly brilliant young acting talent. And she had been a focus and rallying point for the company.

The 1967–68 season was an interregnum between Rosemary Harris's leaving and the decay of the APA. The 1968–69 season featured a peculiarly precious quartet of plays: *The Cocktail Party, The Misanthrope,* O'Casey's *Cock-a-Doodle Dandy,* and a *Hamlet* staged by and featuring Rabb in an unfortunate production which, for the first time, did not trust the play. Only *The Misanthrope* was generally well received by the critics, and the other three productions did very poor business at the Lyceum box office. At the end of April, 1969, the termination of the APA alliance with the Phoenix was announced. The valiant attempt to place rotating repertory permanently in a Broadway theatre had failed. The ending of the alliance was initially blamed on the severe financial strain under which it had always lived and which had caught up with the group in the 1968–69 season. Despite a very successful national tour of *The Show-Off* (which brought in a profit of $240,000) and a total income of $2,229,000, the APA-Phoenix suffered a deficit of $279,000 for the season. The APA-Phoenix board of directors had already borrowed $250,000 to erase the 1967–68 deficit; they could not do the same again. Ending the partnership was the only possible solution, and even that would not erase those previous debts.

While the blame was publicly placed on financial problems, there were other important factors as well. Primary among these was the awkward relationship between the Phoenix management of T. Edward Hambleton on the one side and the APA leadership of Rabb and general manager Norman Kean on the other. Hambleton, a gentle man, had poured much of his own fortune into sustaining the operation on Broadway from 1966 to 1969. Despite this personal commitment, he had not been able to find a modus vivendi with Rabb and Kean; the marriage of the two institutions was hardly made in heaven. The division between them limited not only the administration of the enterprise but also its ability to garner major support. Looking back later on the ending of the company, Hambleton placed the blame on the APA. Maintaining that Ellis Rabb's "insecurity became a source of danger to the enterprise," Hambleton wrote: "Looking back to 1965, many reasons for the termination were already present when we left 74th Street and others developed during the first repertory season, 1966–67; but these might have remained latent if sufficient artistic vitality had developed within the company to share the load and regenerate the artistic leadership of Ellis Rabb."[12] But the Phoenix, too, had its problems. The management was not aggressive, particularly in promotion of the company's productions. The selling of subscription tickets to the APA-Phoenix seasons was lackluster, and—aping the Broadway producers around them—the company devoted far too much money to newspaper advertising and far too little to developing audience interest on more personal and institutional levels appropriate to the nature of the work on the stage.

Above all, the repertoire of the APA hindered it. While the company trusted its literature almost up to the end, that literature was nonetheless of a very special nature. Particularly adept at high comedy (*The School for Scandal, The Misanthrope*), the APA was much less successful with plays which were either realistic or boisterous. The acting company was singularly lacking in the robustness and toughness which characterized less fussy groups like The Guthrie Theater. The APA was superb in pretty plays like *The Misanthrope*; adequate in realistic period plays like *The Cherry Orchard*; striking in esoteric plays like *War and Peace* and *Pantagleize*; and delightfully spirited in the resurrections of *The Show-Off* and *You Can't Take It with You*. But they would have been inconceivable in *Death of a Salesman* or *Who's Afraid of Virginia Woolf?* An American theatre of first rank must be able to perform plays in the major American realistic idiom, and the APA, lacking muscle, was limited by its own specialness. The loss of this specialness is a severe loss, and the powers of New York should be ashamed of their failure to support so tasteful a company as the APA-Phoenix. A city of New York's size needs one delicate theatre enterprise. Still, that is a local need, not a national one. The APA's preference for delicacy finally ruled it out of the National Theatre running.

After the breakup of the APA and the Phoenix, each component went its own way. T. Edward Hambleton held the Phoenix together as a personal producing organization, with John Houseman, now head of the theatre division of the Juilliard School, as the artistic director. His first production, a revival of *Harvey* with James Stewart and Helen Hayes, played first in Ann Arbor and later at the ANTA Theatre on Broadway. He followed this with productions of *The Trial of the Catonsville Nine* and *Murderous Angels*, both first mounted by Gordon Davidson at the Mark Taper Forum and restaged by him for the Phoenix. In 1972, Hambleton restructured the Phoenix and offered touring productions of O'Neill's *The Great God Brown* and Molière's *Don Juan*—the first staged by Broadway producer-director Harold Prince and the second by Stephen Porter, who had staged many APA-Phoenix productions as well as plays in other regional theatres. The tour of the two productions included a brief engagement on Broadway —ironically, in the Lyceum.

135

Regional Theatre: The Revolutionary Stage

The APA, with Rabb still at the helm, left New York in 1969 and appeared in Ann Arbor, then in Toronto, Boston, and Washington. The new production for this tour was a revival of *Private Lives*, with Tammy Grimes and Brian Bedford. Broadway producer David Merrick picked it up and installed it in a Broadway theatre late in 1969, and it had a healthy commercial run. While somewhat hidden under the Merrick banner, the APA was back again on Broadway with a "hit" show, just as it had been in 1965 with *You Can't Take It with You*. However, while the group shared in the financial success of *Private Lives*, their stake was not large enough to save the faltering company, now once more nomadic. By 1970, the company had stopped doing new productions, and there was no group of actors left together. General manager Norman Kean was managing the nude revue *Oh! Calcutta!* in New York. Ellis Rabb directed a Broadway musical version of Truman Capote's *The Grass Harp*, which failed, and later *Twelfth Night* and Gorky's *Enemies* for the Repertory Theater of Lincoln Center, which were praised. Mostly, however, he was associated with the APA's fellow former nomad, the American Conservatory Theatre in San Francisco. For them, he directed *The Merchant of Venice* in 1970, a musical version of *The Selling of the President* in 1971, and *Sleuth* in 1972.

The American Conservatory Theatre has been by far the most swaggering of American regional theatres. ACT (as the company is aptly acronymed) sees the theatre as a bullring—and the matador is William Ball, its founder, master, and eccentric genius.

Until recently, Ball was the enfant terrible of the regional theatre. A graduate of Carnegie Tech, he got his early directing experience at a number of acorn theatres, including the Alley, Arena Stage, and The Actor's Workshop. Later, he was hailed for his off-Broadway productions of *Ivanov* and *Six Characters in Search of an Author*, also staging the latter play in London with Ralph Richardson. He directed productions for the New York City Opera and *Tartuffe* in 1965 for the Repertory Theater of Lincoln Center. Around that time, he was also formulating his plans for the American Conservatory Theatre. From the beginning, ACT for Ball was to be an all-out assault on the need in America for a National Theatre. As he conceived it, it would not only produce the most eclectic repertoire possible but would also train its actors continually in a conservatory setting of the Continental style.

136

A man possessing boundless energy, Ball approached his project with single-minded conviction and determination.

Since he knew Pittsburgh from his student days, Ball decided that his theatre company would burst upon the American scene from there. It was a handy situation. The ancient Pittsburgh Playhouse, a rich community theatre, had a mammoth physical plant that seemed a natural setting for such a venture, and there were rumblings about a connection being formulated between the Playhouse and Carnegie Tech. Ball, securing initial support from the Rockefeller Foundation, proffered his genius as the guiding force of ACT at the Pittsburgh Playhouse. The board of the theatre, realizing that the city was far behind others in the regional theatre movement, jumped at the chance, and in July of 1965 ACT was born in Pittsburgh. The actors in the company included many of Ball's favorites who had appeared in his off-Broadway productions: Michael O'Sullivan (Tartuffe at Lincoln Center), Richard Dysart, Ray Reinhardt, and relatively unknown but highly capable actors, most notably Rene Auberjonois.

The season's debut productions were partly retreadings of former Ball successes (*Tartuffe, Six Characters*) and partly new productions. The most notable of the new was *Tiny Alice*, Ball's operatic rendition of Albee's intellectual melodrama. The offerings were colorful, theatrical, and above all excessive, Ball's special hallmark. Pittsburgh had never seen such theatre, and the citizens were not sure they wanted to see it now. The reaction to the Ball company was often as excessive as the productions themselves, particularly the reaction from the lay leadership and the entrenched professional management of the Playhouse, which stayed on even during the ACT engagement. Acrimony between these old-timers and the new group was severe, and the problem was intensified by the fact that the ACT group never bothered to identify with the community. Their eyes were on larger vistas from the beginning; they were in Pittsburgh because the National Theatre had to start somewhere.

Within six months, ACT left Pittsburgh. Since ACT had garnered many laudatory national reviews while there, it was not difficult for the group to piece together a brief series of engagements in Michigan (Ann Arbor again), Connecticut, California, and Illinois plus training sessions in New York for the company. With his ability to turn the company's insecurity into not only philosophy but also promotion, Ball announced that the nomadic approach was deliberate—in order to find a community interested in supporting his company and worthy of it. During its wanderings from early 1966 through that summer, ACT continued to reap critical praise and public amazement at its versatility, which was genuine. Productions of *Tiny Alice, Tartuffe, Six Characters, Uncle Vanya, Charley's Aunt,* and *Beyond the Fringe*—with actors sharing roles and appearing on alternate nights—showed an ability to handle a range of repertoire unmatched by any other American company. Wherever it went, ACT gave off an air of a new approach to theatre, a new brilliance of actor and director, a new ensemble spirit. That air was properly hailed in the national media, making ACT a major new force in American theatre even while it lacked a home.

Successive repertory engagements at the Stanford University Summer Festival near San Francisco and the Ravinia Festival near Chicago added even more luster to the ACT reputation and resulted in invitations from the city fathers of both cities to settle with them. (Chicago's Goodman Theatre did not yet have a fully professional company and so was not a threat to the larger Ball idea. San Francisco had just lost the remains of The Actor's Workshop, a story which will be told in the next chapter.) Again with characteristic flair, Ball and his associates announced that they wanted to split their year between the two cities, playing six months in each. Obviously it would be a major coup for ACT to be the regional theatre of two of the nation's largest cities. Negotiations began in both, and for a few weeks it looked possible that the plan would be activated. But soon it became clear that the cities were not cooperating with each other on the plan and perhaps that ACT was playing one offer against the other. At the end of the summer of 1966, ACT announced that it would not accept the Chicago invitation because the Windy City did not provide two separate theatres in which to play, a necessity given the size of ACT's repertoire and company (nearly fifty actors). Another reason given for the rejection of Chicago was that Equity would consider such a two-city theatre a touring company, thus raising the cost of maintaining those fifty actors. I suppose that other reasons for not accepting the Chicago invitation were more personal: San Francisco was probably the more attractive city in which to live, and not accepting Chicago's offer would make the company appear all the more committed to San Francisco. Perhaps Ball sensed that self-consciously glamorous San Francisco would not

abide sharing ACT with what it might consider a midwestern meat-
packing town.

ACT opened in downtown San Francisco in January, 1967, in two
theatres—one a commercial touring house and the other the Marines'
Memorial that had housed The Actor's Workshop. The same tried and
true plays that had been performed in Pittsburgh and around the country were shown, and San Francisco welcomed the company ecstatically.
The two theatres gave ACT a combined seating capacity of nearly
2,100—nearly 50 percent more than the capacity of The Guthrie Theater. The fact that more than 222,000 people paid for those seats over
a twenty-two-week season and saw sixteen different productions in rotation indicates the success of the first ACT season. There were 12,000
subscribers, too, more than twice as many as were ever achieved by The
Actor's Workshop over thirteen years in the city. Slangy *Variety* announced, "Ball's ACT in Smash Frisco Bow, with Rave Reviews and
Boff Biz." William Ball seemed to be on the top of the pile.

However, as in other cities where theatres burst upon the scene
rather than evolving slowly, ACT and San Francisco did not enjoy
a permanent honeymoon. The company's spiraling spending almost
immediately incurred large deficits which its sponsor, the California
Theatre Foundation, found difficult to erase. Audience interest, too—
as in Minneapolis with the Guthrie—fell off after the first splashy season, and ACT's practice of regularly repeating its old productions sometimes gave it a déjà vu appearance. Characteristically, San Francisco
had overreacted to the chic vitality of ACT, making it inevitable that
seasons after the first would seem a letdown. Still, ACT's expansiveness
spilled over the stage, even if for fewer people. The theatre simply
assumed its right to overspend, overproduce, and overendear itself,
doing all three with style and unqualified verve.

A major part of the excessiveness of ACT was the wide range of its
repertoire. It was a theatre obsessed with eclecticism. The forty-week
season of 1968–69 was typical: *A Flea in Her Ear* (directed by Gower
Champion), *The Three Sisters*, Aleksei Arbuzov's *The Promise, Rosencrantz and Guildenstern Are Dead, The Devil's Disciple, Little Murders, Staircase*, Arrabal's *The Architect and Emperor of Assyria, In
White America, The Crucible, A Delicate Balance, Hamlet, Room Service*, and two new plays—*Glory! Hallelujah!* and *The Pastime of
Monsieur Robert*. Also, not content with mounting only its own pro-

ductions, ACT co-sponsored commercial productions like *Hair* and *Godspell* and engagements by other repertory companies, including England's Royal Shakespeare Company. While producing such a massive array of plays, ACT maintained its conservatory arm, offering classes not only in acting but also in theatre history and dramatic literature, makeup, hairdressing, wig-making, music, and theatre design, summer and winter, for full-time and part-time students and members of the company, too. (Following his ouster from the Seattle Repertory Theatre, Allen Fletcher joined ACT as the director of the conservatory, also directing major productions of *Hadrian VII, The Latent Heterosexual, An Enemy of the People, Antony and Cleopatra*, and Odets's *Paradise Lost*.) In addition, ACT regularly toured throughout the Bay Area and as far away as Los Angeles in California and even to Phoenix, Arizona, with its production of *Private Lives*, staged by Francis Ford Coppola (the director of the film *The Godfather*). ACT is a theatre that runs at full tilt.

And of course the excess that has informed the work of ACT has been primarily that of an individual. Just as the essential character of the earliest acorn theatres flowed from the character of their leaders, so the excessiveness of ACT has been the excessiveness of William Ball. He is more than talented—he is a genius of theatre, exotic and quixotic. His hold on the company is complete, and this, combined with his ability to attract other major talents (particularly other directors) has enabled him to lead and inspire his company even when absent from San Francisco.

In the early days of ACT, Ball's excessiveness fed his assumption of superiority in the regional theatre. In those days, he tended to expect that naturally money would be made available from philanthropic sources—on the conviction that they could not afford to deny support to his ultimate American theatre. And in the days of greatest financial crisis for ACT in San Francisco, in the late 1960s, this confident expectation of support often charmed that support into being. For instance, in the 1967–68 season, the National Endowment for the Arts gave to ACT a $175,000 emergency grant to help save the company, a grant unprecedentedly large at the time. Likewise, five thousand citizens of northern California pledged $104,282, and an "ACT Now" telethon on San Francisco's educational television station drew over $40,000 from two thousand callers.

Margo Jones, director, Theatre '47–Theatre '55, Dallas

Zelda Fichandler, director,
Arena Stage, Washington

Nina Vance, director,
Alley Theatre, Houston

Jules Irving, *left*, and Herbert Blau, *right*, directors, The Actor's Workshop, San Francisco, and the Repertory Theater of Lincoln Center, New York

By Joseph Zimbrolt

Sir Tyrone Guthrie, *center*, with Peter Zeisler, *left*, and Oliver Rea, *right*, founding directors of The Guthrie Theater, Minneapolis

Arvin Brown, director, Long
Wharf Theatre, New Haven

William Ball, director, American
Conservatory Theatre, San Francisco

Adrian Hall, director, Trinity Square
Repertory Company, Providence

Gordon Davidson, director,
Mark Taper Forum, Los Angeles

Ellis Rabb, director,
APA-Phoenix, New York

Michael Langham, director,
The Guthrie Theater, Minneapolis

Taming of the Shrew, Theatre '48, 1948

Desire under the Elms, Alley Theatre, 1949

Ring Round the Moon, Arena Stage, 1960

The Great White Hope, with James Earl Jones, *center*, Arena Stage, 1967

Jules Irving acted in numerous Actor's Workshop productions
during the early years of the theatre. Here he is seen,
above left, as Lucky in *Waiting for Godot*, 1957, and, *below center*,
in the 1954 production of *Death of a Salesman*.

By Hank Kranzler

Herbert Blau's production of Aristophanes' *The Birds* for
The Actor's Workshop in 1964 was billed as a "classical-lyrical-
vaudeville-jazz extravaganza."

The inclusion of actors Hume Cronyn and Jessica Tandy in The
Guthrie Theater's inaugural company in 1963 brought additional
attention to the new regional theatre. Here Cronyn
is seen in the title role of *The Miser* in 1963.

Two trend-setting productions of Brecht's *The Caucasian Chalk Circle*: *above*, The Actor's Workshop, 1963; *below*, The Guthrie Theater, 1965.

Two monumental productions of Greek tragedies highlighted seasons
of The Guthrie Theater: *above*, Tyrone Guthrie's staging
of *The House of Atreus*, 1967; *below*, Michael Langham's
production of *Oedipus the King*, 1972.

Arturo Ui, The Guthrie Theater, 1968

At the Mark Taper Forum: *above, Uncle Vanya*, 1969,
directed by Harold Clurman, *seated center*; *below, The Trial
of the Catonsville Nine*, 1971.

By William L. Smith

Above, Son of Man and the Family, Trinity Square Repertory Company,
1970–71; *below,* members of the Trinity Square Repertory Company in front
of the Church Hill Theatre (Edinburgh, Scotland), where they
performed as part of the Edinburgh Festival in 1968.

Nancy Walker, *left*, and Uta Hagen, *center*, joined the APA-Phoenix to appear with Betty Miller in *The Cherry Orchard* in 1968.

Exit the King, with Richard Easton, APA-Phoenix, 1967

The Merchant of Venice, American Conservatory Theatre, 1970

Beyond the Fringe, American Conservatory Theatre, 1967   By Hank Kranzler

The Guthrie Theater took its productions of *The House of Atreus* and *Arturo Ui* to the Billy Rose Theatre in New York in 1968. Guthrie, *center*, is pictured under the marquee with (*from left*) Peter Zeisler, managing director; John Jensen, designer; Jon Cranney, stage manager; and Donald Schoenbaum, associate manager.

The Guthrie Theater took its production of *Of Mice and Men* on tour to Bismarck, North Dakota, in 1973.

By Craig Scherfenberg

Still, despite all the support from the local community (which now reaches $350,000 a year), the familiar Ford Foundation was usually the mainstay of ACT support. Since the theatre's San Francisco debut in 1967, Ford has awarded a total of $2,395,000 to ACT—and for general support only, not for theatre construction (as in most other cases of Ford grants over $1,000,000). This major Ford support of ACT is particularly ironic because ACT, in its first excessive years in San Francisco, did not adhere to the rigorous principles of management and even self-denial which Ford support tended to encourage and reward. Unlike the Alley, Arena Stage, The Guthrie Theater, and other major Ford recipients, ACT operated on a luxurious roller coaster and got the big money anyway. Also, Ford's massive support of ACT established a compelling philanthropic precedent. Each large grant to any institution from any philanthropic source tends to assure the next one, because to stop giving could suggest that the source no longer considers the recipient institution worthy.

By pointing out the precedent, I do not mean to suggest that the Ford Foundation still gives money to ACT because it cannot afford to stop (it can) or that ACT is no longer worthy. The ultimate question related to the support of the arts is not whether an institution is modestly managed but rather whether it amounts to anything artistically. On that level, ACT looks like a sound investment. The institution has reduced its program recently, and it is now better managed; yet it is still an exciting theatre because it is still excitingly excessive. Like its predecessor in San Francisco, The Actor's Workshop, ACT takes grand chances.

But—and this is the essential difference between the two—ACT takes mostly physical chances; its excesses are those of action, of flair, of staging. It is a theatre of pyrotechnics. In contrast, the excesses of The Actor's Workshop were intellectual ones which reached beyond *how* something is done to *why*. And that may be the special responsibility of a National Theatre. We shall see. In any case, we are back in San Francisco. It is now time to go back to 1965.

8 To Save the World: The Actor's Workshop Moves East

"The Idea which is *The Actor's Workshop has made its way in the world. The offer from Lincoln Center, as we see it, is the most material certification of that Idea. Our appointment, then, is not a San Francisco issue or a New York issue but a national issue."*

> Letter from Jules Irving and Herbert Blau
> to subscribers of *The Actor's Workshop*

"Something kept us moving: ambition, pride, defiance, foolishness, a sense of Manifest Destiny. . . . I would say the purpose of the Workshop was to save the world."

> *Herbert Blau,* The Impossible Theater

When the time came for a deliberate attempt at creating a National Theatre, the most unlikely regional theatre was chosen for the job: The Actor's Workshop. To understand the irony of this choice, we must go back to the beginnings of the Repertory Theater of Lincoln Center, to understand them as we already understand the beginnings of the Workshop.

Like the American Shakespeare Festival a decade before it, the Repertory Theater of Lincoln Center was a child of the Establishment. At the very top was John D. Rockefeller, chairman of all Lincoln Center. At the top of the Repertory Theater board was Robert L. Hoguet, Jr., vice-president of the First National City Bank of New York. As the first administrative director, there was Robert Whitehead, who had started his producing career with Judith Anderson's *Medea* and Julie Harris and Ethel Waters in *Member of the Wedding* (both co-produced with Oliver Rea, later of The Guthrie Theater) and who had produced a score of other Broadway plays (among them *A Man for All Seasons, Bus Stop,* and *Separate Tables*). Most especially there was artistic director Elia Kazan—prodigy of the postwar American theatre, director

142

of *Death of a Salesman, A Streetcar Named Desire, Tea and Sympathy,* and *J.B.*, and the man largely responsible for the "cult of directors" as it existed in the Broadway theatre of his day. Add to these names those of executive consultant Harold Clurman, designer Jo Mielziner, and house playwright Arthur Miller, and it is obvious that the Repertory Theater of Lincoln Center was created in the first place by taking the top crust of the American theatre of the early 1960s. As Martin Gottfried puts it, it was "designed to be the American National Theatre from the moment it opened its doors."[1] This was assumed, given the fact that it was to join at Lincoln Center such venerable institutions as the Metropolitan Opera (long considered our National Opera), the superb New York City Ballet under America's adopted master, George Balanchine, and the New York Philharmonic under the baton of America's classical music star, Leonard Bernstein. However, unlike these other organizations which came to Lincoln Center after long and honored careers, the Repertory Theater was being created especially and expressly for the Center. It was to be Lincoln Center's only venture into the creation of a performing arts institution from scratch.

And scratch it was. The new Vivian Beaumont Theater, penciled in at Lincoln Center and designed by Jo Mielziner and Eero Saarinen to be a permanent home, was not ready in time, and so the Repertory Theater first opened in a temporary theatre, the ANTA–Washington Square Theatre in Greenwich Village. The theatre was a prefabricated building built by the American National Theatre and Academy on (mostly under) land owned by New York University, and it was the first thrust-stage theatre of any size or consequence built in New York. Despite backstage and lobby limitations, the theatre worked well in its relationship between audience and stage (as noted earlier, it was later purchased in pieces by the Trinity Square Repertory Company in Providence); still, for the debut of such an Establishment venture as the Repertory Theater of Lincoln Center, the ANTA–Washington Square Theatre provided an unusually tacky site.

One problem from the beginning was Kazan's unfamiliarity with theatre classics. He started his task with all the right words—"a world theatre, expressing the way we Americans see the world"—but with none of the classical training which artistic directors even in remote cities could boast. Kazan and Whitehead proclaimed their intention of developing a classical repertory company capable of performing the canon of world dramatic literature. Yet Kazan chose a group of actors known for their singular lack of classical training; among them were Jason Robards, David Wayne, Ralph Meeker, Zohra Lampert, and Faye Dunaway and John Philip Law (both then unknown). Their one-year crash-training program could not bestow upon this group the requisite classical training and discipline, although there is no doubt that these and other actors in the inaugural company had power on the stage in the realistic tradition which Kazan himself had mastered. At the start, the actors were signed to two-year contracts, a new departure on the New York scene.

Another problem from the beginning was the choice of plays. The first three, in rotating repertory, were Arthur Miller's *After the Fall*, Eugene O'Neill's *Marco Millions*, and the premiere of a new play by S. N. Behrman, *But for Whom Charlie*. Except for the O'Neill drama, these were not plays which appeared natural for a repertory company. The Miller play (his first in nine years) and the Behrman comedy were works likely to be produced on the commercial Broadway stage, and their inclusion in the Repertory Theater's inaugural season was scorned by the cognoscenti on this basis. (Actually, Kazan was shrewd to choose modern-dress plays like *After the Fall* and *But for Whom Charlie*, which would not betray his actors' unfamiliarity with and lack of mastery of the classics.)

The opening of the Repertory Theater in its temporary quarters came in January, 1964, with *After the Fall*, featuring Jason Robards in the autobiographical leading role and Barbara Loden as Maggie, the Marilyn Monroe figure. Kazan directed it and *But for Whom Charlie*, and José Quintero, the acknowledged O'Neill expert in the Broadway theatre, staged *Marco Millions* (which featured Hal Holbrook, a more logical choice for a classical company). As might have been predicted, the productions were rejected by critics and audiences—except for *After the Fall*, which satisfied the public's desire for a return of Miller. Kazan's and Whitehead's fellow theatre professionals in New York scorned not only the choice of plays but the season in general (although some of this vituperation must be charged to the inevitable carping of theatre people and the bitterness of those not included). On balance, the first season was without question inauspicious. By the opening of the second season, Kazan was phasing out his involvement with the Repertory Theater, but he did stage the opening production, the bloody Jacobean drama *The Changeling*, his first foray into classical drama. An artistic disaster of almost "camp" proportions, *The Changeling* was not redeemed by either a return engagement of *After the Fall* or the premiere later in the fall of 1964 of another new Miller play, *Incident at Vichy*. The new season, added to the recent embarrassments of *Marco Millions* and *But for Whom Charlie*, was apparently too much for the board of the Repertory Theater to bear. They began to seek new leadership.

Much had been made of Kazan's and Whitehead's so-called "freedom to founder," the right to develop their strengths over a long period unencumbered by demands for either critical or financial success. Kazan, speaking at the first rehearsal of *After the Fall*, had dismissed traditional success: "I'm through with that crap game now."[2] Perhaps the insistence on this freedom by the leaders arose from their awareness of their own lack of training for their jobs. In any case, their dismissal was viewed by many as a failure on the part of the Repertory Theater board to adhere to the concept of "freedom to founder." Critic Martin Gottfried wrote: "This freedom was denied the Repertory Theater of Lincoln Center by nonartistic meddlers who felt it necessary to succeed financially, critically, socially, and immediately. . . . Kazan and Whitehead were denied the right to fail. They were sacked for not 'succeeding.' Repertory theater is so new to this country that, at least at the time, there was really nobody who could say this way is right and that wrong. It was obvious that Kazan and Whitehead were badly prepared for the job in matters of taste and experience, but the values that prompted their dismissal were far more inexcusable."[3]

The reasons for the dismissal of Kazan and Whitehead are not as interesting or as important as the meaning of it. The Repertory Theater of Lincoln Center in this first phase had been an attempt to form a National Theatre out of the best of Broadway, and it failed. If talents like Kazan's and Whitehead's could not create a National Theatre, none from Broadway could—and therefore the talent for the job would have to come from beyond. As a result, the board of directors of the Repertory Theater, led by Hoguet, CBS's Michael Burke, and Schuyler Chapin of the Lincoln Center staff, went out looking for new leaders. They approached many people both in New York and outside it, and they all said no. They asked people in England, and they all said no. The Repertory Theater of Lincoln Center—particularly if one was

145

reasonably content at home—looked like a nest of snakes. Meanwhile, one man who had no home, William Ball, was in New York directing the Repertory Theater's production of *Tartuffe* as the third new bill of the second season. This was a mere six months before he was to form his ACT company. Ball delivered a handsome and giggly production that audiences loved, but apparently his talent was overlooked by the Establishment representatives circling around him, and he was not offered the job.

It has been said that while her husband searched, Mrs. Robert L. Hoguet, Jr., was reading a rare and esoteric book called *The Impossible Theater: A Manifesto,* by Herbert Blau, co-director of the esoteric Actor's Workshop. Blau's book is an extraordinary feat but also dense and full of obscure references; it is slow and difficult reading. The story goes that Mrs. Hoguet got through enough of *The Impossible Theater* to tell her husband about it, and he thus went in search of Herbert Blau, this obscure genius. He found him, of course, and within a few weeks, Herbert Blau and Jules Irving had decided to accept a co-directorship of the Repertory Theater, moving their partnership and many of their actors and staff across the country.

During those several weeks, the Workshop in San Francisco was in a state of total confusion. Given the curiosity of theatre people, Irving and Blau knew that they could not afford to tell anyone outside the most inner Workshop circle about the possibilities being presented to them. Only six people knew of the offer: Irving and Blau themselves, their wives, actor-director Robert Symonds, and Alan Mandell, general manager of the Workshop and later of the Repertory Theater. The rest of us at the Workshop were kept in understandable but frustrating ignorance. Phones would ring in the offices, and suddenly all doors would be shut and locked for ultimate privacy. Irving and Blau, on certain days, would simply not show up for rehearsals of the upcoming *Julius Caesar*, and the only explanation offered was that they had had to make another sudden trip to New York. Strange and elegantly vested older men, looking completely out of place in the dingy Workshop quarters, circulated among ragamuffin actors, nodding among themselves and whispering in corners with Irving and Blau. Finally, on the last day of January, 1965, the news was announced, first to the assembled and tense Workshop company and staff and later that day to the press. The seemingly endless tension was over, and the news was out:

146

Irving and Blau were going to Lincoln Center, and over the next several days they would be talking with each of us about whether we were invited to go along or not.

Apparently theirs was a difficult decision. There were several long meetings for the six people who finally determined a four-way fate: theirs, ours, The Actor's Workshop's, and the Repertory Theater's. At the beginning there was no unanimity of opinion among the six, and the decision changed back and forth several times before final action was taken. However, interestingly and typically, the decision was finally a joint one. In public, at least, it was unanimous.

Although the agreement specified a co-directorship and represented a move for the partnership, the fact is that Blau was the central figure in the negotiations with Lincoln Center. He was better known than Jules Irving at the time because of his recently praised book; his genius was on paper and could be studied in New York, whereas Irving's genius was manifest only in The Actor's Workshop itself. It was Blau's written thinking that had led to this moment. He was the key to the Workshop's disaffection with its city and to its bitterness and negativism around the end of 1964, and his philosophy and personal desires were the central element in the decision to leave San Francisco for Lincoln Center. I am sure that Blau's opinion never wavered through all those long nights of deliberation.

Knowing Herbert Blau, I can imagine his reaction on being approached by the Lincoln Center board: first, a gulp like anyone else's, and then a slightly sly "of course" smile that is uniquely his. Earlier, in discussing the Workshop, I said that it had started without a particular philosophy and that the philosophy came later. Actually, that one philosophy had two coexisting and complementary facets. One was the pragmatic philosophy centered around Jules Irving; this is what kept the Workshop afloat, built it as an institution, and secured money from the Ford Foundation. The other philosophy was the idealistic one of Herbert Blau, which always sought larger social and universal meanings in the tentative activities of the theatre in San Francisco. Looking back now, it is clear that Irving's part of the philosophy held the Workshop together, but it was Blau's part for which the Workshop was known, when known at all. Blau's philosophy was crystallized in his 1964 book *The Impossible Theater*, which climaxed the Workshop's "brilliantly negative" period. (It is revealing that while his book was being prepared for publication, Blau announced within the Workshop that the time had come for the theatre to end its pursuit of alienation and negativism and to embark instead on a period of affirmation in its choice of plays and their mounting—almost as if the Workshop, having served as a case study for the book, could now do something else.) Blau's subtitle is essential: *A Manifesto.* The book defined not only a philosophy of theatre but also Blau himself. In its weight, its bravura, and its absolute hubris—though not at all in its ideas—it seemed a theatrical *Mein Kampf.*

In Blau's book as in himself, there was a basic dichotomy: on the one side, his insistence upon the necessity for theatrical Decentralization (which he tended to capitalize with almost religious fervor) and, on the other side, his assumption of the centrality of his own ideas. In the book, this dichotomy was never resolved.

Blau's frustration with the central Broadway theatre pervades his book: "There is still the assumption of tribute to be paid, and it is that antiquated notion of Tributary Theatre, once so inspiring, of which we must rid ourselves today if a genuine revolution is to take place and Decentralization is not to reverse its course as it once did."[4] So obsessed, Blau was vituperatively anti-Broadway and considered the commercial theatre a "pathological condition." Of many bristling comments in *The Impossible Theater,* one in particular stands out, and in view of what was to come for Blau, it seems particularly ironic: "To talk about Broadway *is* mainly to carp; but we must carp and carp louder, not for Broadway's sake, but because it remains the chief referent for theater in this country and, more outrageously, the chief aspiration for young actors, directors, designers, and playwrights. Bless Broadway, it will survive, if anything does. And nobody would spend his good time beating a dead cow if there weren't so many who still held it sacred, or fed up to the teeth, still buzz like dumb flies around what *they* tell you is a carcass."[5]

Yet like the other acorn creators and even more than they, Blau had banished Broadway only intellectually, in the abstract, and he could still raise a grand cry to arms: "In a revolutionary era . . . I am prepared to believe anything. I am prepared to believe even in the reformation of Broadway."[6] I think that Blau wanted to go to Lincoln Center because he saw himself as the reformer of Broadway. He had become a theatrical Moses, handing down the law. In the beginning, he was out to change his society in San Francisco. Later, his purview widened until it was American thought, and finally the world itself— until he could say, in utter seriousness, that the purpose of the Workshop was "to save the world." The Workshop had started as a little group of anonymous people, in a little situation, scraping to find its own niche. Over years of struggle, it had become for Herbert Blau the answer to the "carcass" of Broadway. Whereas Margo Jones had ingenuously said that she wanted to make the Houston Community Players the "best theatre in America," Herbert Blau, I think, categorically believed that he had made The Actor's Workshop, ideologically, the *only* theatre in America. For him, decentralization had gone so far that the Workshop was the new center of the American theatre. The offer from Lincoln Center provided for him an opportunity to reconcile decentralization and the centrality of his own ideas, that dichotomy in his philosophy. He apparently chose not to notice that the offer and his acceptance of it spurred decentralization to "reverse its course" once again, as he had feared it might.

In the press at the time, Irving's and Blau's decision to go to Lincoln Center was seen as the culmination of the disenchantment with apathetic San Francisco which characterized the Workshop at the end of 1964. This interpretation was correct, but disenchantment was only one of three main factors in the decision. Another was the Workshop's institutional weakness, which rendered it incapable of overcoming San Francisco's apathy. As Jules Irving later explained it, he and Blau had reached "the point of diminishing returns, in which we really couldn't take any step forward. It was beyond survival."[7] Still, I think the primary factor in the decision was the hubris which had also crested by the end of 1964: Herbert Blau's belief that he had founded the National Theatre and his desire to put it before the nation in the one context from which it could speak to all the people—New York. He and Irving maintained that they were not leaving The Actor's Workshop— rather, they were moving it to Lincoln Center. The move was the "Manifest Destiny" Blau had ordered for his theatre.

These ideas and feelings, some realized by the two men at the time and some only subconscious, were present in one of the most revealing documents in the history of the regional theatre: Irving's and Blau's letter of February 2, 1965, to their Actor's Workshop subscribers. It followed quickly upon the announcement of their appointment to Lin-

149

coln Center, and it was designed to quiet a rush of speculation and rumor in the San Francisco press. Blau composed the letter:

February 2, 1965

To our subscribers:

Some of you have been with us for years, some for a short time. But the phone calls and letters from both new and old subscribers confirm our belief that there can be spontaneous rapport between a theater and its audience. If our work has defined us, those who have seen our work may the better understand our actions.

We've made a choice. It is conceivable that the meaning of that choice—to accept the directorship of the Repertory Theater of Lincoln Center—might have been lost in the speculation and wild surmise of this last week. We're writing now to thank you for your faith and forbearance, and to clarify what we can. We also want to outline plans for honoring your subscription during this period of transition.

We say period of transition because we think it important that The Workshop continue in San Francisco under new leadership, and we are currently doing all we can to see that it does. The air, you know, is full of scavengers and quick solutions. But if there has been adventure to the development of The Workshop, there has also been care and logic, and we have no intention of letting the vaguest good intentions, no less sheer bluff and nonsense, guide it through the crisis brought on by our choice.

We are by no means naive about the problems confronting the Board of Directors at this juncture. These problems existed before we were approached by Lincoln Center. While we would have faced them had we stayed, they must certainly be faced now that we are ready to go. No amount of cultural explosiveness is going to expunge Workshop deficits which grow annually. They will only be provided for by firm civic action of the kind we have been soliciting for years—and that we have solicited again today at City Hall.

Our subscribers have done their part by subscribing. But perhaps even they have never been aware that Workshop deficits are immeasurably larger than any budget shows. For the fact is that members of the company—working for the most nominal salaries, half-salaries, or no salaries—have been subsidizing the city's culture for years. They are not complaining, and we are not complaining. Had we chosen to stay in San Francisco, we would have pressed for subsidy, but we would have continued our work under any circumstances, doing what is necessary to survive. If you have created something from nothing, you do what you must with what you have.

But our going has changed the situation for San Francisco. New directors and an augmented company are going to cost the city money. A new theater is going to cost more—as it has, say, in Minneapolis. This is a new period; there is no reason a theater should start or persist the way we did. Culture can afford itself. If the momentum of concern now gathered can collect itself into public financing and the construction of an appropriate building to house it, The Workshop will surely continue. If it doesn't, all your own real devotion—no less the sundry vain wishing suddenly aroused—will have been wasted. We put the issue to you because you have been understanding to begin with. What does take place in this city will need your initiative. Our decision to go opened up a crisis; but crisis alone won't run a theater, as our previous history shows.

Let us emphasize, however, that our decision to accept the offer from Lincoln Center was not based on deficits here or the failure to provide us with a theater building. While we wished for better civic support, the existence of The Workshop was never contingent on it. Even to say that if money is raised The Workshop will continue is misleading. For The Workshop is above all an Idea given substance by the people who believed in it. We should be pleased to have the name perpetuated. We think a new theater should be founded on the traditions we have established. There are people staying behind who can give it substance. But if the new theater is to be worth anything, it must have a point of view of its own.

As for our point of view, it has been obscured by the loose talk. Those who have followed our work from the beginning know that we tended at a very early stage, to put what we were doing in a national perspective. The theater in America was spiritually impoverished when we began. We were among those who tried to prevail against the tawdry habits of mind that made theater in this country an inferior and desperate enterprise. There has always been an evangelistic bent to The Actor's Workshop. Many of you have admired it all the way; some of you have supported us while irritated by it. It has made a few people nearly hysterical. So be it. We have welcomed criticism as we have sometimes fought it, because we have encouraged the notion that the health of a society is measured by the degree of outspokenness it allows itself.

Our theme was to do what you could where you were with the resources that, for better or worse, happened to be at your disposal. It was also our conviction that we and the people with whom we worked were our own best resources. The growth of The Actor's Workshop was a major cultural exercise in the organic development of self-conviction. This was essential in a profession that has had, until very recently, almost no honorable conviction whatever. We have made choices before that were unpopular, but if the theater is entertainment we have never believed it was a popularity contest. All we could finally go by—after the best advice and criticism—were our own best principles. If we've made mistakes, we have proved at least one thing that has become an example to theater people

151

everywhere: that determination and sacrifice could build a meaningful theater from the bare ground up—almost literally out of nothing but ourselves.

Be assured that when the offer came from Lincoln Center, we neither leaped nor took it lightly. We know what our responsibilities are, but we also know what our purposes have been. In the earliest, darkest, and most miniscule days of The Actor's Workshop—against all scoffers and unsolicited "professional" knowhow—we tried to conceive a theater whose influence would extend across the country. (You can find pronouncements to that effect—naive as they must have seemed—in our earliest literature, as in our most recent writing.) Whatever failures of recognition there may have been in San Francisco, the Idea which *is* The Actor's Workshop has made its way in the world. The offer from Lincoln Center, as we see it, is the most material certification of that Idea.

Our appointment, then, is not a San Francisco issue or a New York issue but a national issue. And it is being seen precisely that way all over the world, except perhaps in San Francisco.

And let all of us realize what the opportunity is now. The resources at Lincoln Center are by far the best that *America* has to offer to the Idea developed here. There is no other situation in the American theater which could have induced us to leave San Francisco. We don't underestimate the size of the job, or the difficulties before us in that environment. We appraised them carefully. Danger winks on opportunity. We can count the blocks from Lincoln Center to Shubert Alley as well as anyone, but ideologically we shall remain as we have always been, three thousand miles from Broadway and what it represents. We have been given a mandate to do at Lincoln Center what we have done here, and more so—and there's no doubt that if it can be done, there will have been a revolution in the American theater that will have repercussions everywhere. If there is eminence in our new position, we fully intend to use it to encourage precisely the things to which we have given voice and example before.

Now for immediate matters. We regret that the task at Lincoln Center makes it impossible for us to complete the season here as scheduled. While we shall open a bill of plays at the Encore, *Julius Caesar* has been cancelled along with the other remaining plays on the subscription. But Emlyn Williams is performing as scheduled at the Marines' Theater and will return for the additional week as previously announced. We shall also be keeping our touring commitments.

What we should like to propose for subscribers is the following options:

1) A pro-rated refund of the remainder of your subscription.
2) Application of the subscription to the last two productions of the current season: Harold Pinter's *The Collection* and Conrad Bromberg's *The Rooming House* at the Encore;

152

and/or a return engagement of *Uncle Vanya* at the Marines'.

For either of these your tickets are transferable to friends, or you may request as many as you have remaining on the subscription. Whatever remains on the subscription after that will be refunded upon request.

3) Donation of the remainder of your subscription to a campaign for continuance of The Actor's Workshop in San Francisco.

The Workshop Board of Directors has made an appeal to the Mayor's Office and the Chief City Administrator for a larger portion of the Hotel Tax. We have already made provisions for new directors. They are ready to come if the city is ready to go ahead. That part of the company and staff which remains can be supplemented. Your donation would be used to subsidize an interim operation and to help underwrite the next season.

In any case, those are the options, with our deepest apologies for having to curtail the present season.

The enclosure lists the various options and a schedule of remaining performances from which you can choose if you desire. Please return the form as soon as possible because the action of the Board of Directors—which has approved our choice and is working actively with us to maintain The Workshop—will be affected by the extent and urgency of your interest. If you feel so inclined, we would also like to hear from you on any account. Since this will, in all likelihood, be our last communication to you here, may we close with gratitude for your support and the hope that you will continue to have a theater worthy of your encouragement.

As for ourselves, in view of the task ahead, it would be very helpful, indeed, if we could take your good faith with us.

Sincerely,

Herbert Blau

Herbert Blau

Jules Irving

Jules Irving

Regional Theatre: The Revolutionary Stage

A month after sending out the letter, Irving and Blau had completed their "period of transition" and had moved to New York.* They took with them the leading dozen actors of the Workshop and a similar number of administrative and technical personnel. My wife and I left San Francisco, too, but not for Lincoln Center; turning down both that offer and the inheritance of the Workshop, I had decided to move to Ithaca, New York, and to work with Alan Schneider on starting a new classical theatre festival to be patterned, of course, on Stratford, Ontario.

And so, thirteen years after their underground start in a loft behind a judo academy, Jules Irving and Herbert Blau were chosen to lead what was then thought to be America's best hope for a National Theatre. Their move to New York was the third major turning point of the regional theatre revolution because it marked the first time that the central powers turned to the periphery for help. Surprisingly, the summons to the center did not involve The Guthrie Theater or the American Shakespeare Festival, both of which looked as if they had been created to become the National Theatre. It did not involve the APA or the National Repertory Theatre, both serving the country from touring bases. It did not involve the Alley Theatre or Arena Stage, then the most secure and most professional of the acorns. It involved the little Actor's Workshop—the theatre farthest away, with the farthest-out ideas and the most nay-saying of philosophies. The theatre most ideologically anti-Broadway was summoned to the center, and its decision to go opened up a new world for the regional theatre form. Now it had reason to see *itself* as the solution for the central theatre's ills; it could hope to be a savior. Decentralization, as a goal and a way of life, would never be the same again.

Whether The Actor's Workshop would become the National Theatre was far from sure, of course. One thing was sure: the move to the

---

* It was generally assumed that the departure of Irving and Blau would spell the end of The Actor's Workshop. However, an energetic young actor-technician in their company, Kenneth Kitch, took up the reins with Irving's and Blau's moral support and began to rebuild the group. Hiring director John Hancock, Kitch reopened the theatre in the summer of 1965 with a production of Tennessee Williams's *The Milk Train Doesn't Stop Here Anymore*. But Hancock soon left San Francisco for the Pittsburgh Playhouse, and Kitch went with him. When Hancock left Pittsburgh, Kitch went on to Arena Stage. The Actor's Workshop was gone from San Francisco. Its records and old photographs were stored by Irving and Blau in the recesses of the Repertory Theater of Lincoln Center.

East was not only an exhilarating experience but a bittersweet one as well. There was more than a touch of irony in something that happened on the opening night of *Danton's Death* in 1965 at Lincoln Center, Irving's and Blau's debut at the center. My wife and I had flown from Ithaca to New York to join our Workshop friends in their moment of joy and triumph. A party was held after the opening performance, and a dance floor was set up in the lobby of the theatre. The dance band sat down to start playing. Their opening song was the most popular of that year—"I Left My Heart in San Francisco."

9 Up against the Marble Wall: The Loss of The Actor's Workshop

"The climate is no longer right for me to do what I came to do in the form I had in mind."

> Herbert Blau, explaining why he left the
> Repertory Theater of Lincoln Center

"I obviously feel that the climate is right for me."

> Jules Irving, explaining why he remained

"Our dramatic heritage is being strangled by indifference. To have great theaters, there must be great audiences, great donors and great statesmen."

> Jules Irving, upon his resignation

For those regional theatre leaders who had been hoping that the National Theatre of America would evolve out of their individual theatres, the move of Jules Irving and Herbert Blau to the marble splendor of Lincoln Center was a severe jolt. Many felt that Irving and Blau had deserted the movement which had made them what they were and that they had also betrayed their colleagues in the movement. They may also have resented the fact that they had not been chosen instead. Among ambitious people who have risen from anonymity in hostile situations, there is sometimes little room for genuine pride and pleasure in the sudden propulsion of others. All regional theatre leaders had gloried in the advent of Tyrone Guthrie several years earlier because he had added legitimacy and class to their crusade, but they could not bring themselves to bask in the propulsion of two men considered their mere equals (and by some their inferiors). In the minds of other regional theatre leaders, the National Theatre prize seemed to have been suddenly and surreptitiously snatched from them.

Irving and Blau arrived in New York in the spring of 1965 with neither the unadulterated good wishes of those friends they had left

156

behind nor the high hopes of the commercial New York theatre crowd lying in wait for them at the center. The fact that they brought with them many San Francisco actors who seemed neophytes in the eyes of New York theatre personnel also caused friction. Added to this was the fact that both Mrs. Irving and Mrs. Blau were to be actresses in the company, which looked like nepotism at the very least. Through the spring and summer of 1965, the New York theatrical fraternity sharpened its claws for the upcoming debut of Irving and Blau, which would be further complicated by being the debut as well of the new marble Vivian Beaumont Theater in Lincoln Center, built for the Repertory Theater at a cost of $9.5 million. Still, Irving and Blau continued their planning despite the ill will, which did not ruffle them outwardly; as Blau said, "Some people have implied that 'The knives are out for you.' That's nonsense, the knives are always out for you. The only way to deal with the knives is to be powerful in your art."[1] Two friends of Irving and Blau fed the fires of controversy. Professor and novelist Mark Harris (a fellow San Franciscan whose play *Friedman and Son* they had produced at the Workshop) wrote a Sunday *New York Times* feature article depicting the pair as young Lochinvars come out of the West to save the fabulous invalid. And Theodore Hoffman said, in a *Show* magazine article entitled "Who the Hell Is Herbert Blau?": "The theatre of Blau and Irving wasn't exactly the toast of San Francisco, and Shubert Alley probably won't like them either, until someone—probably Norman Mailer—discovers that they're really sweet gutsy guys. But they'll flutter the dovecotes all right, attract plenty of violent partisans, make lots of provocative copy for the Sunday drama sections and probably drive the board of directors to as many secret discussions as the last regime."[2]

The early approach and actions of Irving and Blau in their new position were naive, a fact that Jules Irving realized in later days. Looking back on those early days after five years on the job, Irving noted that "Coming here was an overwhelmingly complex move. It was a difficult time. Both the personal and the artistic adjustments were difficult and challenging. We had to inaugurate a new plant and integrate some actors we had brought from San Francisco with a number of New York players. The best way I can describe the period is as one of deep travail, of trying to make a theatre work at the top of the mountain."[3] That "top of the mountain" was another way of saying that the Repertory Theater of Lincoln Center could become the National Theatre of America.

The personal adjustments he mentioned reflected the hectic and disorienting nature of the move. This was a group of people very western in their habits and attitudes, and generally they found New York an alien environment. In some instances, the people brought from San Francisco were simply unable to deal with the greater tensions and demands of work in the limelight of New York. For example, the Workshop technical director, José Sevilla, was brought to New York to serve in a similar position at the Repertory Theater. In San Francisco, his special talent had been in accomplishing mammoth feats on short notice all by himself, a one-man-whirlwind technical department. This was just what the helter-skelter Workshop needed. In New York, he was not able to lead a technical department of other people who needed direction rather than the opportunity to watch a whirlwind at work. A fairly large number of young people brought from San Francisco could not cut the New York mustard; it was a tough and merciless world for which they were simply unprepared. They either fell by the wayside or soon returned to more relaxed and congenial California.

Irving and Blau, while no doubt feeling many of the same personal doubts and insecurities, still forged ahead. They announced a four-play season which was rightly praised for its esoteric quality: Büchner's *Danton's Death* (not performed in New York for many generations), *The Country Wife*, Sartre's *The Condemned of Altona,* and *The Caucasian Chalk Circle*. While the small experimental Forum Theater in the basement of the Beaumont building would also be ready for production, the two directors chose to leave it dormant during the first season while they tried their wings on the main stage.

The responsibility of staging the inaugural production naturally fell to Blau, the primary figure in the move to the center. Irving, less known as a director and by personality more suited to the management side, would wait to direct a play. Blau's *Danton's Death* provided a suitably colorful opening, but it was a dud as a production. Typically, the work was conceptually outsized, but it was unfocused on the stage. The reviews were not good, although *New York Times* critic Howard Taubman was indulgent: "Not all the problems of 'Danton's Death' . . . have been solved, nor all the problems of forming a strong company and using the impressive new stage. But there are heartening

158

signs of a viewpoint and a commitment. One could not ask for more this early in the game."[4]

The second production, *The Country Wife*, staged by actor-director Robert Symonds, was no better received than the first; what had been a delightful success at the Workshop only a year before was dwarfed by the vastness of the new theatre. *The Condemned of Altona*, also staged by Blau, was another critical failure, and the first season was saved only by the final production, Jules Irving's remounting of *The Caucasian Chalk Circle*. Audiences appreciated it, its run was extended into the summer, and its moderate success allowed the new directors to catch their breath. But for anyone privileged to have seen the Carl Weber mounting in San Francisco two years before, the Lincoln Center re-creation was no comparison—again, the new and gleaming theatre dwarfed what had been an exciting underdog in that dirty servicemen's YMCA.

One example of the difference between the San Francisco and New York productions of the same plays (*The Country Wife* and *The Caucasian Chalk Circle*) was the surprising experience of young actress Elizabeth Huddle, who played the leading role in both productions in both cities. In San Francisco, Miss Huddle, a full-blown girl with a winning insouciance, was warm and gutsy and delightful—and I for one fully expected that she would take New York by storm. In the Lincoln Center productions, she was pleasant and all right, but no more. One had the feeling that almost any young, full-blown, insouciant actress, of which New York has many, could have done the roles as well. In this, I think Miss Huddle's experience paralleled that of the Workshop as a whole in the transfer to New York, despite the expectations for both held by many knowledgeable people. Like the Workshop itself, Miss Huddle had seemed brilliant in the musty YMCA, but she simply could not command the stage of a multi-million-dollar marble theatre in New York. Eventually she returned to California.

Jules Irving and Herbert Blau could afford no such solution to their first season's problems, nor did they seek it. In the midst of the first season, the board of the Repertory Theater must have pondered its own solutions, but it could ill afford any flare-up after the bad press of the Kazan-Whitehead fracas. Besides, there was *The Caucasian Chalk Circle* to redeem the first season, and a record-breaking 40,000 subscribers supporting the theatre. Though this number dropped off for the second season, there was still a mandate, still a willingness, albeit cautious, to give Irving and Blau a chance. The two Lochinvars would be indulged while they continued to learn the inscrutable ways of the East. They still had far to go to satisfy the New York critics, who were by now thoroughly disenchanted with their regime. In fact, the once-indulgent Howard Taubman had changed his tune as early as the opening of the second production: "It is, indeed, not too soon for an agonizing reappraisal. . . . Acting is not the only problem at Lincoln Center. Directing is another. . . . The problem of the stage and theater can be solved as the acting company and direction are improved. And improve they must if the great potential of this institution is to be realized."[5]

The second season was announced: *The Alchemist*, Lorca's *Yerma*, Leo Lerman's new play *The East Wind*, and Brecht's *Galileo* (apparently an attempt to duplicate the saving-grace success of the first season's production of *The Caucasian Chalk Circle*). Rod Steiger was announced for the role of Galileo, and John Hirsch, then director of the Manitoba Theatre Center in Canada and guest director at Stratford, Ontario, was chosen to direct the Lorca play. Irving, fresh from his success with *The Caucasian Chalk Circle*, opened the second season with a heavy-handed production of *The Alchemist*. Hirsch's *Yerma* was somewhat more successful. Robert Symonds staged *The East Wind*, which failed to amount to much as either a play or a production. Meanwhile, Rod Steiger, claiming illness, bowed out of *Galileo*; it was more likely that he blanched at the prospect of Blau's directing him.

Near the beginning of 1967, the small Forum Theater was to open with a premiere production of Wilford Leach's *In Three Zones*. Just as he had staged the inaugural production on the main stage of the Beaumont, so Blau was directing the Forum's opening bill. *In Three Zones*, like *The Birds* in San Francisco, proved Blau's brilliance of mind but also his incapacity to mount his ideas in a workable fashion. In its use of film and other media, it was ahead of its time, but by the time *In Three Zones* reached its preview performances, Blau had spent on that one production almost the entire Forum budget for the whole season, and the production itself was a mess. The premiere was cancelled. Shortly thereafter, Blau's resignation was announced. The matter was handled delicately and cryptically: "The climate is no longer

right for me to do what I came to do in the form I had in mind,"
explained Blau. It was further announced that Irving, at Blau's urging,
would stay on as sole director of the theatre and that they would remain
personally close.

Certainly the disaster of *In Three Zones* was the final straw for Herbert Blau, but it was hardly the main reason for his departure. The
change in the "climate" really was the major reason, and that change
was an extreme one. The climate had altered from one of high hopes
and exalted pronouncements to one of tension and acrimony between
Blau and the Repertory Theater board. Blau insisted that from the
beginning he had made very clear to the board members his idiosyncrasies and his ideas and had warned them that they would find him
difficult. Blau also maintained that they had obviously understood and
accepted these ground rules. However, they did not really understand
what Blau was saying in his involuted way, or else they did not choose
to hear him; at the same time, Blau did not see that he was not getting
through to them. Blau and the board were never on the same wave-
length, not from the day they first met. They lived and thought in
different worlds. When Blau announced to us in San Francisco that he
was leaving for Lincoln Center, he said in amazement that he had discovered that "there really is an Establishment in this country, after all."
I think that he had never really believed that it existed, and while he
was going to join it he had no idea of how to deal with it or use it. Blau
was as innocent as he was brilliant.

Nevertheless, Blau still had the ability to understand himself and
therefore his own predicament. The essential change in the "climate"
was, I think, Blau's realization that he was in over (or under) his head.
He had come into a situation that was intellectually not ready for him,
and for which he was not ready politically or dynamically. Despite the
acuity of his mind, he proved unable to function in the maelstrom that
is the New York theatre scene. His idealism could not accommodate the
details, let alone the plays of power. He and Irving had decided to
manage the Repertory Theater as a team (unlike the arrangement at
the Workshop, which Irving managed alone), but Blau turned out to
be not only uninterested in management but unsuited to it, too. He
might have stayed on to function as a literary manager for Jules Irving,
as Kenneth Tynan served Laurence Olivier at the National Theatre in
England—and he would have been superb in his job—but having stood

161

in the primary spotlight, he could not accept such a supportive function. The hubris which had brought him to the center could not accept less than the ultimate job. In short, Blau achieved the centrality he desired, but he could not handle it. His genius got lost at Lincoln Center, which makes his story one of the saddest in the history of regional theatre—particularly because Herbert Blau was one of the few real intellectual geniuses in all of the movement.

And so he was gone—the man whose mind had conceived in The Actor's Workshop what he had thought to be a National Theatre and who had come to New York to put it before the nation. Despite his realization that he had to leave, it must have been a bitter experience for a man as proud as Blau. After a year of teaching at the City College of New York, Blau too returned to California—this time to Los Angeles, as dean of the new Institute of the Arts which had been created through funds from the estate of Walt Disney. However, Blau's ideas proved unacceptable to the Disney powers, and he was dismissed from this position; later he turned back to college teaching.

With Blau gone, Jules Irving was left alone at the Repertory Theater helm. At least in the beginning, it must have been a lonely job for him. In the eyes of Actor's Workshop people as in the eyes of other leaders in the movement, Jules Irving had always been the day-by-day leader of the Workshop. When W. McNeil Lowry of the Ford Foundation offered Jules Irving grants to study in Europe, Irving would reply that Blau instead should go and that he himself should stay and run the theatre. This was sensible. If Herb Blau had left the Workshop, it would have changed but it would have gone on; if Jules Irving had left, the Workshop would have collapsed. Irving was the essential institutional figure. But in the move to Lincoln Center, Blau played the principal role; the partnership changed from Irving-Blau to Blau-Irving. Irving "went along" to Lincoln Center. However, being a natural scrapper, he soon began to feel his oats and to like the rough-and-tumble of New York producing. He ingratiated himself with the Repertory Theater board at the same time that Blau was alienating it. It was inevitable that in New York the rigid idealism of Herbert Blau would become a liability for the more pragmatically adaptable Jules Irving. In San Francisco, where their primary goal was not simply to "make it," their opposite personalities and approaches complemented each other. In more competitive, do-or-die New York, there was no room at the top for two even complementary personalities. The New York maelstrom could accommodate only the more resilient Jules Irving. In short, Irving could get over any initial loneliness because in the New York atmosphere it was natural for him to be in charge by himself.

Irving's first task was to complete the 1966–67 season and particularly to replace Blau as the director of *Galileo*. He chose John Hirsch to direct and Anthony Quayle to replace Rod Steiger in the title role. *Galileo* turned out to be the best Repertory Theater production yet, and it provided a strong start for Jules Irving on his solo path. He had been careful to point out to the board that he did not assume that he himself would be retained beyond the end of that season, but when, at the end of the season, he was offered a new extended contract, he accepted wholeheartedly.

Irving's planning for the next season included a radical departure from previous policy—an invitational production of *The Little Foxes*, mounted by Broadway producer Saint Subber, featuring an all-star cast (Anne Bancroft, Margaret Leighton, George C. Scott, and E. G. Marshall), and directed by Broadway's new prodigy, Mike Nichols. After the Repertory Theater engagement, *The Little Foxes* was transferred by Subber to the Barrymore Theatre on Broadway, where it was presented in association with the Repertory Theater of Lincoln Center "under the direction of Jules Irving." The fact that Nichols misdirected the play for Lincoln Center (staging it not for the Beaumont's thrust stage but for easy transfer to the Barrymore's proscenium) did not dim the box-office success of the production or the Broadway prestige which Irving himself gained from it. The other productions of Irving's first solo season were creditable renderings of *St. Joan* (with Diana Sands); *Tiger at the Gates*, directed by Anthony Quayle; and *Cyrano de Bergerac*, staged by Carl Weber. Never again would a production be mounted that was as embarrassing as *The Country Wife*, *The Condemned of Altona*, or even Irving's own *Alchemist*. Devoting himself exclusively to managing the theatre, Irving ruled himself out of directing for the main Beaumont stage; instead he hired guest directors (including, frequently, John Hirsch) for all major productions. In a related move after *The Little Foxes*, Irving opened the doors of the Repertory Theater to commercial stars who could conceivably handle the demands of the classics. The idea of a continuing company of actors forever banded together—a key factor at The Actor's Workshop—was dropped. Irving explained his approach as pragmatic: "I think it's going to be a question of time before the identity of the company emerges fully. . . . During that time of development I must maintain the highest standards possible. . . . I'm committed to a policy of slow growth and maintaining an open door, while the company evolves. Each season the company is exposed to new actors, to keep it revitalized. Out of that exposure and continuum of work—just as with The Actor's Workshop—the identity of the company is emerging."[6] Irving was hoping that actors would come to the Repertory Theater for several plays, leave for a while, and then come back for several more. This open-door policy was his attempt to build a pool of actors such as that used by Olivier's National Theatre in England. Irving was taking an approach which appeared to be a reasonable one in his situation. He used the power of the Lincoln Center location to cast his productions with stars who would attract audiences, and he used his power well.

Related to the emphasis on name actors for the main stage was a parallel decision to relegate the few remaining actors from the Workshop to the Forum Theater in the basement of the Beaumont. Only Robert Symonds of the Workshop group continued to play important roles on the main stage, including Cyrano and the title role in *The Miser*. In the early days of the regime, in *The Condemned of Altona* and *The East Wind*, about half of the actors were from San Francisco. By 1969, with such plays as *The Time of Your Life* and *In the Matter of J. Robert Oppenheimer*, only 10 percent of the acting company were Workshop alumni.

Reopening the small Forum Theater in late 1967, Irving obtained a $25,000 grant from the Rockefeller Foundation to mount exclusively new plays there. The Forum gained a rightful reputation as an open-door theatre for experimentation by new young playwrights. Irving himself sometimes directed plays in the Forum, but generally he was more and more the producer. By the 1968–69 season, he was beginning to hit his stride. That season boasted four critical and box-office successes in a row: *King Lear* and William Gibson's *A Cry of Players* in rotating repertory for half of the season and *In the Matter of J. Robert Oppenheimer* and *The Miser* in successive runs for the remainder. For the Gibson play, Irving brought back Anne Bancroft, and for Lear, he achieved the casting coup of his career—Lee J. Cobb. Both were box-office dynamite. The third play of the season, *In the Matter of J. Robert Oppenheimer,* was Irving's first unqualified artistic success at the Repertory Theater. It was transplanted from an earlier Mark Taper Forum production, with Gordon Davidson again directing. The play, a courtroom drama in modern dress with an all-male cast, fitted the stage and the resources of the Beaumont perfectly, and it was the first production offered by the Repertory Theater which obviously deserved a permanent place in theatre annals. Not only was the production brought back for a summer run but also it embarked on a national tour in the fall of 1969, this time restaged by Irving himself.

The 1968–69 season ended in glory for Jules Irving. When *Oppenheimer* was followed immediately by an effective staging of *The Miser,* the *New York Times* critic Clive Barnes rather offhandedly ventured the idea that the Repertory Theater "is—like it or lump it—at present, our national theatre."[7] Jules Irving, who had been striving "at the top of the mountain," now seemed to belong there, at least as a visitor. Interviewed in Boston upon the opening in that city of the touring *Oppenheimer,* he referred to "our image as the National Theatre of America" and said, "If this country is to have a national theatre—and it will be a disgrace if it doesn't—now is the time to throw away the crystal ball and get on with the huge job at hand."[8] At that point he appeared to have as much right as anyone to assume that the job could be his. Interviewing him early in the 1969–70 season, Lewis Funke of the *New York Times* caught the essence of Irving's success: "Sitting in his simple though spacious office in the administrative wing of the Beaumont the other afternoon, the immaculately groomed Mr. Irving looked the picture of a man on his way. His hair is considerably grayer than it was when he first took over his assignment. But the energy remains, and his eyes still glisten as he discusses grosses, management problems, and artistic aspirations."[9]

However, the order of these last three considerations reflected the core problem of the Repertory Theater of Lincoln Center. Grosses and management problems had to take precedence over artistic aspirations because the Repertory Theater always operated at the edge of an economic precipice. There were constant and daily trials, not eased by either the growing critical acceptance of the company's work or the relatively steady audience (which averaged 84 percent of capacity over the years). In so large a theatre at the center of the storm, even minor nuisances seemed to be major crises; and the Repertory Theater, as the youngest and poorest member of the Lincoln Center family, lacked power and prestige within its home context. This weakness was intensified by the basic ineffectuality of the Repertory Theater board of directors, which, while composed of rich and influential people, never rallied fully to the financial needs of the company. By trimming his program, by mounting more royalty-free and smaller productions, and even by laying off most of his administrative staff during the summer months, Irving was able to keep his yearly operating budget in the early 1970s to approximately $2,000,000; but in the same period, contributions to erase the deficit were less and less each year—and Irving himself raised most of the money in government and foundation grants. The board was standing back, not pulling its weight to secure the theatre.

In 1971, the delicate hold on life was almost snapped by a complicated and melodramatic incident—the near take-over of the Vivian Beaumont Theater by the City Center of Music and Drama, helped by Lincoln Center itself. The City Center, started in 1943 by Mayor Fiorello La Guardia, is the sponsor of both the New York City Ballet and the New York City Opera, both of which perform at Lincoln Center; until the mid-1960s, it was also the sponsor of a traditional drama series at low prices. Early in 1971, it was announced that the City Center, an institution much more powerful than the Repertory Theater of Lincoln Center, would take over the operation of the Beaumont Theater and would reconstruct it to house its emerging film program. The Repertory Theater would become a tenant of the building, with exclusive use of the main Beaumont stage for its winter season of plays. The rationale behind the move was that the Repertory Theater was unable to support the maintenance of the Beaumont building (which in itself exceeds $600,000 each year) and that by becoming a tenant it would vastly improve its financial position and ability to continue. The plan seemed logical and feasible on the surface, and all appeared in accord until it became clear that the City Center was planning to gut the Forum Theater and replace it with a film auditorium. The New York theatre community, which by then had grown accustomed to the good experimental work of the Forum and which cherished the theatre itself as a small but unique "gem," was horrified at the prospect of its loss and responded by mounting a campaign to save the Repertory Theater from City Center and Lincoln Center wreckers. The fight grew heated and intense, but Jules Irving was strangely silent in the controversy. Finally, after the battle had been waged by others on his behalf, he presented an impassioned plea to the New York City fathers (who had ultimate jurisdiction in the matter) and was able to stem the tide so that the Repertory Theater could continue on its own. His ultimate success in defeating the plan was ironic in view of the fact that in the beginning he and his board had officially endorsed it: "For the first time since our inception, our creative energies can be wholly devoted to our regular four-play subscription seasons on the Beaumont main-stage and in The Forum. . . . The proposed plan assures the continuity of The Repertory Theater as the prime tenant of the Vivian Beaumont and a far more financially stable constituent of Lincoln Center. The proposed plan would be good for The Repertory Theater, good for the City Center, and good for Lincoln Center."[10]

While Jules Irving may not have wanted to support the take-over plan in the beginning, he was obligated to go along with it until he got lucky, until others joined the battle to fight with him. He could not have won it alone because his institution was at the mercy of its environment, obligated to react to forces rather than being a force in itself. Even in triumph over the City Center take-over attempt, the economic crisis continued unsolved; the victory was Pyrrhic. Irving himself described his operation as "a particular brand of brinkmanship and insanity."[11] His former partner Herbert Blau sympathetically suggested that the Repertory Theater, in the midst of opulence, was still "up against the marble wall."[12]

A less pragmatic person might have tried to destroy the wall, like Joshua—or might have left in disgust. But Irving was a realist, and by the end of the 1960s I think realism and the accommodation it engendered were beginning to take a personal and institutional toll. Irving's pragmatism, which had made it possible for him to function at Lincoln Center, was turning into conciliation. Unlike his leadership of The Actor's Workshop in far-away San Francisco, his direction of the Repertory Theater at the center of the storm had to be filled with compromise in order to survive. And that staying power was exacting a severe price: the deferment of long-range goals, the artistic aspirations referred to by Lewis Funke in the *Times* article. To many observers, the Repertory Theater appeared to be a theatre without an ideology—the opposite of The Actor's Workshop. The need and indeed the choice of compromise meant that Jules Irving had to give up the "Idea" that had been the Workshop; and this loss, I think, was painful for him personally. For instance, Irving seemed to enjoy climbing the mountain more than being a monument at the top—even after he reached the top. In his office at Lincoln Center hung photos of Actor's Workshop productions and a painting of him as Lucky in *Waiting for Godot*. Behind his massive Repertory Theater desk sat the old rolltop desk from which he managed and sustained the Workshop. He wanted to believe that "the objectives are reasonably the same as they were in San Francisco,"[13] that his was still a regional theatre in a region that happened to be New York. He sincerely hoped that despite all the changes, despite all the conciliation, the Repertory Theater still represented a coming to the center of The Actor's Workshop. Not quite. Jules Irving had come to the center, but in order to stay there he had had to leave the Workshop behind: "If I've learned anything during these continuing years in Wonderland, it's that there's always room for one more at the Mad Hatter's tea party. What does it take to create and run New York's major classical theatre on $5 a day? A little madness coupled with nerves of steel, a bullet-proof directing shirt, that Ph.D. in brinkmanship and a steady and shining dream."[14]

In the end Jules Irving proved to be a man unwilling to give himself up to compromise. Eventually and greatly to his credit, when he was forced to choose between the dream and survival, he chose the dream. Faced with a growing and supposedly unobtainable deficit for the 1972–73 season, the Repertory Theater board decided to close the Forum Theater. By then, the Forum had become the one part of the Repertory Theater operation where Jules Irving could pursue an Actor's Workshop kind of dream, and he was unwilling to go on without it. Bluntly and firmly but with a diplomat's tact, he resigned his position, pointing out that he hoped his action would prove that theatres like his had to be more fully and dynamically supported. The board accepted his action with seemingly little chagrin; president Clarke Coggeshall said, "Mr. Irving has been an exceptionally imaginative and resourceful artistic director for the past seven years and he has steadily developed the Repertory Theater artistically in the face of the most difficult economic conditions."[15]

Once he resigned, Irving seemed relieved; he was freed of the burden of compromise. Perhaps it was the Actor's Workshop part of Jules Irving that left the Repertory Theater; perhaps his heart had always stayed in San Francisco; or perhaps he was just worn out. Whatever the deepest personal reasons, in the act of quitting he won a respect which never had been accorded him during the years of struggle.

Meanwhile, it was up to Lincoln Center, in 1973, to find his replacement. Amyas Ames, chairman of the complex, announced that "We're going to search the country for an idea."[16] It was the same approach they had taken in 1965 when they had gone to find Jules Irving and Herbert Blau.

10 The Establishment Theatre

"In 1960 we were practically without a non-commercial theatre, and within five years the theatres had joined the symphony orchestras and art museums on a super-institutional cultural binge."

Martin Gottfried, A Theater Divided

"They come to represent the city's image of itself, rather than the artist's image of the city."

Michael Murray, The Drama Review

By 1965, there had been three major turning points in the regional theatre revolution: the entry of the Ford Foundation in 1957, which legitimatized the form and set it on the course of institutionalism; the opening of The Guthrie Theater in 1963, which gave the form national attention and introduced the hope of a single National Theatre; and the move to Lincoln Center of The Actor's Workshop in 1965, which encouraged the assumption that the regional theatre could be the savior of the American theatre overall. Also by 1965, there had developed a change which was much more subtle, much less specific, but for individual theatres much more significant: their achievement of Establishment status in their respective communities. In other words, they had reached a position in which their civic value was assumed and from which they could call upon the power structure to defend and support them.

The early regional theatres, in the late 1940s and 1950s, started as reactions to the theatrical Establishment of their time—Broadway. They sought to dislodge the overwhelming psychological power of the New York commercial theatre which the leaders saw as moribund and perverse. Opting for classical repertoires and for companies of actors working as self-contained units, they went against the American grain. They were a new anti-Establishment revolution. And yet from the beginning the leaders yearned for personal recognition and acceptance. After all, these early people were young and lacked resources of personal power, fame, or wealth; they came out of decidedly middle-class surroundings and upbringings. In each of them, besides the passion for innovation and reform in the arts, there existed a need for making a public mark for themselves. At the same time that they were rebelling against the Broadway Establishment, they were seeking to establish their theatres and themselves in their own communities.

As already noted, their first major hurdle in gaining public acceptance was the fact that the public considered theatre a get-rich-quick profession. With only Broadway as a standard, people tended to think of theatre as a somewhat naughty game that the Shuberts, Rodgers and Hammerstein, and Mary Martin played and won. Anyone not playing in their league was apparently not very good at the game. The public did not realize that there could be other forms of winning and that the game could even be played for its own sake. Partly to counteract the narrowness of the public's viewpoint, the early leaders enshrined their theatres as soon as possible in an institutional form which lent propriety. An entity larger than the leader but growing out of him, the institution took on an identity of its own and sought loyalties to itself. The leader may have stood for the institution within it, but in public the institution stood taller and said to the community around it, "Look, there is no one getting rich off me. I'm here to serve not Mammon but you." Almost all regional theatres, then, chose a structure which their local Establishments already understood because it was like the structure of the university, the hospital, the symphony orchestra, and the community chest. Once the regional theatres gained acceptance as institutions, their movement from outsider to official status was inevitable.

Between 1960 and 1965, regional theatres took on more and more characteristics of Establishment power and influence. The theatres sought to justify their existence (and their need for financial support) less by pointing out their intrinsic worth than by listing the various ways in which they served the community. Service had all the respectability that mere production of plays did not have. The ways in which the theatre could serve the community other than by producing great

171

plays well seemed legion. For instance, The Guthrie Theater worked very hard in its early years to serve not only theatrical but civic needs as well. There was a Guthrie Theater Boy Scout troop, a teen council to advise the management on the desires of the young, and even a plan for actors to instruct area preachers in the reading of Holy Scripture for maximum dramatic effect. The overall community service goals of regional theatre were best summed up by Tyrone Guthrie's lieutenant, Douglas Campbell: "When you give something of importance to every part of your community, the community will not let you fail."[1] In other words, you can count on payment for services rendered.

The educational role of the regional theatres was one of their most carefully developed aspects of community service. As nonprofit organizations, the theatres were expected to serve educational functions. Beyond this, the school system represented a primary link with the theatre audience of the future. Serving educational needs appeared to be an excellent investment in the future. The relationship between theatre and school was usually initiated by the theatre in making available low-priced tickets to groups of students coming to performances. For a theatre like the American Shakespeare Festival, special spring and fall performances for students from throughout the Northeast provided financial support for the main summer festival season; by 1970, the festival was serving 112,000 students from a thousand schools in twelve eastern states—big business in itself. Even at the anti-public Actor's Workshop, tours to schools throughout northern California and performances for students in San Francisco were carefully developed. One of my most vivid memories of Workshop days is the picture of Jules Irving standing in the midst of a vituperative school board meeting in Napa, California, defending the Workshop's ribald production of *The Country Wife* against the attacks of outraged parents. Characteristically, he received a standing ovation from the self-appointed vice squad and managed to sell tickets for the production to the parents themselves!

The regional theatre's role in educational service was greatly furthered by the passage in 1965 of the federal government's Elementary and Secondary Education Act, a "Great Society" bill. The legislation, among other provisions, offered money to local school systems for cultural enrichment, including performances either in the theatres themselves or by professional actors visiting the schools. Realizing the finan-

172

cial potential of this legislation, theatre leaders throughout the country persuaded (and in some cases had to plead with) superintendents to make application for funds under the act. Here was a built-in audience for the theatre and also dependable revenue. For the regional theatre, the new legislation was manna from heaven. The variety of educational service programs soon became so great that some theatres added special staffing to handle them. Scores of proposals arrived at the United States Office of Education in Washington for grants to schools to purchase theatre services—nearly all of them engineered, I daresay, by the theatres, to keep the dependable revenue coming in.

The plethora of educational programs fostered many instances of strange bedfellows. The bureaucracy of the school systems was often unbearable for the theatre artists, and the mercurial vagueness of the theatre people sometimes alienated the educators. Also, in common with community service programs generally, the easy availability of funds prompted many regional theatres to promote programs far beyond their own capacity to deliver. It is difficult enough to mount six or eight large productions in a nine-month period, let alone to divert time, staff, and resources to activities which are extracurricular to the theatre's main purpose. Nevertheless, the service programs carried with them sure money, and no theatre could afford to say no to any idea which might make its operations more secure. Also, no theatre would deliberately refuse to perform those services which, even if performed only passably, still tended to legitimatize it.

As theatres became active community resources and so more and more proper, it was natural that the power structure of communities would enfold and support them. Most early acorn theatres which had started out with boards of directors composed of the leader's friends later sought out and obtained the participation of more influential community leaders. The later sapling theatres and of course the oak tree theatres took care to seat influential community leaders on their boards of directors from the beginning. The greater involvement of the power structure was a key building block of Establishment status, for the community leaders brought that status with them, and it was a social, financial, and psychological boon. At the same time, the greater involvement introduced a new problem: conflict between the artist and the Establishment as represented by the theatre's board of directors. The early leaders had had the problem of being shunned by the Establishment, but the later leaders had the problem of the Establishment getting inside the institution and disagreeing with them. The involvement of the power structure was an external advantage but an internal threat, and where artists and the Establishment have clashed, the struggles between them have often been public and sometimes ugly.

Interestingly, there have been few crises of this kind in the acorn theatres (one exception occurred in the early years of the Fred Miller Theater in Milwaukee). At the Alley and Arena Stage, there appear to be no tensions between the artist and the board; in fact, members of the boards stand in awe of the artists. This is so because the artists came first and created the institution and its rules. Only then was the Establishment board admitted—to a world where the power was held by the artists.

The conflicts have been frequent in oak tree and sapling theatres, where usually the boards came first and defined the rules and so hold the ultimate power. Stuart Vaughan and Allen Fletcher in Seattle, André Gregory in Philadelphia, Jon Jory in New Haven, Richard Block in Louisville, Word Baker in Cincinnati, Elia Kazan, Robert Whitehead, and Herbert Blau in New York—all clashed with the Establishment boards and all lost their battles. Always, I suspect, the problem arose because neither party really heard what the other was saying over long periods of time, and so they did not understand each other. Those artistic directors who do understand and use the situation are those who direct their board members in much the same way as they direct their actors—motivating them, showing them the way, knowing when to step back and let them perform on their own. Of course, actors expect to be directed; boards do not. To direct a board like an ensemble is a very difficult task. Those who are good at it are the ones suited to the institutional life, even though being good at it can lead to a personal identity crisis. Those unable or unwilling to do it have often been the more interesting creative personalities; the loss of them has been a severe one for the regional theatre movement. Yet no artist should be discredited because he is unsuited to the institutional life; some artists simply cannot accept the fact that their destiny can be controlled by people with little or no knowledge of their art. For example, in explaining recently the upheavals in his theatre, one board member suggested to me that any artistic director, in the course of three or four years, is bound to have used up his "creative juice" and so is bound to be of no further value to the theatre institution. In the presence of such an attitude, it is not surprising that many theatre leaders have found it difficult or impossible to commit themselves to their institutions. Why should an artist go to a place where he may be almost automatically discarded before he settles in? Also, in the artist's defense, there *are* problems of philistinism, and the outlook of boards is frequently narrow. The Establishment's narrowness is self-protective, for it has much to protect—including all that it has inherited and accomplished. Artists, on the other hand, must change the status quo in order to accomplish their goals. The basic conflict between the artist and the Establishment is simple: The artist is asking the Establishment to pay for his personal vision which often tends to deny the values of that power structure. Gordon Davidson crystallized the problem in quoting a member of the Los Angeles Establishment: "I refuse to give money to support plays which tear down institutions which I hold dear."[2]

Still, boards of directors are not the primary constituency whose institutions a theatre cannot afford to tear down. In any community, the audience exercises final control and represents the ultimate Establishment. Indeed, some theatres have disappeared because they did not answer the needs of their audiences, as defined by those audiences. Certainly the Theatre of the Living Arts in Philadelphia and the Charles Playhouse in Boston collapsed in part because their increasingly exotic repertoire did not interest an audience even in a city of several million. Conversely, the Studio Arena Theatre in Buffalo changed from a marginal operation to a more healthy one by serving the conventional tastes of its audience. For instance, a Studio Arena news release of February 21, 1969, illustrates its approach:

Neal DuBrock, Executive Producer of the Studio Arena Theatre, has announced that Neil Simon's laugh jackpot, *The Star-Spangled Girl*, will be the next Studio production, running from March 6 to 29, and presented as an "experiment"....

One certainly would not think to label Neil Simon an "experimental" playwright, and since a presentation of a Simon comedy is usually a guaranteed, solid hit, what makes the presentation of *The Star-Spangled Girl* an "experiment" for Buffalo's Studio Arena? It certainly is related to the dilemma of selecting a season of plays, compatible to all types of theatregoers, from sensitive Pinter worshippers to Simon laugh fans. The experiment was actually triggered by the storm of controversy which has raged in print, by mail and phone and in after-play panel discussions, over the theatre's current productions of Harold Pinter's *The Homecoming* and *The Killing of Sister George* which preceded it. Therefore, *The Star-Spangled Girl*, the complete antithesis

175

of *The Homecoming*, is scheduled to play immediately after it as an "experiment" to better determine Buffalo's audience support for the type of play they most prefer.

Since the theatre is currently in the process of planning next season's schedule of plays, this experiment is a most timely one in that it is sure to have a bearing on the plays selected for next season.

Of several collapses because of failure to heed the audience's demands, only one has been documented: the Front Street Theatre in Memphis. Working on a grant from the Rockefeller Foundation, Jack Conrad, a professor of anthropology at Southwestern University in Memphis, created a demographic and more importantly a psychological profile of the Front Street audience. Any regional theatre in the country could more or less match Conrad's demographic portrait.[3] The men worked primarily in professional and managerial positions. The median income was $18,000 a year. Thirty-two percent had incomes in excess of $25,000, and 9 percent in excess of $100,000. The audience was 60 percent Protestant, 23 percent Jewish, 6 percent Catholic, and 11 percent agnostic. (The Protestant percentage matched that of the general population; the Jewish percentage was 8 percent higher, and the Catholic 15 percent lower.) It had had 3.82 years of college education. Approximately 65 percent had worked as volunteers with underprivileged and handicapped persons. Over 90 percent had headed or participated in charitable fund drives. Clearly, the Front Street Theatre audience was composed of the upper middle class and above.

The overall purpose of Conrad's profile was to uncover the personal reasons for attending the theatre and secondarily to show how the Front Street Theatre perished by failing to serve those reasons. Conrad's thesis is that people attend plays which relate to their personal needs. His conclusions, while hardly startling, are still worth noting: "This group goes to the theatre primarily for aesthetic and entertainment reasons. . . . To a far lesser extent they are concerned with plays that have a message or purport to provide a new insight into themselves or the world. . . . It appears that the Front Street audience rejected emotion-laden, heavy drama, not so much because of intellectual lethargy, but because *it fulfilled no central emotional need for them*."[4] Conrad is saying nothing that a theatre manager cannot sense by comparing his box-office receipts for *You Can't Take It with You* with those for *Waiting for Godot*. Nor does he deal with the possibility that the Front Street audience's lack of need for heavy drama might betray a massive case of dullness in the Memphis population. What Conrad does prove is that audiences want primarily to be entertained and that if you do not give them what they want they will desert you.

Conrad's study is effective in its analysis of the audience but offensive in the solution it offers:

The basic structure of any eight-show season in Memphis should include the following range and ratio of plays:
1. One relatively new and popular musical—such as *Kiss Me Kate*;
2. One older and well-liked musical—such as *The Student Prince*;
3. One relatively new and popular comedy—such as *The Seven-Year Itch*;
4. One older and well-liked comedy—such as *Private Lives*;
5. One Shakespearean play—preferably alternating tragedy with comedy;
6. One well-known drama—such as *Who's Afraid of Virginia Woolf?*;
7. One experimental or avant-garde piece—such as anything the director wishes to try;
8. One children's favorite—such as *Alice in Wonderland*.[5]

Meanwhile, of course, the artistic director has thrown in the towel and left town because this is a season of plays which says absolutely nothing. The only thing it accomplishes, besides alienating the artists, is to save the theatre by allowing the audience to call the tune. Fortunately, no regional theatre has gone as far as Conrad suggests in allowing the audience to control its program. Still, the tendency to be ruled by audience preferences is very strong and is bolstered further by the dependence of regional theatres upon subscriptions. Indeed, the growth of such dependence parallels the theatre's emergence as part of the Establishment.

Once the Ford Foundation appeared on the scene in 1957, stability of theatres became a key goal; and Ford's solution was that stability should be achieved through the theatres' own box offices: "The overall aim of the program is to help the participating theatres ultimately sustain themselves through box-office receipts."[6] The systematic development of a regular and committed subscription audience seemed a theatre's proper hope for stability. The Ford Foundation applied to audience-building the evangelistic talents of Danny Newman, press agent extraordinary for the Chicago Lyric Opera. Advising and cajoling theatre staffs, Newman set out in the early 1960s to build a major theatre constituency in America. In the first several years of his work, subscription rolls grew on an average of 75 percent each year, and today 10,000, 20,000, even 30,000 people in a city will subscribe to sea-

177

sons of plays in advance and on faith in their theatre's ability to deliver.

It was Danny Newman who came forth with the fact that in any community 1½ to 3 percent of the population will respond to a theatre by subscribing. His primary rule was to saturate the community with hard-sell appeals in order to isolate and capture that small percentage of the population. In Newman's mind, attempts to attract a broad cross section of the population were not only too costly but also fool-hardy; they would simply not respond, he said. His was a purely elitist approach to building audiences; he was seeking the upper middle class. It was hard to fault Newman's approach because it delivered an ever-growing audience to fill each theatre's seats. There was no regional theatre working with Danny Newman which failed to make gains under his tutelage. And despite disaffection among some patrons (who subscribed because it was obviously the "thing to do" and then dis-covered that they hated the plays), there were always more upper-middle-classers to take their places in the seats.

Still, while enjoying the fruits of Newman's approach, regional the-atre leaders felt constricted by it as well. The predictability of Newman audiences in their look and their reactions fired frustration in those who dreamed of more widely representative audiences. These dreams were given voice in a 1968 book, *In Search of an Audience*, by Bradley Morison and Kay Fliehr, audience developers for The Guthrie Theater in its first years: "Despite the guaranteed nucleus that subscribers con-stitute for a company, does year-after-year sellout to the same people result in artistic stagnation? Does it prevent the accomplishment of one responsibility of a theatre: the introduction of new people to the the-atrical experience? Does it perpetrate the 'arts-for-the-few' tradition in the arts in an age when the arts should be moving from the periphery to the center of society?"[7] Morison and Fliehr took a populist approach to building audiences for the arts. The two Minnesotans were on the side of the angels, and they were guided in all they did by their convic-tion that the audience of a theatre (or any other performing arts insti-tution) must represent the total community around it, not only better to serve that community but also to ensure the growth of the institu-tion and even its intrinsic worth. Morison and Fliehr were the ones who conceived the Guthrie's Boy Scout troop and teen council and planned to send actors to work with ministers on reading Scripture—

all because they believed that a theatre exists primarily to serve its community.

Through their approach and their success with it, Morison and Fliehr provided a focus for all who sought to broaden the regional theatre constituency across class lines. By deliberately keeping open avenues to all people, by insisting that patrons should "come as you are," by trying to get the theatre's name off the society pages and onto the sports pages of newspapers, the populist promoters were being non-Establishment in order to attract the "common people" into the theatre. Such approaches reflected the egalitarian call of the 1960s on all fronts of our society; and in the years of the "Great Society," there was much money available to theatres for projects to democratize their audiences. Many an actor ventured forth on a special assignment into the ghetto and got on famously with the young people there. Still, the rapport they found did not ensure that the young people would come out of the ghetto to attend a play in the gleaming theatre that was the actor's own ghetto. And de-emphasizing the Establishment aspects of theatregoing did not necessarily encourage the average Joe to come. After all, even at the *anti*-Establishment Actor's Workshop, the audience was not a blue-collar one; it was an ascotted and turtlenecked audience.

In short, noble as the egalitarian approach was in the abstract, it simply did not work. A large part of the reason for the failure was the fact that the approach was based on making upper-middle-class western European culture available to all classes. The egalitarian approach was very much a "white man's burden"; it assumed that the classics were good for everyone, almost like medicine, and that every person's life was incomplete without them. The egalitarian approach was based on the now discredited and discarded but then still-strong "melting pot" theory, which did not recognize the virtues of ethnic and social diversity which our arts now enjoy. Then, less than a decade ago, we were all supposed to be basically the same and to enjoy the same pleasures; and so the theatres were saying to the "common people," in effect, "We want you to come over and play our game in our yard." Looking back now, it is clear that this invitation was not only naive but also offensively elitist; there is no one more elitist than an aware and educated person seeking to aid those he regards as disadvantaged by imparting to them his own cultural tastes. The leaders of the theatres, wanting to be liberal and perhaps not daring to question a simplistic egalitarian craze, had to assume that every kind of person in society would respond to classical theatre. When they did not, the leaders reacted by scourging themselves for failing to serve the new age. The leaders should not have blamed themselves; their only mistake was in allowing their genuine social concern to cloud their judgment and common sense. They were wrong in assuming that a theatre concentrating on the world's classics *must* appeal to everyone and in feeling guilty when it did not.

To say this is somewhat heretical even today, for the official liberal Establishment rule is to distrust anything that is not obviously for all people. Yet there is no reason why the *classical* theatre must appeal to everyone; that is unlikely so long as it concentrates on literature as its medium. Literature, after all, is something enjoyed by an intelligent elite. That elite may grow larger (and I hope it does) as more people are educated further, but it will never embrace *all* people. In other words, 3 percent of the people is too low, but it is not *immorally* low.

The overemphasis on theatre for everyone and the guilt feelings when it did not emerge grew partly out of the artist's reaction to his absorption into the Establishment. And yet the regional theatres were being sustained by Establishment money and elitist audiences, and "he who pays the piper calls the tune." Without major federal, state, or civic subsidy, theatres could simply not afford to cut the umbilical cords to the Establishment represented by both boards and audiences. Also, I think in the end the theatre leaders themselves, while espousing the egalitarian approach, were nevertheless not interested in devoting their strongest efforts to broadening their audiences. For them, the most important matter was not who was in the audience but that the audience kept growing and supporting the theatre. The Newman approach achieved that while the Morison-Fliehr approach did not.

Besides, Danny Newman was heeded because he came from the Ford Foundation, the original catalyst of legitimacy for the regional theatre and its primary benefactor. From the beginning of Ford interest and support, arts director W. McNeil Lowry had hoped that theatres could become self-supporting. However, the deficit pattern remained constant as inflation and ambition pushed expenses ever higher. Theatre leaders kept saying that deficits were inevitable and that therefore there was justification for permanent subsidy, but in the first half of the 1960s Lowry was either not free or not ready to provide massive and permanent general support. Instead, he carefully and regularly warned all recipients that the foundation would not support any theatre indefinitely. Ford grants before 1965 were usually not for subsidy but for new programs and projects which would broaden or improve the work of the individual company.

While money from Ford always went technically to the nonprofit institution, it was the ability and approach of the person in charge that determined which institutions would be the recipients. Lowry was investing Ford's money in people, and it was obvious from his grants who his favorite people were. Evidence of this personal emphasis was the fact that in several instances—most notably, the Milwaukee Repertory Theater and The Actor's Workshop—grants previously awarded to an institution were discontinued by Ford when people whom Lowry liked and respected either left or were ousted. Such actions may seem cavalier on the surface, but I believe that Lowry was right to consider each situation personally and to make grants on the basis of personality and talent—far better that than a bland and general mathematical formula for the awarding of money. Of course, awarding grants on the basis of personal preference encouraged a "cult of personality." The enigmatic Lowry became a father figure within the regional theatre movement; he was Mr. Money and Mr. Establishment, and "what Mac might say" became a consideration in every important decision of theatre leaders. Actress Nan Martin, sent by Lowry on a fact-finding junket in 1961, sensed the awe that influence like his conjured up around the country: "I always feel that the acquisition of money from foundations is a daily routine with most of these people. They know how to handle themselves in polite disagreement. They are subtly tenacious. . . . Caution. Now that is the key word. Oh how they practice it constantly. They know that whatever they say will be recorded on paper, and every word they say seems to be with that thought in mind."[8]

In the middle years of the 1960s, Lowry began to become much more receptive to the need of theatres for general support. I suppose that there were several reasons for this change, not the least being that by then Lowry had become a foundation vice-president and his arts program a more visible and heftier part of the total Ford program. The arts were no longer an experiment within the foundation itself. Another factor in Lowry's change was, I think, the new general acceptance of the inevitability of income gaps in the performing arts, especially as proved by Baumol and Bowen in their Twentieth Century Fund study *The Performing Arts: The Economic Dilemma.*

I suspect that a third factor in the change at Ford was the emergence of the National Endowment for the Arts in 1965 as a source of direct federal support of arts institutions. The Endowment, entering the field long after Ford had set the pace, was not blazing any new trail in its support of regional theatres; also, because it was giving out tax monies, it was obligated to support American theatre broadly and could not, like Ford, single out a small group to support exclusively or massively. Still, under the able direction of Ruth Mayleas, the theatre department of the Endowment soon made its presence and influence felt among regional theatres. At first, it did not support theatres already receiving funds from Ford, acting on the theory that other theatres needed help more urgently and that the wealth should be spread. Eventually, however, the Endowment also bestowed money on the Ford theatres, in part because they too were serving taxpayers and certainly also because many of them were doing some of the most interesting work in the country. By the beginning of the 1970s, the Endowment was working with considerably more money than in its first years (almost $3,000,000 for theatre in fiscal 1973), and it was able to provide support comparable to Ford's. As a rule, not more than $100,000 went to any theatre in a given year, but a goodly number received support in nearly that amount. In 1972, for instance, the federal agency granted $2,045,500 to forty professional theatres across the country; Arena Stage, The Guthrie Theater, the American Conservatory Theatre, and the Mark Taper Forum each received $100,000, and the Alley and the Long Wharf received $75,000 each.

The advent and growth of the Endowment's theatre program meant that the Ford Foundation was no longer the only significant outside benefactor of many regional theatres. Since the Endowment was giving money only for program purposes and not for general support, Ford was partially freed of the program responsibility and was challenged to address the new area of general support, which fitted in with Lowry's decision that general support was justified. By 1967, he was saying publicly that deficits were inevitable and worthy of support. In announcing several large grants (including $870,000 to The Guthrie Theater), Lowry pointed out that despite growth the future of regional theatres remained uncertain. The factors accounting for the uncertainty, he felt, were inflation and the realization that "nonprofit professional theatres, like symphony and opera, will have to be operated on a deficit basis."[9] Speaking in the same period at a national conference of regional theatre managers and board members at the Studio Arena Theatre, Lowry underlined not only his acceptance of deficit funding but also the arrival of the regional theatre within the Establishment: "For the first time in America, the theatre is generally recognized as a cultural necessity. Leaders of industry and business and government leaders, municipal, state, and federal, acknowledge the theatre's claim to share in the esteem and material support traditionally given the other arts."[10]

For Lowry as for the Establishment generally, the regional theatre's legitimatization was complete. From then on and especially for a certain group of theatres, Lowry provided sustaining funds to erase deficits. In the ten-year period from the start of 1962 through the end of 1971, the Ford Foundation (as part of a much larger total arts program) awarded $16,126,291 to seventeen regional theatres:[11]

Alley Theatre	$3,500,000
Arena Stage	2,659,450
American Conservatory Theatre	2,395,000
Mummers Theatre	1,785,000
Guthrie Theater	1,207,000
APA–Phoenix	900,000
American Shakespeare Festival	699,800
Mark Taper Forum*	500,000
Actors Theatre of Louisville	360,000
Trinity Square	357,606
Playhouse in the Park	350,000
Center Stage	320,545
Seattle Repertory Theatre	305,240
Washington Theatre Club	250,000
Hartford Stage Company	239,650
Actor's Workshop	197,000
Milwaukee Repertory Theater†	100,000
Total	$16,126,291

* Originally awarded to predecessor, Theatre Group, UCLA.
† Awarded to predecessor, Fred Miller Theatre.

In general, the Ford money was awarded intelligently and often imaginatively. Lowry, the first and for a time the only national supporter of an unprecedented theatre movement, was as daring in his way as those he supported. Without him, there would have been no regional theatre movement, and his support allowed the form to mature in the 1960s. Ford's position as a decisive force is clear in Peter Zeisler's public question: "Does . . . anyone think for a minute that the resident theater could have developed without foundation support? Let resident theaters rely on their local communities entirely for all funding (direct and indirect) for just 90 days and see what happens to growth and development—let alone existence!"[12]

However, to acknowledge the vital importance of Ford and other foundation support is not to discount the problems which accompanied it. The persuasive power of Ford support tended to homogenize and codify theatres, although the villain in this was not really or directly Ford but rather those theatres which homogenized themselves in hopes of thereby gaining Ford support. In this homogenization, they had Ford's indirect help through its creation and underwriting of Theatre Communications Group, a service organization for regional theatres. TCG, as it is commonly known, was an outgrowth of Ford's 1959 meeting at which the early leaders met each other and discussed joint concerns. From its start, TCG's goal was to "improve standards" in production, administration, and the training of personnel. In the beginning, professional regional theatres and some community theatres and university programs were included, but after 1964, citing the divisions of purpose between professional and other forms, TCG limited its purview to the professional regional theatres and committed its resources to the movement. Thereafter, TCG's major program became a casting service to ferret out New York actors to join regional companies and to select college graduates to start their careers in the companies. TCG also became the employer of Danny Newman and the official provider of his services. The visitation program enabled staff members of regional theatres to visit their counterparts around the country and share experiences for mutual benefit. Through most of the 1960s, TCG was led by Michael Mabry as the executive director. I joined him as the associate director in 1966 and replaced him in 1968 for one year.

The fascination of TCG came from its being a synthesis of the regional theatre movement, providing an overview of the revolution.

TCG's emphasis as a service organization was always on structure and stability in regional theatres. It shied away from distinctions among theatres based on quality of production, offering its services to theatres which adhered to administrative rules and manners. For example, when we decided in 1967 to limit our services to thirteen theatres, we chose them for their "administrative and economic structure capable of gaining support, continuity of artistic and managerial leadership, and cooperation with other theatres and with TCG programs."* In promoting stability through sound structure, we were saying to the theatres, in effect, "If you do things in this way, you will survive and be one of the group that lasts." Looking back now, it is clear that what seemed to be synthesis was really homogenization and that the chief agent was again not Ford but TCG itself. (Ford, with its immense resources, could support any theatre it chose, even on the basis of quality alone and without regard to TCG's finicky rules. A case in point was the American Conservatory Theatre, which Ford was supporting with large grants while we were ruling it out of our thirteen because it did not meet the criteria of stability and sound structure.) TCG homogenized theatres through its casting service, which prompted the appearance of the same actors in various theatres over the years; through its visitation program, which encouraged artists and managers to think and act alike; and through Danny Newman's peregrinations, which provided promotional tools that looked and worked alike. We helped theatres to become more stable but at a high cost to them—a threatened loss of individuality.

The sameness encouraged by TCG was the natural result of over-structuring, and it contributed to a malaise that plagued the regional theatre in the latter half of the 1960s. Once-rugged individualists found themselves so codified and pigeonholed that they felt their uniqueness endangered. Sameness did not serve each theatre's desire to make its own mark and to triumph in those National Theatre sweepstakes. The malaise was also caused by a natural frustration of each theatre leader

* Howard Taubman, "Emphasis of Communications Group to Be on Strengthening Best Troupes," *New York Times*, February 15, 1967. The theatres included in the TCG "Demonstration Unit" were: Alley Theatre, Arena Stage, APA-Phoenix, Mark Taper Forum, Front Street Theatre, Repertory Theater of Lincoln Center, Goodman Theatre, Milwaukee Repertory Theater, Guthrie Theater, Mummers Theatre, Playhouse in the Park, Seattle Repertory Theatre, and Trinity Square Repertory Company.

with his peers. After all, people who had banded together into a movement, initially for protection and corroboration, did not necessarily like each other personally. The leaders were willing to cooperate for the common good for a time; but eventually, as all became more stable, the naturally competitive spirit of each reasserted itself and found itself in conflict with the others in the contest for a primary national position.

Another cause of the malaise was the achievement of Establishment status itself. For those who had eked out their theatres' existence against almost insurmountable odds, the achievement of full recognition was itself unsettling. There was no struggle left that was as dynamic as the tortuous—but in retrospect attractive—fight for sheer survival. The specter of boredom loomed very large. Looking back on the period from the perspective of the 1970s, Zelda Fichandler described its uneasy feelings: "The malaise is a malaise of doubt: in the audience, in oneself to create and lead a meaningful artistic entity, in the 'relevance' of our repertory, in the validity of theatre itself within a technocratic society. For some of us it felt (or feels) that a whole artistic life had been misdirected and that, somehow, we were part of a great betrayal, with no one to blame but ourselves."[13]

The malaise pervasive in the regional theatre in the last half of the 1960s was caused by the fact that the form had reached Establishment status through institutionalization in structure and especially in philosophy. The institutional approach had been the means of survival, but it had also become a curse. Theodore Hoffman, usually ahead of the movement intellectually, caught the essence of the problem as early as 1967:

My thesis is that regional theatre has institutionalized itself, perhaps in the least productive fashion, and that the impulse to imagination may have passed elsewhere, to off-off-Broadway, to happenings, multi-media, street theatre, poor people's theatre, even to universities. Be that as it may, the matrix of regional theatre is still clearly before us, its behavior still fairly pristine. . . . In the meantime, regional theatre exists, expands, agonizes. There have been surprisingly few failures; such is the power of institutionalization.[14]

This was not necessarily a disaster; as Hoffman himself pointed out, "Regional theatre can best survive and grow by recognizing itself as another institutional resource of commodity culture."[15] Still, no one believed that. Michael Murray, writing a year after Hoffman and after leaving the Charles Playhouse, spoke for the disaffected artist caught in the malaise:

I think few artists have any institutional instincts or any but the vaguest sociological impulses; most of them simply want a place to do their work. The appeal of regional theatre to people like me is not that it is regional (in fact the more regional or remote it is, the less we like it) but that it is a place to do our work. In the process we may incidentally develop all sorts of missionary zeal about our role in the community along with the orchestra and the public library, and our concern for the high school student, but most of that is essentially beside the point.[16]

Institutionalization seemed to have backfired for those who had sought it. At the same time that they were stretching their wings in the hope of being a national solution, they were bound by their Establishment status at home. Their frustration came out of the realization that in ten short years the movement had become, like all elements of the Establishment, a *preserver of the past* and that they were no longer innovators. Their main innovation had been the form itself, which was now twenty years old.

Yet despite their fatigue and doubts, despite their suspicions and fears, this was a hardy group with energy still to spare. Perhaps they could overcome their malaise with another innovation, one that could free them from being mere preservers of the past.

11 New Plays and New Ploys

"The production of classics is healthy, but . . . the seed of progress in the theatre lies in new plays."

Margo Jones, Theatre-in-the-Round, *1951*

"Later on, when both the management and the audience know better what we can and ought to attempt, and also what we can and ought to afford, then we may take the risk of producing, and even commissioning, new work."

Tyrone Guthrie, A New Theatre, *1964*

"Let's find a new play that will be a success and so get us out of the regional theatre."

Jon Jory, Theatre Today, *1970*

More than any other artistic element, the attitudes toward the production of new plays in the regional theatre have undergone sweeping change in the twenty-five-year history of the form: from dream through lip-service to a major emphasis. The changing attitudes toward new plays are directly related to the regional theatre's changing relationship to the Establishment.

It must have been clear to those early leaders who learned from Margo Jones that the emphasis in her theatre was upon the production of new plays. Yet for most of the twenty-year period between 1947 and 1967, American regional theatres reversed her doctrine, concentrating on classics instead of on new writing. This reversal gave to most stay-at-home New York critics their principal defense against the burgeoning regional theatre: that while regional theatre was filling a need for the classics, it was not actively developing and nurturing new playwrights of consequence or propelling them into national prominence. This had always been Broadway's special ability and function (a fact which even Margo Jones had recognized and used), and Broadway's sovereignty in this area seemed secure.

188

New Plays and New Ploys

There were logical (financial) reasons for the paucity of new plays in the early years. As mentioned earlier, the first and largest obstacle which the regional theatre had to overcome in the 1950s was the fact that it was unfamiliar and therefore insecure. Given this obstacle, the presentation of classics was innovation enough. Anything more obscure and unknown, regularly presented, would have blunted public interest and assured financial collapse. Theatres had to be careful to sneak new plays into their seasons, neatly sandwiched between more acceptable classics. Still, while the early forays into new work were rare, they were sometimes notable and showed that the early leaders had a natural sense of what might work on the stage. For instance, the first new play presented by the Alley Theatre, Ronald Alexander's *Season with Ginger*, was produced in 1950. Later retitled *Time Out for Ginger*, the play became a Broadway success starring Melvyn Douglas. Another Alley premiere, in 1955, was James Lee's *Career*, which the Alley dedicated to the memory of Margo Jones. That play later went on to off-Broadway success and was made into a film starring Dean Martin and Shirley MacLaine. But the later success of both plays was unrelated to the Alley, which did not propel them beyond its stage as Margo Jones had propelled the plays she premiered. At the Arena Stage during the 1950s, however, Zelda Fichandler's interest in new plays was steady. In the early years of her theatre, she presented the premiere production of Robert Anderson's *All Summer Long*, which, following his later success with *Tea and Sympathy*, went to Broadway (and took director Alan Schneider and actor George Grizzard away from Arena Stage with it). Robinson Jeffers's *The Cretan Woman* and Josh Greenfeld's *Clandestine on the Morning Line* (the latter financed by a Ford Foundation grant) also had their premieres in Washington. The loosely structured and more radical Actor's Workshop pursued new work with the most steady energy, producing plays by Sidney Michaels, Mark Harris, David Marks, and poet James Schevill along with the cerebral, discursive plays of Herbert Blau himself. However, none of the Workshop's new plays went far beyond their San Francisco premieres, and they always brought disaster to the box office.

As stability became a formal goal, the production of new plays continued to be rare and even foolhardy from an institutional point of view. The growing number of subscribers—essential for stability—tended to foster so constant and homogeneous an audience that new plays had to be viewed as a threat to their continued loyalty and patronage. Because the audience was so important, it could and did rule out any concentration on new plays. One theatre leader summed up the dilemma: "I had the feeling that when we offered one play free out of seven, and one new play out of seven, the subscribers felt they were coming out even—one free miserable evening." Another pressure to perform mostly classics and not new plays arose from the growing dependence on student audiences. The familiar and teachable classics proved a highly marketable commodity, and the emphasis upon them tended to relegate new plays to isolated workshop situations—strange, unknown little plays mounted almost in secret by the actors and sometimes only for each other.

The price paid by regional theatres for making themselves seem familiar to their audiences was to make their programs predictable. In the first half of the 1960s, new plays occupied the main stages of the theatres only rarely, although again a high proportion of those that were produced were notably well chosen. In 1960, the Alley had its first playwright-in-residence, Frank Gagliano, whose play *The Library Raid* was produced in Houston. The play later went to off-Broadway as *Night of the Dunce*. Another Alley playwright-in-residence was Paul Zindel, then an unknown writer of novels and plays. His play *The Effect of Gamma Rays on Man-in-the-Moon Marigolds* was premiered by the Alley in 1965. The play then disappeared, except for a showing on educational television, until it was mounted at the Cleveland Play House in 1969 and went on from there to off-Broadway success and the Pulitzer Prize.

In the early 1960s, new play efforts were sometimes supported by the Ford Foundation, which paid the expenses of playwrights in going to regional cities to work with directors on their plays in rehearsal. Another Ford program, initiated in 1963, provided fellowships for poets and novelists (including Philip Roth and John Hawkes) to spend long periods in residence at regional theatres, in the hope that the exposure would encourage them to write plays. It is regrettable that most of the writers spent most of their time working on their own poems and novels and came up with few plays for the theatres they were observing (although in their defense it should be pointed out that some of the writers, including Roth and Hawkes, later provided plays for other theatres).

190

Generally, all reasons for the scarcity of new plays through 1965 stemmed from the regional theatre's emergence as a preserver of the past, a function underlined by the advent of the Guthrie and most other oak tree theatres as almost exclusively classical theatres. Opening his Seattle Repertory Theatre in 1963, director Stuart Vaughan called it a theatrical "library," providing a broad sampling of dramatic literature. Most people go to the library less to browse than to pick up what they have already decided to read; what they want to read is literature, not mere writing. And literature is what regional theatre audiences were served. For instance, between 1965 and 1970, *Twelfth Night* and *The Importance of Being Earnest* were the two most popular plays in the regional theatre. A study of the repertoire around the country in those five years shows that Shakespeare received twice the number of productions of Shaw, the next most popular playwright. After these two, the most popular in descending order were Molière, Pirandello, Brecht, Chekhov, O'Neill, Thornton Wilder, and Tennessee Williams.

Nor did the coming of the new breed of theatre leaders in the mid-1960s bring any surge in new plays; their sapling theatres, with few exceptions, were particularly biased toward the classics. One reason for this has been pointed out by Jon Jory: for young directors, even the classics were new, since they had never mounted them before. In the few instances where sapling theatres emphasized new plays, the experience was often painful. At Jory's Long Wharf, for instance, he and Harlan Kleiman followed their first winter season with a summer festival of new plays in 1966. While the season earned the Margo Jones Award for the theatre, the large financial loss incurred by the experiment was the first element in the crisis that led to Jory's leaving the Long Wharf. At the Theatre of the Living Arts, André Gregory's contract specified that he was to have free choice of one new American play each season. When he chose *Beclch* and mounted it in the shocking mode, he was ousted. New plays continued to be the exception to the rule. The rule remained the recognizable and safe classics, and the primary reason for it was the audience's refusal to accept more than a token emphasis on new plays. As Allen Fletcher explained it: "Seattle audiences are artistically unsure of themselves; they want to be certain that what they see is 'good' art—proven by critics and audiences before them. They are afraid to make their own artistic or intellectual judgments, and they are suspicious of the avant-garde and unproven drama.

They are wary of anything that they have not heard of because they are not sure that they ought to like it."[1]

By the middle of the 1960s, theatre leaders were becoming dismayed with the public's unofficial but pervasive insistence on mostly classics. The malaise that accompanied the arrival of respectability included boredom with the standard classical repertoire—what came to be known as "*Uncle Vanya* and *Charley's Aunt* in rotating repertory." The actors, too, were becoming restless with the steady classical diet, and artistic directors began to look to new plays to infuse new life into their companies and to keep their actors happy. Another reason for the change of attitude toward new plays was that new theatrical groups were springing up to challenge the Establishment regional theatres just as these had challenged an earlier Establishment. Some of these new groups were the Theatre Company of Boston challenging the Charles Playhouse, the Washington Theatre Club challenging Arena Stage, and the Firehouse Theatre challenging the Guthrie. These younger and more adventurous groups, generally dedicated to new plays, represented a threat to the older, more solidified theatres. Also, among the young a new audience was developing for new theatrical forms and new writing, and the smaller theatres were attracting that audience. Perceptive leaders in the older regional theatres began to see that in order to hold their audiences and develop younger ones, they would have to compete on new terms, with new plays. In short, so long as the regional theatre was insecure and a cultural underdog, it could not afford to emphasize new plays. Once it had gained a surer foothold in the community and was being attacked as an Establishment theatre, it could not afford not to emphasize them.

In the middle of the 1960s, there were a number of modest but provocative attempts to stimulate new plays. These programs were supported largely by the Rockefeller Foundation instead of the ubiquitous Ford Foundation. Rockefeller supported the start of the Theatre for Tomorrow series at the Milwaukee Repertory Theater, the New Theatre for Now series at the Mark Taper Forum, the efforts of the Theatre Company of Boston, and other programs for the development of new plays. Also, Rockefeller was instrumental in the genesis and continuance of two organizations apart from the regional theatre but closely related to its interest in new plays: the Office for Advanced Drama Research and the O'Neill Foundation. Located at the University of

Minnesota, the Office for Advanced Drama Research was designed to unearth new plays of merit, to circulate them, and to get them produced throughout the country. Headed by Professor Arthur Ballet, the OADR developed close relationships with several regional theatres which were willing to premiere the plays. Some of the most controversial were presented in Minneapolis by The Guthrie Theater, notably Terrence McNally's *And Things That Go Bump in the Night* and Rochelle Owens's *Futz*.[2] Passing on up to 1,500 plays each year, the OADR also arranged premiere productions at the Playhouse in the Park, the Theatre Company of Boston, and the Hartford Stage Company.

The O'Neill Foundation was founded by Yale Drama School graduate George White in 1965, and it has been more visible than the OADR largely because its location near New York (in Waterford, Connecticut) has enabled it to involve a larger theatrical constituency. The O'Neill Foundation has sponsored many new programs (including the National Theatre for the Deaf, a critics' institute, and a training institute for college students), but its primary program has been the presentation of new plays each summer in its casually idyllic setting beside Long Island Sound. Each summer the leaders of regional theatres have trekked to Waterford to mingle with new playwrights and to see their work performed. Out of this very civilized annual event have come frequent productions of the plays of John Guare, Frank Gagliano, Megan Terry, Lanford Wilson, Leonard Melfi, and others in the new wave of playwrights. Above all, the O'Neill Foundation has enabled the regional theatre to keep abreast of new developments in playwriting which otherwise would have been left in only an off-off-Broadway context. As such, it has provided for the regional theatre an important link with the central theatre in New York.

These various developments in the mid-1960s served the regional theatre's growing interest in new plays. However, a stunning leap forward was needed to give prominence to that interest, and it came with the premiere of *The Great White Hope* at Arena Stage in Washington in 1967. This one premiere was the fourth major turning point of the regional theatre revolution because it proved the national power of new plays.

Howard Sackler's *The Great White Hope* came to the attention of Arena Stage when the theatre was presenting a one-act play by Sackler in 1966. Zelda Fichandler read the sprawling biographical play about black boxing champion Jack Johnson, liked it, and agreed to present it in her 1966–67 season; but as she and Sackler worked on the script, it became clear that the revisions to be made would necessitate a delay to 1967–68. Indeed, Zelda made a total personal commitment to the play's development, working long hours with Sackler on honing the piece. As director Edwin Sherin later pointed out, "It all happened because of the whimsical and radical genius of Zelda Fichandler. . . . Zelda has the vision of a seer. She didn't give a goddam if it failed and we all floated down the Potomac. She believed in it!"[3]

The Great White Hope was a gargantuan undertaking for Arena Stage—scores of actors, hundreds of costumes, many thousands of dollars. Despite a special grant of $25,000 from the National Endowment for the Arts, Arena Stage lost $50,000 on the two-month *Great White Hope* premiere, but it gained something that could not be measured in dollars. It gained for itself a place in the forefront of the modern American theatre as representatives of the nation's media flocked to a regional theatre to report on the latest rage. Among them was Henry Hewes of the *Saturday Review*: "The great bright hope of the resident-theatre company movement is that these organizations will be able to tackle large, serious works that would be financially prohibitive in the current Broadway economy. Therefore, one has nothing but admiration for Arena Stage for attempting Howard Sackler's enormous new play, *The Great White Hope.* . . . Beyond that one must applaud the integrity of the whole venture."[4]

The Great White Hope was a major turning point because, as Zelda Fichandler says, it "swung the dominance for the production of new plays away from Broadway to the resident theatres outside New York."[5] Now regional theatre leaders had powerful ammunition to assault Broadway's hold on the American theatre. Indeed, the regional theatre's interest in new plays was only a secondary interest until *The Great White Hope* proved that new plays could be a savior's most effective weapon.

Of course, the power of *The Great White Hope* depended on its ability to move beyond Washington; as Zelda notes, "We just produced a play that was viable in a way that was recognized by the dominant culture—that is, it went to Broadway."[6] And it went with a vengeance. In the fall of 1968, it opened on Broadway (after being sold in the interim by Sackler to the movies for nearly $1,000,000, some of which provided the capital for the Broadway production). In moving to Broadway, it became a major American play rather than merely a significant regional event, but Arena Stage had no part in this. Herman Levin, producer of *My Fair Lady*, secured rights to the play for Broadway through a contract with Sackler's agent, with no reference to Arena Stage. Levin hired the Arena director (Edwin Sherin), the Arena star (James Earl Jones), and a large portion of the Arena company, who left Washington to ride with the play onto Broadway, many of them for the first time. *The Great White Hope* opened to laudatory reviews and quickly became the "thing to see"; it then went on to win many theatre awards, including the Pulitzer Prize. Arena Stage was left behind.

A bitter and mutually incriminating controversy raged for several weeks in *Variety* between Sackler and Levin on one side and Arena Stage on the other. The main point of dispute was that Arena Stage had sought and was denied a percentage of the play's Broadway earnings. Sackler and Levin maintained that Arena was too late and was simply trying to cash in on the play's New York success. Apparently Sackler and Levin did offer the theatre a share of the play's profits up to $50,000, which the theatre rejected as piddling. Ironically, the sum would have erased Arena's loss on the Washington premiere, and in a less charged atmosphere it might have been graciously and gratefully accepted. As matters stood, the entire affair ended in bitterness and ill will.

Yet bouncing back from this sad experience, Zelda Fichandler began to concentrate more and more on mounting premieres. The season after *The Great White Hope*, she premiered Arthur Kopit's *Indians*, featuring Stacy Keach. It too went to Broadway, and this time Arena Stage took care to obtain a 5 percent interest in the possible profits (which turned out to be nil). In the next three seasons, Arena Stage offered premieres of Arthur Giron's *Edith Stein* (directed by Zelda herself), Stanley Greenberg's *Pueblo* (based on the naval incident), Jay Broad's *A Conflict of Interest*, and Michael Weller's *Moonchildren*. Of this group, however, only the last went to Broadway and again did not succeed financially. It was possible that the lightning of *The Great White Hope* would not strike twice in Washington, but a major part of Arena Stage's programming seemed an attempt to encourage just that. For her efforts in new plays, Zelda was given the Margo Jones Award in 1972, by then long overdue.

Arena Stage's new emphasis on new plays was matched by many other regional theatres. By the 1969–70 season, 15 percent of all plays presented on the main stages of theatres were new plays—triple the percentage in the two seasons before *The Great White Hope* paved a new course. And over a two-season period, 1968–69 and 1969–70, many plays traveled from regional theatres to New York for runs either on or off Broadway. In addition to *The Great White Hope* and *Indians*, they included *We Bombed in New Haven* from the Yale Repertory Theatre; *Red, White, and Maddox* from Theatre Atlanta; *The Sudden and Accidental Re-Education of Horse Johnson* from the Milwaukee Repertory Theater; Albee's *Box* and *Quotations from Chairman Mao Tse-Tung* and Lanford Wilson's *Lemon Sky* from the Studio Arena Theatre; *The Gingham Dog* from the Washington Theatre Club; *Don't Shoot Mable It's Your Husband* from the American Conservatory Theatre; *Beclch* from the Theatre of the Living Arts; *Park*, a musical from Center Stage; *Inquest* and *The Effect of Gamma Rays* from the Cleveland Play House; *A Whistle in the Dark* from the Long Wharf; and *Who's Happy Now?* from the Mark Taper Forum. The fact that only *Gamma Rays* proved both critically and financially successful did not lessen the pride felt throughout the movement, and even *Variety* was obliged to concede the commercial theatre's new dependence on the "hinterland" by emblazoning across its front page, "Sticks Making Hay on B'way."

Of course, they were "making hay" only psychologically, not financially. In no instance was a regional theatre taking its production into New York on its own; in each case, a commercial producer picked up the play and reproduced it, as Herman Levin had done with *The Great White Hope*. Nevertheless, primarily through the battle surrounding that play's move, most theatres whose plays were going to New York had learned the importance of protecting their interests in possible future profits. While nearly all the plays failed to make money in New York, their original regional producers fought for their rights in case they might. Again, Zelda Fichandler spoke for the whole movement: "Let it be known that I am no high priestess of the arts. I am dedicated, fanatic even and, after a good night's sleep and with a production on the boards that I like, I may even exude a certain charisma.

But I am of the world, not above it. I require and now have learned to demand a worldly portion of what we help to bring about. I speak for my brothers and sisters in this I am sure."[7]

Some regional theatre leaders overreacted to the possibility and hunted for new plays that looked like future Broadway hits. In 1970, critic Martin Gottfried, alternately a defender and castigator of the movement, attacked the new emphasis: "These theaters are now starting to think in terms of Broadway potential. Once proud that professional theater could exist outside New York, they now look for a piece of the action. Once scornful of the 'Broadway marketplace,' they now see the advantages of selling there."[8] Indeed, the effort sometimes became obsessive—both for those theatres which had not yet enjoyed New York visibility for their new plays and for those which had and now hungered to duplicate it. Still, the hunger was not so much a financial hunger as a psychological one. In the *Great White Hope* controversy, it was not the loss of the money that most rankled Arena Stage; it was, I think, instead the fact that even the acknowledgment it received was not as large or as public as it might have been. The theatre as an institution could be proud of having first mounted the play; but that pride is private, whereas history records only the public phenomenon of the play itself.

The key word here is "history." To act as a preserver of the past is to serve history; to premiere new work is to create it. The mounting of a new play is partly an attempt to create something of historical importance. Indeed, regional theatres may find their ultimate justification not in quantities of productions and audiences but in the quality of those new plays which, through them, become works of art. This is so because, of all theatrical elements, only literature can be permanent. Buildings will crumble, productions will come and go, actors will fade away, but plays can last in the history of man and his arts. Under ideal circumstances, a new play entering history can take its theatre with it. After all, through Shakespeare we still know the Globe, through Molière the Comédie Française, and through Chekhov the Moscow Art Theatre. The desire to mount new plays in a regional theatre is at least in part a desire to move the theatre *itself* into a context of national importance and historical influence. What regional theatres of today will the world know a hundred years hence, and through what playwrights? After *The Great White Hope*, that question became a primary one in the minds of regional theatre leaders, who saw new plays as one key to unlock a place in history for them.

But, as evidenced by *The Great White Hope*, to achieve a place in history a play must live in a national instead of a regional context. As Gordon Davidson points out, "I do a new play—it still has to come to New York"[9]—because New York remains the number one battleground. Reviewing the Arena Stage production of *Indians, New York Times* critic Clive Barnes put it down in black and white: "When a regional theatre makes national news with a major premiere, it deserves national attention. Without this attention, our regional theatres will always be regarded as second-class citizens, a kind of off-off-off Broadway wasteland."[10] Many people working in regional theatre at the time understood keenly—and felt personally—what Barnes was saying.

12 The Regional Dilemma

> *"The appeal of regional theatre to people like me is not that it is regional (in fact, the more regional or remote it is, the less we like it) but that it is a place to do our work."*
>
> *Michael Murray*, The Drama Review

> *"We are not regional (I think the term is second-class sounding). . . . Until we aim our own thinking toward a conviction that we have some international importance—whether we do or don't—we are downgrading our goals."*
>
> *Nina Vance*, Players

The development of the regional theatre can be viewed as a series of three spiraling thrusts. Each thrust overlapped the next, but each had its own period of primacy. While primary, each thrust was synonymous with the compelling dream of the theatre leader whose personality shaped his or her institution.

The first thrust of the regional theatre was toward *stability*, and it was primary from the beginnings of the form until the middle of the 1960s. The stability thrust was characterized by the overriding concern of each theatre for its own survival and security. This was the period of struggle for a foothold, a period which saw the development of huge subscription audiences, community service programs, and foundation support. The thrust was climaxed by the emergence of the theatre as part of the Establishment. Today, even though no regional theatre is completely secure financially, the thrust toward stability is no longer primary. Now the dreams of theatre leaders are made of more heady stuff.

In the middle years of the 1960s, the thrust toward *quality* was uppermost. Once regional theatre leaders dared assume that their institutions would still be there when they woke each morning, they could turn more of their attention to the quality of productions. This was also a period in which better known and more experienced talents were introduced into the regional theatre. As a result, the quality of the work improved significantly during this period.

After 1968, and particularly after *The Great White Hope*, the third thrust became evident: the thrust toward *centrality*. Having survived and having improved the overall quality of their productions, regional theatres grew concerned about what the world knew of them and thought of them. In their eyes, through professional decentralization they had created a solution to the problems of the American theatre. The leaders now had a new though perhaps subliminal goal: to achieve for their theatres a central place and so to influence the future rather than simply preserving the past. For the leaders themselves, who had had to scratch out niches in often hostile environments, the achievement of a central place became a kind of last frontier. It was also synonymous with each theatre's striving for acceptance as the National Theatre of America. The thrust toward centrality paralleled and complemented the striving for supremacy.

In personal terms, the three thrusts also contributed to the regional theatre's malaise. The thrust toward stability bred uneasiness over the theatre's service function in the community. The thrust toward quality bred a horror of sameness among theatres. The thrust toward centrality bred fears that the thrust itself might not succeed. These last fears constitute the regional dilemma: the nagging suspicion in people who have given their lives to the movement that they might have thus relegated themselves to a minor position on the periphery.

As I noted earlier, to gain a place in American history, one must function in a national context rather than a regional one. Politically, this is one reason for the exceptional alderman's striving to be mayor, then state assemblyman, then United States congressman, then senator, even President. In the realm of American culture, the best of regional writers—a William Faulkner, a Tennessee Williams—must be read by a national audience to achieve a place in American letters. As we have seen, a play like *The Great White Hope* can be premiered and noticed in a regional context, but it can win the Pulitzer Prize and become the best American play of the year only by entering the national arena in New York. The real prize—the chance to change America's direction—

is reserved for those phenomena which attain a national context. Through the 1960s this meant one thing: despite all efforts to save the American theatre by decentralization or institutionalism, the achievement of national *power* remained a primary goal, and so the thrust toward centrality was power-oriented.

In order to acquire national power in America, one must concentrate on what is new, and one must change almost daily to do so. Our country's obsession with the new governs all elements of our national life—our politics, our commerce, our fashions and fads, our arts. We plan obsolescence in order to accommodate the dizzying rate of change, and as a nation we make no room for enduring values or institutions. The inventor, not the sustainer or the refiner, is the romantic American hero. What has been carefully preserved will always be overshadowed by what is new today, and what is new today will be overwhelmed by what comes along tomorrow.

Our obsession with the new is stimulated by the American media— our newspapers, magazines, radio, and television, which play a significant role in focusing public interest. Their first responsibility, after all, is to tell the nation what is new and therefore noteworthy, a responsibility which is inimical to preservation. The media, pursuing the new at all costs, not only must ignore all forces of preservation but must also undercut them whenever possible because there is not equal room for novelty and preservation in the span of our national attention. This poses a special problem for regional theatres. There was a grace period during the 1960s when preservation was itself a new idea and so was newsworthy. In order to be reported now, however, most regional theatres must premiere a new play; the preservative function of the regional theatre stands alone, unnoticed, and unheralded in the organs of national expression. In short, preservation is dull copy.

Among the media, several publications tend to hold sway over the regional theatre as they do over all American life. For example, the *New York Times* is read by all concerned theatre people no matter where they are. Its critical views of the theatre, for better or worse, are considered gospel, and its assessment can make or break the individual production. It is no wonder that Herbert Blau, faced with a San Francisco critic who had called The Actor's Workshop a "little theatre," responded that "it was true that we were a little theater, but he, compared to us, and his paper, compared to *The New York Times,* were infinitesimal."[1] In the 1960s, the *Times* was generous and sympathetic in its coverage of the regional theatre, particularly in articles and reviews by drama critics Howard Taubman and Clive Barnes. In this, the *Times* was fulfilling its national responsibility to report to the nation what was new in that decade.

The regional theatre's psychological dependence on the *Times* is great. A favorable mention of a particular theatre in the Sunday drama section can send the leader of that theatre to heights of joy; an attack on his theatre can send him into the depths of despair. Even more seriously, the *Times*'s opinion of a particular theatre is noted by members of the theatre's board and by the community, who react to that opinion by adopting it. Recognition by the *Times* often turns the tide in local support of productions. According to Long Wharf Theatre artistic director Arvin Brown, "We can get brilliant local reviews; we can saturate the area with television and radio publicity; and yet it will still not make the difference that one notice in the *Times* will make."[2]

The recognition accorded by the *New York Times* and its sympathetic attitude proved to be major factors in the growth of theatres outside New York. However, other voices and opinion-shapers were harsher and more cynical. Among these, *Time* magazine is most noteworthy; there is also no more obvious example of the power of the media and the location of that power. *Time* has covered the regional theatre scene rather frequently but often from a condescending point of view: "The rank mediocrity of most resident companies has been camouflaged by some New York drama critics, who put down Broadway commercialism and confect gorgeous fictions about the distinguished dramatic art and high esthetic integrity that they have discovered in Nome, Keokuk, and the lower Gaspé Peninsula."[3] Any art form which is by definition struggling to survive cannot easily ignore such a dismissal. The destructive power of the dismissal is heightened by the fact that a magazine like *Time*, unlike a newspaper like the *Times*, sits for weeks on coffee tables and in doctors' waiting rooms across America, its opinions burrowing into the minds of the power structure. What *Time* says tends to shape the thinking and the actions of the American upper-middle-class Establishment, and when *Time* scoffs at the regional theatre, even the power structure which has been supportive may start to question its commitment.

The Regional Dilemma

Time stands not only for the power of the media but also for the insularity of that power. The magazine has correspondents throughout the country and the world, and they report on significant events in all places. But their dispatches are filtered through a skyscraper on the northwest corner of Sixth Avenue and 50th Street in New York City, where they are edited for American consumption. *Time* is circulated from Chicago, in the physical center of our country, as a matter of efficiency, but it is conceived and put together in New York, the most powerful intellectual center in the country.

Obviously, a national magazine like *Time* or a national newspaper like the *New York Times* cannot be created either everywhere or nowhere; it must be put together and controlled in some one place. We all accept this necessity, but we find it very difficult to accept what follows from it—namely, that this one place is bound to be the center of our nation. The media are such a powerful force in American life that the city where they are concentrated is the fulcrum of the nation. Because a single American city has our primary newspaper, all three television networks, and the majority of our magazines and publishing houses—in short, because it has our national voice—New York is that fulcrum, and it is deciding what America should read and hear. This is an awesome and presumptuous responsibility for any one city to undertake, and we Americans are loathe to allow it. Our democratic urge has its own geography. Deeply imbedded in the American dream is the notion that all large cities, like all men, are created equal. In so wide a country, no one city is supposed to play the arbiter, particularly no city on the edge of the land. As a nation we have always wanted to believe, as Herbert Blau once wrote, that "the same things that make it easy to get to New York make it just as easy to get away."[4] Or rather, as Herbert Blau wrote before he went to New York.

It is pleasant to believe that all large cities are equal, and it is no doubt a popular idea in Kansas City, Indianapolis, and Denver; but it is simply not true. Probably all other cities in America are nicer to live in than New York, but still it is the only ultimate American city. We may love it or hate it or both, but we need it and use it, and it needs and uses us. Insular *Time* understands this: "Cincinnati and Phoenix, to cite two typical American provincial cities, may be agreeable places to live in, but they are simply not large enough to contain, as does New York, the wide variety of types and temperaments that form the American character. Americans and foreigners alike call New York the least American of cities. In fact, it is the most American, reflecting as does no other all aspects of national life. . . . New York, the cultural, financial, and commercial capital, is thus the only truly great city in the U.S."[5]

Those who maintain that America is far too large to have only one focal city usually invoke the smallness of European countries as the reason why they have only one. It is true that England and France, for instance, are no larger than some of our states. It is also true that people even in the farthest reaches of those countries who want to enjoy the cultural riches of London or Paris can drive to those cities in a long day at low cost. Because the countries are small, London and Paris can be focal cities for whole nations. Yet it does not follow that America will have more than one focal city simply because it is so large. The supremacy of one city is a result not of a nation's size but rather of its very structure. The American dream has blinded us to what should be obvious—that any nation, as a social mechanism, must have a motor located in some one part of it. In America, New York is that motor because it is the center of our commerce, finance, media, and culture— in short, the center of our American power. That power is based on three properties of New York: its novelty, its volume, and its brains.

According to Alvin Toffler, author of *Future Shock*, New York's "principal product is not rags, words, or money. It is novelty."[6] This is directly related to the fact that the national media are located in New York and are devoted almost exclusively to what is new. Because the media use New York as a testing ground, the city is the nation's purveyor of the new. It is where the latest in everything must surface and be accepted in order to become American. Every day New York is the newest place in America—what scientist René Dubos calls "the experimental city par excellence."[7]

Secondly, New York's volume of activity encourages quality as diffusion elsewhere cannot. The best emerges through survival of the fittest, simply because there is so much competition. There are occasional extraordinary events in other cities (in theatre, a *House of Atreus* in Minneapolis, an *Oppenheimer* in Los Angeles, a *Great White Hope* in Washington), but they are isolated, not part of a sustained volume of activity. Lacking that, no other city can assure the regular quality that is inevitable in New York. Again, in its insularity, *Time* happens to be correct: "How well a city is doing in many fields is often measured against New York, which is really the commercial and cultural marketplace of the United States. For better or worse, any artist anywhere has to meet the criteria of New York before he can claim real stature."[8] Volume of audience is also a key factor. New York is one of only two cities in the nation with so many millions of people in and around them that the approximately 3 percent who will support classical theatre can still provide a huge constituency. (The other city is, of course, Los Angeles; but Los Angeles lacks the ethnic variety and concentration of special interests which are necessary for full cultural flowering.) In New York, plays of many different cultures and persuasions can be mounted and can compete with each other, and each can still find an audience. It is the only American city with a population both large enough and diverse enough to embrace a total theatre.

Finally and most importantly, New York is supreme among American cities because it is where the brains of the country are most concentrated. Many of these brains control our media, and through our media they control us. Others are involved in experiments of all kinds in every facet of society, because New York is where ideas are tested and synthesized. It is where problems surface first—for example, the problem of absorbing immigrants from overseas or from the American farmland; the problem of massive welfare; the problems of drug abuse and of legalized abortion. Because it is the first city to face many problems, it is also the first to seek solutions to them. Therefore many of the best brains of the nation are attracted to New York because it affords for them the first opportunity to apply their solutions to society's ills.

The novelty, volume, and brains of New York make it unique among American cities. This is the great difference between it and the cities in which the regional theatre took root. The regional dilemma is partly the fact that, as Michael Murray noted, "We are mainly operating in cities which do *not* want to be unique."[9]

In the beginning, the creators of regional theatre considered New York's unique power to be its unique perverseness. Philosophically rejecting New York as a cultural Gomorrah, they sought to save the American theatre by decentralizing it. This created a centrifugal theatre, moving away from the New York center, and later the dream of a single National Theatre to come out of it. Yet through the 1960s, New York's uniqueness held the whole experiment in a kind of thralldom. Audiences and critics all over the country judged productions on the New York standard. New York's media alternately noticed and ignored them. The motor would not reverse direction, and the fulcrum of power could not be shifted—simply because New York is where the *mind* of the country is most concentrated. If there is to be one National Theatre company in America, it will have to be located where the nation's mind is—in the central city of New York. The regional dilemma, then, revolves around the fact that the development of a single National Theatre company has nothing to do with decentralization. In fact, the two goals contradict each other.

It is easy to theorize on the dilemma in the abstract, but sooner or later it can become a personal problem. For instance, by working outside the center of activity, the professional actor, director, designer, or manager is taking himself away from the largest concentration of people with similar talents. Theatre people are notoriously narrow in their social intercourse and do not mix often or well with non-theatre people. Sometimes the only close relationships the theatre professional develops are with people with whom he is already working day and night. Sometimes these relationships are ingrown and intense; sometimes they sour and, in souring, harm his work. Moreover, the narrowness of acquaintance in a regional city can be a severe psychological problem because it limits corroboration. Theatre people, like all artists, tend to concentrate in one place for corroboration of their own individual talents. The larger the corroborating group, the easier it is to satisfy one's ego needs. In regional cities, the smallness of the group can breed doubt about one's own talent. Every person in the theatre, hoping that he is talented, also hopes that that talent will get to function in an ultimate situation. Therefore, when they are relaxed or when they cannot sleep, the professional people in the regional theatre may feel that they are missing something by being where they are, by not being in New York. So every week you buy the Sunday *Times* (in some cities it is not available downtown until Tuesday), and you devour the theatre section, reading about what is happening in New York—what is opening, and closing, and succeeding—and where are you? *Marat/Sade*, for instance, opens in New York—one of the truly great productions of our time, and you cannot get there to see it. Maybe you can if you are rich enough to fly in to catch a performance on your Monday off; but that may mean flying in from Houston or Minneapolis or Seattle. Eventually, of course, you will see some production of the play; you may even be in the play someday. But in the meantime you are probably unable to go and participate in that original, seminal theatrical event, and so there is a chink in your experience, your consciousness, and therefore perhaps your professional worth. No matter how satisfying your work and how proud of it you might be, you are also harboring fears that you may be missing out. As playwright William Gibson wrote, "It is not dominant in the American grain to regard less money, less glory, and for that matter [poorer] working conditions or less technical finish, as preferable to more, merely for the sake of internal scope."[10] No matter how much better the working conditions and the technical finish get, you may still hunger for the money and the glory.

It was in the late 1960s, during the era of malaise, that the regional dilemma as a personal problem became most intense and pervasive. The only theatre people whom the dilemma did not touch were the older ones (primarily actors) who had once functioned in the commercial theatre but who had rejected it for the more civilized regional form. They knew what they had given up (in some cases, poverty); and while they may have missed the conviviality and excitement of New York, they relished more the comfortable life and often the better roles offered by the regional theatre. About the worst thing that could happen to them was an incident like the one that happened to Peter Zeisler after the inauguration of The Guthrie Theater. In New York on business, Zeisler happened to meet an old theatrical chum from his Broadway days. The chum grasped Zeisler's hand and inquired, solicitously and delicately, "Peter, have you been . . . working?"

Those hit hardest by the regional dilemma in the late 1960s were the young theatre people who had grown up in an increasingly mobile society and who had many more options open to them than had those who came earlier. Young directors wanted to be loyal and wanted to develop their companies, but many were embarrassed and frustrated by never having worked in the central theatre, and they also lacked professional clout because they had not. For these directors, the dilemma also revolved around the second-rate nature of many regional cities; the more aware the director, the more severe the problem. For he was often going to New York, seeing not only *Marat/Sade* but also many experimental plays, talking to intellectual leaders at meetings, going to Europe to see theatre on his vacation, and reading scholarly journals. Then, when he went back to his city, wanting to bring all he had discovered to his stage, he found that his city was not ready for it. Some few select people may have been ready, but then they were the people who also were going to New York, going to Europe, and reading scholarly journals. And so the director was often frustrated by seeing what could be but always having to return to a situation which was not ready for it. Therefore, as we have seen, some bright young directors did not commit themselves permanently to the regional theatre; they tended to view it as a personal training ground, a way station on a longer career journey. And frequently this lack of commitment seriously jeopardized their theatres as institutions.

Like the young directors, actors who began their careers outside New York may have wondered whether they were wrong (or weak) not to go to New York to live in the Village and wait on tables while seeking fame and fortune. They imagined only the excitement of the New York experience, never the awful frustration; and if they could have realized that frustration, they probably still would have wanted to chance it. Actor Rene Auberjonois, a truly distinctive acting talent to come out of the regional theatre, described the problem with knowing humor: "I am convinced that most actors involved in regional theatre are schizophrenics in the sense that they cannot reconcile the feeling that they should be fighting the fight of commercial theatre with the feeling that they are chosen members of some great and holy theatrical crusade. This dilemma gives rise to a working climate which could be compared to a monastery filled with self-consciously zealous monks suppressing the desire to ravage the neighboring village."[11]

Among those most deeply and poignantly affected by the regional dilemma were the leaders of some of the earliest theatres. After all, the movement had begun with their banishment of Broadway, but the banishment had been only philosophical and somewhat automatic—for most of them had never tried it. For these leaders, I think, the regional dilemma was an inevitable result of that willful rejection. Now that they had proved their talent to themselves and to their world, it was natural to wonder what they might have missed.

As the 1970s approached, nearly everyone was caught in the dilemma: the noble mission on the periphery versus the attraction of ultimate power which was available only in the center. Gaining that power was equated with becoming the one National Theatre; the problem, of course, was simply that that one theatre could not be on the periphery. Long-banished Broadway had become the final frontier of the revolution. The time had come to storm the citadel.

13 Storming the Citadel: The Theatres Go to New York

"We aspire to go to New York because that is where the competition is. To be a champion you must play against champions."

Barton Emmet, New York Times

"As I see it, the regional theatre actor's greatest problem is to pick the right moment to get out of the womb."

Rene Auberjonois, The Drama Review

Two distinct but intertwined desires assured the attempt to centralize the decentralized theatre. One was the desire of individual theatres to function in a national context that could spell permanent influence. The other was the hunger of individual artists for the corroboration, the acclaim, and the power that only recognition in New York can bring. For the theatres, of course, approval in the tough New York marketplace could prove their worth and justify their requests for financial help and loyalty at home. In the words of Barton Emmet, a former manager at both The Guthrie Theater and the Trinity Square Repertory Company, "One of the best ways to please the locals is to go to New York."[1]

For a select few in the regional theatre, the movement in fact became one of *re*centralization; having once succeeded in various capacities in the central commercial theatre and having rejected it, they were now interested in coming back—and in glory. However, for the vast majority of people in the regional theatre who had either never worked in New York or had worked there anonymously, it was centralization for the first time. It took two forms: the propulsion into New York of new plays which had been premiered in regional theatres and the booking of limited engagements by regional theatre companies on Broadway.

Centralization actually started with individuals rather than with institutions, beginning in the earliest years of the regional theatre; the move of George Grizzard and Alan Schneider from Arena Stage with *All Summer Long* was a notable example. The most striking example, of course, was the Irving-Blau move to Lincoln Center in 1965, which included not only the two leaders but also a dozen or so actors from their San Francisco theatre, none of whom had made a mark previously in the New York theatre (and only two of those actors made a significant mark after arriving—Robert Symonds, as a leading member of the Lincoln Center company, and Edward Winter, who soon left the company and won featured roles on Broadway).

About the time of the Irving-Blau move, other actors in other regional theatres started slowly and quietly to leave for New York. One of the first was one of the most exotically talented—Zoe Caldwell. An Australian, she had first scored at the Stratford festival in Ontario and on the English stage. As a protégée of Tyrone Guthrie, she was a leading member of the original Guthrie company in Minneapolis. Playing Frosine to Hume Cronyn's Miser, she captivated audiences with her front-and-center, knock-'em-dead talent. She showed her slightly more subtle side in *The Three Sisters*. In 1965, she was nearly the only appropriate element of the Restoration comedy *The Way of the World*, and she also played the pivotal role of Grusha in *The Caucasian Chalk Circle*. When the 1965 Guthrie season ended, Miss Caldwell left for New York. There, early in 1966, she substituted for the ailing Anne Bancroft in *The Devils* on Broadway and caused a sensation within the theatrical profession for her strong and very different portrayal. Then, in a short-lived Tennessee Williams work, *Slapstick Tragedy*, she outshone both Margaret Leighton and Kate Reid and won a Tony Award. Zoe Caldwell was becoming known as a highly theatrical actress, and an intellectual claque was forming for her. In 1967, she returned to Stratford, Ontario, to appear in *The Merry Wives of Windsor* and in *Antony and Cleopatra* (opposite Christopher Plummer). Meanwhile, through fellow Guthrie actor Hume Cronyn, she had met producer Robert Whitehead (Cronyn's cousin). Whitehead, returning to Broadway producing after his Lincoln Center debacle, was planning *The Prime of Miss Jean Brodie*, and it looked just right for Miss Caldwell. He produced it; she appeared in it; they married; she won a Tony Award again and became a full-fledged star. Zoe Caldwell is too much of an acting whirlwind to be easily contained within a repertory company situation; her talent and sometimes simply her mannerisms dwarf those around her. Old-style in her theatricality, like Bernhardt, she serves a function in a national context that could appear grotesque if confined to a regional one. She is the most starrish acting talent that the regional theatre has produced, and it is perhaps this very star-ism that keeps her now away from the regional theatre.

Other actors as well known as Miss Caldwell have come out of the regional theatre, although their participation in it was more accidental than hers. Both Dustin Hoffman and Jon Voight served early apprenticeships in theatres outside New York—Hoffman at the Theatre Company of Boston, Voight at the Old Globe Theatre in San Diego. Another actor with a longer list of regional credits is Stacy Keach, one of the few young actors in America who has the requisite voice, energy, intelligence, and arrogance on the stage to develop into a great classical actor. Regrettably, like many other actors of his generation, Keach now spends more time working in films than in the theatre (although he found time for *Indians* at Arena Stage and, in 1972, for *Hamlet* at both the Long Wharf Theatre and the New York Shakespeare Festival).

Less well known actors have moved more quietly from the regional to the central theatre and have managed to continue their associations with their former life. Jane Alexander, who began at the Charles Playhouse and then moved to Arena Stage, was the leading lady of *The Great White Hope* in Washington; she then left the Arena company to play the same role on Broadway and in the film version. Now, despite further work in films and on Broadway, she has spent two summers at the American Shakespeare Festival. Len Cariou, out of Canada through Stratford, Ontario, and The Guthrie Theater, came to New York with the Guthrie on tour, switched to the American Shakespeare Festival for *Henry V*, and then moved on to the musical *Applause* as Lauren Bacall's romantic interest and the Broadway mystery play *Nightwatch*. Nevertheless, the 1972 season found him back at the Guthrie, playing Oedipus Rex there and directing *Of Mice and Men*. Toward the end of the 1972 season, he flew back and forth between performances as Oedipus in Minneapolis and rehearsals for a new Harold Prince musical in New York. Apparently some actors (and directors) cannot get the regional theatre out of their systems after centralizing themselves, and this is good.

One of the most interesting examples of a young actor's move from regional to central theatre is the case of Rene Auberjonois. In his teens, he carried spears and received limited training at the American Shakespeare Festival. After college at Carnegie Tech, he began his acting career at the Alley Theatre. In the early 1960s, he moved to Arena Stage for a season of leading roles. When William Ball founded his American Conservatory Theatre in 1965, Auberjonois was one of the original members. In San Francisco, he distinguished himself as Tartuffe and in *Charley's Aunt* and *Beyond the Fringe*; he began to be noticed and praised by the national critics covering ACT. However, the exigencies of that theatre and its very regionalism were beginning to bother Auberjonois. He left Ball's company, and shortly thereafter he wrote a brief article for *The Drama Review* on the problems of the actor's life in the regional theatre:

> There is, undoubtedly, much to be said for the "womb of the rep" which affords the freedom to make those mistakes which may lead to brilliance, but one must also contend with the nagging fear that one is copping out and losing perspective. There is the danger that the constant pressure to create leaves no time to stop and take stock of one's work—to learn from those mistakes. Doing 16 shows in 22 weeks is about as satisfying and creative as grinding out a weekly TV series. The problem of perspective is furthered by the league of well-meaning critics rallying to the cause of "culture in the provinces" and heaping hysterical praise on the "good-ole-college-try" productions.
>
> I do not mean to deny that the training and exposure afforded by regional theatre is the only practical way for a young actor to mould himself into a useful artist. I mean that most actors will admit that they are actors because of a driving desire to be loved. It follows that to be loved on the grandest scale by the greatest number of people is an important, if not primary, objective.[2]

After leaving ACT, Auberjonois appeared with Hume Cronyn in *The Miser* at the Mark Taper Forum, then with Lee J. Cobb as the Fool in *King Lear* at Lincoln Center. Joining the drama faculty at the Juilliard School in New York, he still managed to appear on Broadway in the ill-fated *Fire* and to make an auspicious film debut in *M.A.S.H.* In 1969, he caused a minor sensation as a fey dress designer in the musical *Coco*, won a Tony Award, and left to make more movies. And while he did later appear as Malvolio in *Twelfth Night* at the Repertory Theater of Lincoln Center, he has not, as of this writing, returned to work in any theatre outside New York.

Regional Theatre: The Revolutionary Stage

Auberjonois is like Zoe Caldwell in the very high degree of his talent. They represent the best of regional theatre actors who left to go to the center. They are also the least likely to go back to stay because that extremity of talent lends itself most to personal stardom and least to company work. They are the exceptions to critic Walter Kerr's description of regional theatre actors in general: ". . . all professionals though none are charismatics on their way to screen contracts."[3]

Among those "professionals"—the blander, more serviceable actors— some have left the regional theatre, failed at the center, and now seek to go back. The theatres will take them back, probably, or other theatres will hire them, and they will become like those older actors in the regional theatre, happy to have tried the commercial theatre but grateful now to have a steady wage. At that, they are better off psychologically than those who have never tried it and who sit in frustration wondering if they should try it now or if they should have done so before. When an actor leaves a regional theatre to try his fortune elsewhere, however, the theatre can suffer. There may be many more actors than there are jobs in the American theatre, but so few actors have the requisite classical training and group adaptability that theatres still have problems recruiting their companies. Sometimes these problems are aggravated by propulsion of the theatres themselves into the national idiom. For example, in the winter of 1970, the Long Wharf Theatre in New Haven presented the American premiere of Maxim Gorky's *Country People*. When the play received universally complimentary reviews (including the essential review by Clive Barnes in the *New York Times*), the theatre considered taking the production to New York. While the plans never materialized, the occasion prompted artistic director Arvin Brown to voice his concern about what the results might be for his theatre: "I must say that the principal value . . . is for the actors. And naturally I feel very ambivalent about that. . . . I feel that because their work is good, that it should be seen in New York, and that they should have the excitement of going to New York. I feel bad about it because I know that some of their work is so good that they are going to be snatched up right and left when they get there, and I am probably not going to be able to get them all back next season."[4] Had *Country People* gone into New York, some of the Long Wharf actors would no doubt have been "snatched up," and I suspect that most of them would have loved it.

Of course, the same opportunity to function at the center is often welcomed by the up-and-coming director—for example, Arvin Brown himself. While one of the most sincerely devoted of young directors, Brown is also keenly aware of the possibilities that exist beyond his immediate sphere. For instance, after Brown took over the direction of the Long Wharf and had mounted a good production of *Ghosts* with Mildred Dunnock, there appeared in the *New York Times* a simple ad for the theatre bearing a quotation from *New Yorker* critic Brendan Gill: "In New Haven the other evening, at the Long Wharf Theatre, I saw a production of Ibsen's *Ghosts* that was as near-perfect as no matter, directed by a brilliant young man of twenty-eight named Arvin Brown."[5] So everyone in the New York theatre found out that Arvin Brown was not only twenty-eight but also brilliant and, I daresay, available for occasional assignments. Within several months, Arvin Brown was in New York, directing his own production of Thomas Murphy's *A Whistle in the Dark*, which had premiered at the Long Wharf early in 1968. The production brought acclaim to both Brown and his theatre. In 1970, he made his Broadway directing debut with a commercial production of Noel Coward's *Hay Fever*. In 1971, he directed *Long Day's Journey into Night* off-Broadway (with Stacy Keach) and Robert Anderson's *Solitaire Double Solitaire* on Broadway (another production transferred from the Long Wharf).

Brown has a very solid talent backed up by common sense and the good fortune of being strategically located. Less than a hundred miles from New York, he can command the attention of the New York national media for his new plays and his own work, and he can function occasionally at the center of the American theatre as a commuter. Other directors are not so lucky. They cannot dash into New York for a day at a time to develop relationships, nor can they get producers and critics to come up for an evening to see their work on their home stages. If even despite these odds they obtain an assignment in New York, they cannot easily keep track of their home fires from great distances. Fragile organizations have a way of tottering when their leaders are off pursuing their own separate careers elsewhere. Also, even when the theatre survives its leader's absence, he may not have any increased reputation to offer upon his return. Among productions staged in New York by regional theatre directors, the percentage of critical success is so far no higher than among productions generally. Arvin Brown is an exception.

Another director who has consistently brought home glory with him is Gordon Davidson of the Mark Taper Forum. His first important experience in directing in New York was *In the Matter of J. Robert Oppenheimer* at the Repertory Theater of Lincoln Center, a transplant of his original production in Los Angeles and a major critical and audience success. (The central prominence that *Oppenheimer* brought Davidson was an indirect accident. When the play first came to his attention, it was through English director Peter Coe, who intended to direct it in Los Angeles. Shortly before rehearsals were to start, Coe called to say that he had been offered a film to direct and asked to be let free. Davidson decided to stage the play himself and from that decision came his central career.) After *Oppenheimer*, Davidson directed two plays in New York for T. Edward Hambleton's Phoenix Theatre—*The Trial of the Catonsville Nine* and *Murderous Angels,* both again transplants from the Mark Taper Forum. Later, Davidson was chosen to stage Leonard Bernstein's *Mass* as the inaugural production of the Kennedy Center in Washington. Through these assignments, he has developed into an American director rather than just a Los Angeles one. One reason that Gordon Davidson has fared well directing in New York is that he has always gone there with proven plays which he has already mastered at home. Another advantage for him, both at the Repertory Theater and the Phoenix, was that he was able to work with institutions like his own and with associates and personal friends. In effect, he was bolstered and protected by the familiar while working in the New York maelstrom.

Edwin Sherin, the original director and later the Broadway director of *The Great White Hope,* also had a proven play but the context was different. He had staged the play first in that most efficient of theatres, Arena Stage; in New York he was engaged by an old-line Broadway producer, Herman Levin. Here was a typical commercial situation, and Sherin proved equal to it. His move to New York was more a recentralization than that of most regional theatre directors because, before going to Arena Stage in 1964, he had spent nearly a decade as an actor and director in New York. He was going back with an impressive list of directing credits from an additional five years at Arena Stage. With the extraordinary success of *The Great White Hope* on Broadway,

Sherin became a new celebrity in the New York theatre, and he came on very strong, waving the banner of the regional theatre. The real fun and achievement of his life, he said to the press, began when he went to Arena Stage, finally to function as a real artist. In nineteen productions, he came into his own as he could never have done on Broadway or even off-Broadway. Clearly, he said, the regional theatre was the only real theatre; the New York theatre was moribund and corrupt. "Get with it," he was saying to the central theatre. "Get off it," the central theatre replied. When awards time came around, Edwin Sherin was totally ignored by those in the New York theatre who decide such things. While his work was worthy of all awards available, he had talked himself out of any. He had overreacted to his central debut.

Perhaps it did not matter to Edwin Sherin. Immediately after the New York opening of *The Great White Hope,* he returned to Arena Stage, where he was still the associate director and heir apparent to Zelda Fichandler. There he directed Frank Silvera in *King Lear* and then departed to make films. While he occasionally returned to regional theatre work (notably, at the American Shakespeare Festival and the American Conservatory Theatre), his emphasis was on the central theatre; the new real fun and achievement of his life had taken a commercial turn.

Fortunately Sherin is not typical of all young directors from regional cities who succeed at the center. Gordon Davidson and Arvin Brown, for instance, have gracefully accepted their central success and then have returned to their home cities and used that success to the advantage of their theatres. This is a particularly important attitude in directors like Davidson and Brown who are in charge of their theatres; if they were to desert them at the first signs of central acclaim, those theatres might not survive. By contrast, Edwin Sherin was not in charge of Arena Stage; he worked for another strong-willed director, Zelda Fichandler. There was no reason for him to think that by leaving the theatre he was threatening its future. He was free to answer his commercial urges. Such urges are no weaker in directors at the helm, but they are less free to pursue them. This, of course, constitutes an aspect of the regional dilemma—a conflict between institutional responsibility and personal ego and ambition.

However, there is one possible solution to the dilemma for the leader at the helm: he can centralize his theatre itself, even if only briefly and temporarily. This allows him to propel himself without abandoning his theatre, and so perhaps he can enjoy the best of both worlds. In the last years of the 1960s, this solution took the form of limited engagements by regional theatres in New York. It was natural that the first regional theatre to experiment with this approach was The Guthrie Theater. As we have seen, after a highly touted opening and strong audience acceptance, the Guthrie was in decline by 1966. Subscriptions had dropped from a 1963 high of more than 21,000 to fewer than 16,000, attendance had fallen from 85 percent of capacity to about two-thirds, and there was a déjà vu feeling about the theatre in its own community. Another key change in the theatre by 1966 was that two of the original three leaders—Tyrone Guthrie and Oliver Rea—had resigned, leaving the third, Peter Zeisler, as the managing director. Zeisler, while a dynamo in production management, had never administered a major theatre institution, and he had no reputation for it. He was forging ahead without any extensive background in the field. But he was determined to succeed, and he managed to salvage the theatre in the 1967 season, with significant assistance from guest-director Guthrie's production of *The House of Atreus*. This production was so well received that it was brought back into the repertoire in the 1968 season, which turned out to be one of the theatre's most successful years to date. In fact, the 1968 season boasted three of the five most popular plays in the theatre's first six years (*Atreus, Arturo Ui,* and *Twelfth Night* in 1968, *The Three Sisters* in 1963, and *The Miser* in both 1963 and 1965). The 1968 season played to 87 percent of capacity, a Guthrie record at that time. Apparently the downward trend had been reversed and The Guthrie Theater was riding a new wave. While the number of regular subscribers continued to drop, the total number of people attending the theatre was growing—which meant, of course, that more and more individuals were being introduced to the theatre's work.

It was during the exceptional season of 1968 that the decision was made to tour the company to New York. Actually, the New York stop was one of two; the other engagement was to be at the Mark Taper Forum in Los Angeles. To help in subsidizing the tour, Zeisler obtained two major grants: $75,000 from the National Endowment for the Arts and $50,000 from the Billy Rose Foundation (the company was scheduled to perform in the Billy Rose Theatre on Broadway as part of that house's nonprofit season in 1968–69). For the tour, Zeisler chose *The House of Atreus* and *Arturo Ui*, both from the 1968 season and two of the most popular productions in Guthrie history. There was no question that one of the selections had to be *Atreus*. It was a theatrical milestone; it was representative of the company's best ensemble work, staged by the director who had created the theatre; and it had already been praised by two *New York Times* critics in its Minneapolis premiere: "The company's collective strength is more impressive than individual actors. The ensemble style so long sought by the Guthrie Theater is becoming an actuality, and this massive 'House of Atreus' is one of its finest accomplishments."[6] "This 'House of Atreus' is a remarkable achievement. The unpredictably imaginative Guthrie has taken a heady leap forward in exploring the outer reaches of the stage."[7] *Atreus*, in short, looked like a sure bet for New York laurels. The other production, Edward Payson Call's staging of *Arturo Ui*, was as fine in its way as *Atreus*, but as a pair they provided fare somewhat heavy for a rotating repertory engagement in "Fun City." While not nearly as admirable a production, Kaufman and Connelly's 1920s potboiler *Merton of the Movies*, another 1968 success in Minneapolis, would have been a more logical choice for a second play to add balance and joy, particularly at a time when New York audiences were beginning to rediscover (and overreact to) the delights of simplistic plays of bygone eras. The choice of *Arturo Ui* was a strictly artistic one—and why not, given the subsidy provided for the tour? There could be no doubt that The Guthrie Theater was going to New York with its best foot forward; it would be seen as an intelligent alternative to the crass and shallow commercialism of Broadway. In the plays it was bringing and the way it was bringing them, the Guthrie was living up to its reputation as the preeminent regional theatre.

The Guthrie company opened at the Billy Rose Theatre on December 17, 1968, and presented *Atreus* and *Arturo Ui* in rotation through January 11, 1969. It then played an engagement of six weeks in Los Angeles, where the large number of Mark Taper Forum subscribers assured a sympathetic and enthusiastic audience. In New York, however, the company was greeted by a resounding thud of critical and audience apathy, which was not helped by the fact that the engagement started at the beginning of what is always the worst box-office week in the New York theatre, the week before Christmas. While some New York critics found merit in the flagship *Atreus* production, the essential

New York Times did an about-face on it. This time Clive Barnes was the reviewer; first apologizing for his review (and so maintaining his reputation as a supporter of regional theatre), Barnes then leveled his guns: "It is a bundle of stage tricks by the director, Sir Tyrone Guthrie, noted founding father of the Minnesota company. The production has two great virtues: it is lavishly spectacular and it gets more laughs out of a Greek tragedy than any other production I have previously encountered."[8] *Arturo Ui* drew reviews only slightly better, although it did draw more patrons than *The House of Atreus.*

In an attempt to minimize the negative Barnes review, Zeisler took ads in newspapers reprinting the favorable Walter Kerr review of the Minneapolis *Atreus* production, but this did not help appreciably. In a theatre with potential weekly ticket sales of $55,000, the Guthrie receipts never rose above $27,049, less than 50 percent of capacity.[9] In another effort to stir up interest in the company's visit, Zeisler announced an extension of the limited engagement at the Billy Rose (the productions, originally announced to run through January 4, were extended through January 11). Actually, there was no public demand prompting this extension. The extra week had been reserved in case audience interest should require it; the company therefore had nowhere else to go between the New York and Los Angeles engagements, and so it extended the New York visit rather than wandering or dispersing. When January 12 finally came, the Guthrie company left New York with its collective head down and severely in debt despite the subsidy of the tour.

If it is true that "one of the best ways to please the locals is to go to New York," then it is also true that the way to displease them is to go back home without great honor. It was difficult in Minneapolis in 1969 to believe that The Guthrie Theater was the best regional theatre in the United States—not after that scalding in New York. The 1969 season in Minneapolis was a disaster compared to illustrious 1968: attendance was down 20 percent, income was down 22 percent, and the deficit was more than doubled. The theatre was again in decline; it was as if the 1968 season and the tour it had spawned were freaks. The wind was out of many sails, most notably out of Peter Zeisler's. He was the one who had conceived the tour to New York, and in retrospect it appears to have been not only an institutional but also a personal venture. Zeisler, after all, had been relatively anonymous when he left New

220

York to help two more famous people form the Guthrie. When known, he was known (and respected) as a production manager, that fellow in shirt sleeves who gets the backstage work done. Through circumstances in Minneapolis—the resignations of his original partners and the fact that he stayed on and knew the scene—Zeisler moved into a position of solo leadership. There he was obligated to prove himself publicly and institutionally; he moved from backstage to front and center. He was a fast learner and he liked that position at the top; but the institutional mantle did not sit easily on him. The Guthrie tour was perhaps in part an attempt to improve an awkward situation by showing New York (and therefore Minneapolis) that the mantle could be borne. Also, Zeisler may have been going to New York for many of the same reasons that Herbert Blau had gone, perhaps with the hope that he was taking the National Theatre with him; but when the company got there, it was not acclaimed widely as the National Theatre or even as the best regional theatre in America. And the tough commercial theatre that Zeisler had mastered but had then rejected did not acknowledge and cheer the Guthrie's superiority. When January 12 came, it was Peter Zeisler's duty to lower his gaze and lead his company out of town. It must have been a painful exit.

Within a year, faced with the continuing decline of local interest and support and haunted, I suppose, by the psychological and financial failure of the New York tour, Zeisler left Minneapolis on a year's leave of absence, ostensibly to conduct a study of the repertory theatre form and prepare a major report to the Guthrie board of directors. No one would say whether he would return or not, but as one of his former associates suggested, "If things are going badly in Minneapolis, he won't want to go back; and if things are going well, they won't need him back." Things continued to go badly in Minneapolis, but still the members of the Guthrie board decided that they did not need him back; they sent word that there was no reason to return. The tour to New York had turned out to be Peter Zeisler's albatross. He was one of the first casualties of centralization, and there would be more.

Since the days when the regional theatre started to take its place as part of the Establishment, and particularly after the move of Jules Irving and Herbert Blau to Lincoln Center, there had been growing interest in New York in the work of theatres beyond. This interest encouraged the suggestion that a place be set aside in New York for the exhibition of the best of regional theatre. In fact, when Herbert Blau left Lincoln Center and specific plans for the Repertory Theater were not yet known, *Times* critic Walter Kerr came up with a possible solution for the Lincoln Center woes:

The Vivian Beaumont stage might be made available for a season to any and all companies from outside New York that are willing to come in on a Festival basis and are able to adapt themselves to the particular stage at hand. . . . There is activity buzzing all around us, there is bound to be talent in it, there are plays of all sorts being mounted to provide variety, there is a curiosity about the quality of work being done that can only be satisfied by seeing it shoulder-to-shoulder in competition, there is no doubt an eagerness—the facts of life being what they are—on the part of companies outside New York to be seen in New York.[10]

However, Jules Irving seized the initiative, and the Vivian Beaumont stage was not available for visiting troupes. Still the idea kept being presented. Not long after the failure of The Guthrie Theater at the Billy Rose, another Broadway theatre was set aside for the use of regional companies interested in centralizing themselves. As noted earlier, the American National Theatre and Academy, over nearly forty years, had succeeded only in burying its head in the New York sand while theatres developed throughout the country. Although its National Theatre Service had focused on theatres outside New York, both professional and amateur, the Service director, Ruth Mayleas, had left ANTA to join the National Endowment for the Arts. ANTA was purposeless and still burdened with a Broadway theatre bearing its name. The theatre, appraised at $2,300,000, was subject to a first mortgage of $715,000, due in 1976, and a second mortgage of $375,000, due in 1969. Lacking substantial funds, ANTA was facing almost certain and certainly deserved death.

Meanwhile, Roger Stevens was leaving his post as the chairman of the National Endowment for the Arts after four years of admirable service. Returning to New York, he was looking for a way to facilitate New York engagements for those theatres he had been supporting with government funds. The idea of limited engagements for regional theatres in New York and ANTA's desperate need for funds came together, and Stevens developed a plan. The idea seemed neat and clean: through a special contract between ANTA and the Endowment, the ANTA Theatre was donated to the Endowment as a "gift to the American people."[11] A grant of $438,000 from the Endowment to ANTA provided for the retirement of the 1969 mortgage and the planning of an invitational season in the ANTA Theatre. Stevens's reasoning to President Johnson was straightforward but unintentionally patronizing to the very groups he hoped to help: "We plan to make this theater available as a performing arts center in New York City for many nonprofit groups throughout America, many of whom have never before had the opportunity of presenting their creative talents in a truly professional atmosphere."[12]

The donation of the ANTA Theatre to the Endowment made Uncle Sam the absentee landlord of a Broadway theatre, but Uncle Sam wanted none of that headache, particularly with Stevens leaving government service. Also, with all that money, ANTA still had no purpose to spend it on. Therefore the Endowment pumped enough life into ANTA to enable it to manage the theatre for the Endowment, the government, and the American people. Stevens made a personal project out of the restructuring of ANTA and the use of its former theatre as a showcase for regional companies.

The restructuring of ANTA constituted a severe jolt for an organization long ridiculed for its geriatric, incestuous, and Broadway-oriented ineffectuality. One of the first things Stevens did was to eliminate the large and unwieldy ANTA board. In its place, he installed a new group of seventeen, including a few former members and four new members from theatres outside New York: Zelda Fichandler, Gordon Davidson, Adrian Hall, and Peter Zeisler. Also among the seventeen on the new board were three leaders of institutional theatres inside New York: Ellen Stewart of the Cafe La Mama, Richard Barr of the Playwrights Unit (and also a commercial producer), and Joseph Papp of the New York Shakespeare Festival. It seemed a motley group, given the presence of the seven institutionalists plus representatives of the commercial theatre: designer Oliver Smith, Warren Caro of the Shubert theatre chain, agent Audrey Wood, and producers Stuart Ostrow and Robert Whitehead (who, despite his commercial position, had done his share of institutional suffering). Yet it was not a group of strangers—not with the decentralized theatre trying to centralize itself.

Having rebuilt ANTA, Stevens then persuaded the Endowment to give ANTA more money. A second grant of $694,000 was provided to administer ANTA through the end of 1970 and to underwrite a 1969–70 season of guest engagements by institutional theatres on the ANTA

223

stage. The organization came out of Stevens's wringer with a total of $1,132,000 to spend as the regional theatre's home in New York. The new ANTA then did a strange thing. It hired two of the brightest theatre people of the 1940s—Jean Dalrymple (to manage the operation) and Alfred deLiagre (to mount the season). DeLiagre had produced on Broadway with regularity (among other plays, *Voice of the Turtle, Janus, The Royal Hunt of the Sun,* and *J.B.*). Miss Dalrymple had managed the City Center drama seasons for many years, and she was well known for her conventional ideas. No more traditional people could have been chosen, nor people less familiar with theatre outside New York. The commercial theatre members of the new ANTA board seemed to be appointing from within their own ranks, while the regional members were selecting people who might enhance their own centripetal ambitions. Naturally, the new board was closely involved in the planning of the 1969–70 invitational season. By serving theatres whose leaders were on its board, ANTA had built-in conflicts of interest; yet there was no problem of a few institutional theatre leaders on the ANTA board squeezing others out of the ANTA season, as critic Martin Gottfried has suggested.[13] Peter Zeisler, for one, probably wanted nothing to do with the ANTA season after his company's roasting at the Billy Rose Theatre the year before. Zelda Fichandler, wiser in the ways of New York after *The Great White Hope,* astutely demurred. Besides, most regional companies could not easily pick up and go to the ANTA Theatre during the winter months; they had their own subscription seasons to fulfill at home. ANTA was left scurrying around New York to find enough tenants to fill up the winter weeks. Board members Ellen Stewart, Richard Barr, and Joseph Papp agreed to take productions from their experimental stages into the ANTA Theatre to take up the slack.

By the end of its invitational season, ANTA had used up its $694,000 but had succeeded in bringing into New York only four regional theatre companies: the American Conservatory Theatre, which inaugurated the series with William Ball's productions of *Tiny Alice* and *The Three Sisters* and Gower Champion's staging of *A Flea in Her Ear*; the American Shakespeare Festival's *Henry V*; the John Fernald Company of Oakland University outside Detroit, with *The Cherry Orchard*; and the Trinity Square Repertory Company of Providence, with *Wilson in the Promised Land*. Gordon Davidson's Mark Taper Forum was scheduled but had to give up its engagement when the State Department canceled the international tour that would have taken the company to the East. Once in the fall and once in the spring, productions using surefire stars attracted attention and brought in sorely needed receipts (and for these two sure successes, the ANTA organization provided no subsidy): the Plumstead Playhouse's *Our Town,* starring Henry Fonda and first produced on Long Island by Alfred deLiagre, and the Phoenix Theatre's *Harvey,* starring James Stewart and Helen Hayes. These two productions did ringing business, allowing ANTA to wander through the rest of the season.

Despite the nearly $700,000 in federal money being applied to itself and its invitational season, the new ANTA was covering only part of the costs of each engagement, and theatres from outside New York had to bear large costs themselves. Also, the new ANTA did little to promote the non-star productions or to sell them to the public as a subscription package. Miss Dalrymple and deLiagre simply opened the plays as if they were commercial ventures; when most of them received negative or noncommittal reviews, there was no choice but to close them down. The American Shakespeare Festival's *Henry V* was able to survive because of heavy student audience bookings, and ACT, with its controversial productions and self-promotion, lasted its full four-week run. But many other productions (including the Playwrights Unit and Trinity Square, both of which came with ANTA board representation) were closed even before completing their limited engagements. Trinity Square's experience was particularly grotesque. It had been scheduled for a six-week run, and to accommodate Adrian Hall's staging a nearly $100,000 renovation of the theatre was undertaken. Despite critical interest in *Wilson in the Promised Land,* ANTA closed the production after one week, and the second Trinity Square production, James Schevill's *Lovecraft's Follies,* never opened at all.

In general, the ANTA season was a clumsy affair and a distinct embarrassment. The planners had been unable to provide a steady stream of good work from outside New York, which was the original stated purpose. Most work presented was either rejected by the critics and the public or withdrawn before it could find its audience. Except in the case of *Our Town* and *Harvey,* two productions in the Dalrymple-deLiagre idiom, little attention was paid to the necessity of filling seats with paying customers. Those theatres that came to be centralized through ANTA met with apathy. Those that could not come, would not come, or were not invited to come, ended up breathing sighs of relief.

The ANTA season was an officially sanctioned assault on the citadel of New York and an inevitable one, given the development of the regional theatre form by the late 1960s. By then, the movement had enjoyed enough national attention and had caught a taste of enough national power to assume that from it could come a national savior. The movement was ready to try to seize the primary theatrical power, to try to return in triumph to save the Broadway it had banished. Yet the storming of the citadel was really an overreaching; like Coriolanus when he tried to invade Rome, the regional theatre was cut down. The revolution was cheapened into a mere coup d'état and an unsuccessful one at that. It was the more embarrassing because the citadel hardly noticed that there was an attempted coup going on. The thrust ended in ignominy.

The ANTA season debacle was the fifth and final turning point of the regional theatre revolution, and the first negative one—because through it the regional theatre's dreams of centralization were dashed. Combined with the earlier failure of The Guthrie Theater in New York, it seemed to prove that Broadway would not be conquered and particularly that no *one* regional theatre was likely to be dubbed the savior. At the start of the ANTA season, Walter Kerr of the *New York Times* had written: "If there is one dream more secret than another, but likely very pervasive, it is the quiet little dream on the part of every outlying company that one day—one triumphant, miraculous day—it will come into the center and be so remarkably good that it will be asked to stay, turning then and there into the American National Theater. Don't say that you don't dream it, directors, actors, and producers. You do."[14] The failure of the theatres in storming the citadel ruined that dream for all. Some talented people, on their own, came out of the experience with greatly enlarged personal horizons and careers, but no one institution emerged as finally preeminent. By the middle of 1970, the race for National Theatre supremacy had been neutralized.

The race on the outskirts, that is. At the center, in New York, a new and separate force was running a race of its own and was beginning to gain extraordinary strength and to attract much attention. The new force was Joseph Papp and his New York Shakespeare Festival, which by the early 1970s was the one institutional theatre in America able to command constant attention and to make its own rules.

For nearly twenty years, Papp's theatre had paralleled the regional theatre movement. It too had started as an acorn, a unique and particularly audacious one. In 1953, while a stage manager for CBS television, Papp began working with unknown actors in a Shakespeare workshop at a church in lower Manhattan. In 1956, he presented a season of Shakespearean productions in an outdoor amphitheatre (the plays were staged by Stuart Vaughan and cost a total of $750 to mount). The next year, he moved his festival to a platform on a truck in Central Park and began to attract attention. From the start, Papp insisted that all of his summer productions had to be offered free to the audience—their right as citizens. The festival was a belligerently popular undertaking, and it thrived on adversity. In 1959, for instance, New York parks commissioner Robert Moses issued an edict demanding that Papp charge admission to the summer plays to provide funds to replace the grass being trampled by his audiences. Papp categorically refused and turned the disagreement into a public crusade from which he emerged the champion of both the people and the art of free theatre. In 1961, he began to receive steady funding from New York for his summer productions, and in 1962, with city and private money, he commissioned a new open-air theatre for the festival in Central Park. He attracted major actors to appear on the stage: Julie Harris, James Earl Jones, Stacy Keach, and both Colleen Dewhurst and George C. Scott—a pair whose early experience had been with the festival in its first years. By the middle of the 1960s, the New York Shakespeare Festival had become permanent in the city, and Papp was an acknowledged force not only theatrically but even politically because he was on the people's side and they were on his.

Many others would have been satisfied to continue producing a summer festival of Shakespeare's plays, but Papp yearned for more. Citing both the need to keep his institution fresh and its public responsibility to offer not only classics but also new work, Papp embarked in 1966 on a winter program which did not emphasize Shakespeare. For $575,000, his festival purchased a cavernous 112-year-old building in lower Manhattan which was originally the city's first free public library. Over the next six years, he turned the space into five small theatres for the production mostly of new plays and soon was spilling over into additional space which he annexed in the neighborhood. Papp named his new space the Public Theater, which pointed up his commitment to the theatre as a public art; but, unlike the summer Shakespeare festival, the Public Theater sold its tickets. Uptown in the summertime, Papp was drawing a polyglot audience as various as New York itself; downtown in the wintertime, he was attracting an audience that was interested in new ideas and new ways of doing theatre. He was balancing the two worlds and making them feed each other.

The Public Theater side of Papp's operation brought his New York Shakespeare Festival to new heights. Whereas the summer productions continued to be broad and robust and highly physical, the winter productions were more specialized and deeper in their purposes. And yet the Public Theater plays were rarely esoteric and in fact were often very conventional and recognizable in form. Papp maintained his popular touch, and he combined that touch with a promotional sense very much like that of a hot-shot Broadway producer. For instance, the theatre downtown opened with the world premiere of *Hair*—not the flashy nude version but a smaller and quieter one. When another commercial producer saw a bonanza in the production and bought it for Broadway, Papp made sure that his festival shared in its earnings; therefore, in each year that *Hair* raked in money on Broadway, some of that money went back downtown to support Papp's burgeoning theatre projects. But *Hair* was not the only bonanza to come out of the Public Theater. Charles Gordone's *No Place to Be Somebody*, one of many black plays produced by Papp downtown, became the first off-Broadway play to win a Pulitzer Prize. Several other plays which were premiered at the Public Theater were sold to the movies. The downtown theatre came to be regarded by critics and audiences as New York's theatrical fountainhead; Clive Barnes called it "a great theater."[15] In a city bursting with all kinds and styles of theatre, the institutional New York Shakespeare Festival was in a class by itself.

Joseph Papp was beginning to cut a very wide swath. When financial straits threatened the festival with extinction in 1971, Papp pointed out that the problem was caused by the renovation and operating expenses of the Public Theater as a public trust; he got the city to buy the building from the festival for $2,600,000 and to rent it back for $1 a year. When other institutional theatres in the city were threatened financially (including the Repertory Theater of Lincoln Center), it was usually Joseph Papp who rose up to spearhead attempts to save them, thereby placing himself in a position almost above competition. His emergence was climaxed in 1972, when virtually all attention was focused on him and his festival. On Broadway, his productions of David Rabe's *Sticks and Bones* (transferred from the Public Theater) and his rock musical version of *Two Gentlemen of Verona* (transferred from Central Park) won Tony Awards as the best play and the best musical, and the profits of the latter were subsidizing the losses of the former. (Papp was also grandly turning back 5 percent of *Verona*'s Broadway profits to the city as a gesture of gratitude for the more than $5,000,000 in municipal support over the years.) Two more productions—Jason Miller's *That Championship Season* (from the Public Theater) and *Much Ado about Nothing* (from Central Park)—were installed on Broadway in the fall of 1972. Miller's play, realistic and even old-fashioned, was Broadway's only sell-out. *Much Ado* was put into a theatre usually reserved for huge musicals and was set in turn-of-the-century, small-town America; it had the aura of a smash-hit comedy about it. Meanwhile, CBS television engaged Papp and his festival to produce thirteen "specials" in prime time over a four-year period and provided more than $7,000,000 for the project, starting with a taping of *Much Ado*. This development more than any other put a national constituency at Papp's disposal; it was a startling and brilliant coup (and particularly impressive because CBS had fired Papp from his stage manager's job when he refused to testify before the House Un-American Activities Committee about his alleged former Communist leanings). One after another, the traditional and even the special awards were bestowed on Papp. *Newsweek* featured him in a major article and put his picture on the cover with a banner headline: "New Life in the American Theater."

Indeed, by 1972, Papp and his theatre were being heralded as a national solution. He called in the spring for the establishment of a "national theatre service" (presumably under his leadership) to bring the best of his world to the nation as a whole. To tour productions throughout the country was the basis of the idea, and in this Papp was suggesting a plan much like former proposals, but it was implicit that he was really proposing to send out his own work to the rest of the nation. In short, he and his institution had succeeded in doing what no regional theatre had been able to do. They were occupying Broadway as conquerors; they had seized the initiative, and they seemed to be getting (or taking) the power. They looked like a national force, and they were acting like a national savior.

In one sense, the regional theatre revolution started with Margo Jones and ended with Joseph Papp, and yet Papp was not really part of that revolution. The New York Shakespeare Festival was much like the regional theatre in its institutional bias, in the fact that it faced many of the same financial and social obstacles, and particularly in its dependence on one leader to give it character and purpose. It differed, however, in three very important ways: in its scope, in its leader, and particularly in its context.

Its scope was simply broader than that of any regional theatre. The New York Shakespeare Festival embraced a wider range of work—the elemental, gutsy work in Central Park and the finer, more seminal work at the Public Theater. Unlike the APA, it mastered a wide diversity of styles. Unlike the Guthrie, it made the classics more American and more accessible to a broad public. Unlike the American Conservatory Theatre, it reached beyond the pyrotechnics of theatre to the why, but, unlike Arena Stage, it did not intellectualize it. Unlike The Actor's Workshop, it both wanted to popularize the theatre and succeeded in doing so without sacrificing quality. More than any regional theatre, the New York Shakespeare Festival merged entertainment and art.

This was possible, I believe, primarily because of Joseph Papp himself. Unlike most leaders of regional theatres, Papp did not come from a middle-class background. He was born Joseph Papirofsky, the son of immigrant Jewish parents in Brooklyn. His youth during the Depression was one not of hardship but of poverty. His education ended with high school, and so he was not changed by the abstractions of college classrooms or the socialization of college dormitories. He was of the streets, and when he came in off them he brought with him a common touch. Popularization of the theatre for him was not a "white man's burden" or something pursued on a grant from some foundation; rather, it flowed out of his own being, not as a fashionable experiment but as the essence of his approach to theatre.

Most of all, the New York Shakespeare Festival differed from the regional theatre in its context—both where it was not and where it was.

230

It was not within the regional theatre movement; while his institution qualified structurally, Papp remained an outsider. He was not legitimatized by Ford Foundation support. He was not homogenized by Theatre Communications Group. He was neither pigeonholed by the movement's overstructuring nor haunted by its malaise. He shared its dream, but he lived outside its rules; he lived and worked by the rules of the New York game. His region was within the central situation, a psychological rather than a physical region. He was able to banish Broadway and still rub against it. Strengthened by institutionalism but unencumbered by decentralization, he had to fight only half the battle. Therefore, his success came not from doing better work than the regional theatres did but from doing it in a context where it could reach furthest and matter most—the central situation. He was able to storm the citadel from within.

Finally, then, the New York Shakespeare Festival differed from the regional theatre in its opportunity to combine *power* and *popularization* and so to reach for a National Theatre that could be organically a people's theatre. In this, Papp looked like the only leader who might meet the challenge with which Norris Houghton ended his *Advance from Broadway*: "The theatre of tomorrow will be a people's theatre. Whichever has the most to contribute to that—the college or the community playhouse, Broadway or the labor stage—will be the leader of the American theatre of the future."[16]

The aggrandizement of Joseph Papp and his New York Shakespeare Festival was a distinct embarrassment to the regional theatre, and it caused sparks throughout the movement (which were fanned by the announcement that the Rockefeller Foundation had granted Papp funds to explore his national theatre service idea). The leaders of other theatres around the country countered by pointing out that a National Theatre for America had to be not just one company in one place but instead an interconnected grouping of theatres whose whole was greater than the sum of the parts—in other words, the regional theatre movement itself. Now that none of them had emerged as a single National Theatre, the regional theatres as a group were hoping to become a collective National Theatre.

There was both logic and virtue in this concept, but it could be only informal (and unfunded) talk. Also, the talk was going on only outside New York. Within the capital, Joseph Papp was less and less involved in talking about a National Theatre for America and more and more involved in staking his claim on it. In early March of 1973, he assumed even more power with the surprising announcement that his Festival would replace Jules Irving's Repertory Theater at Lincoln Center. The Festival would become, in effect, a new constituent of the cultural complex and yet would continue all its other activities in Central Park, at the Public Theater, and on Broadway. Papp was not so much joining Lincoln Center as annexing it.

Papp's extraordinary record and the sway he held over the New York theatre scene led most observers to feel that Lincoln Center was lucky to get him and that he would be able to solve the Repertory Theater's woes. Papp, of course, assumed that indeed he could solve them (as Irving and Blau had assumed in more innocent days). He set a high price for his involvement: acceptance by Lincoln Center of an income gap for the Lincoln Center Festival of double what it had been under Irving and provision of $5,000,000 to cover two-thirds of that gap over a five-year period—in advance! Unlike Jules Irving, the powerful Papp could make such a grand demand. While it was unclear at first exactly *who* was supposed to meet the demand (Lincoln Center or Papp himself), it was nevertheless assumed that the money would be found— either by Lincoln Center (because the Establishment could not afford to fail to meet the challenge), or by Papp (because Lincoln Center was a new world to conquer and so a new desire), or by both working together. In any case, Papp had turned the tables and was writing his own rules. His latest coup, however, was not so much an artistic advancement as it was a broadening of his personal and institutional *power*. When asked why he was willing to move some of his operation to Lincoln Center, Papp answered that he was doing it "for personal aggrandizement and to establish a cultural power base here in New York so as to take over the rest of the repertory theaters in the country, and to create a liaison with China and Russia."[17] Supposedly he was joking, but probably theatre leaders elsewhere in the country were not laughing.

Power had become Papp's theme, and in achieving a form of ultimate power within the center he had brought to an end the regional theatre revolution. Yet only in one sense; by seeming to preempt the revolution, he actually helped to redefine it. He preempted, after all, only the *power* part of the revolution—the part involving the hunger for a single National Theatre and the storming of Broadway and New York itself. All that was a necessary part, natural and psychologically essential; indeed, if the leaders had not tried to seize national theatrical power, the world could have dismissed them as peripheral and their movement as inconsequential. Still, while necessary, the power part of the revolution was really secondary. It was not only a detour but also an aberration, and it kept hidden the really important part of the revolution—the plain, almost homely fact that the American theatre has been decentralized, and the regional theatre has survived. There may not be much glamour in that, but there is a lot of simple magnificence.

The failure of the regional theatre's thrust toward centrality and power was the climax, and it marked the end of the revolution. However, it did not defeat it. The revolution, after all, was far larger than any aberration that obsessed it along the way. The aberration was inevitable, but it was not the point; the point of the revolution was the creation of new theatrical alternatives. At the same time that the thrust toward power was failing, those new alternatives were becoming clear —and the climax can open up new vistas for the regional theatre. It can turn from a secondary *national* purpose to a primary and greater *regional* purpose. Now, I hope, each theatre can concentrate not on power but on strength, not on being an ultimate solution but on being an alternative, not on overcoming other forms of theatre but on refining and securing itself at home. That is a less glamorous but more difficult challenge, and it will require a new and more suitable dream.

14 A More Suitable Dream

"I am unconcerned with forming a national theatre. It is much more important for us to grow stronger in our own areas."

Arvin Brown, New Haven Register

"The man who contends that our theatre will be great only if superior people lead it is quite right. But the question is, from whence come these superior beings? We believe in this country that they come from the people, that they may be anywhere."

Norris Houghton, Advance from Broadway

As in a well-made play, there came, after the climax, a catharsis. Once it became clear that no one institution from outside New York would be hailed as the American National Theatre, the regional theatre movement could become a more civil and polite world. There had been intense competition among theatres during the late 1960s—for talent, for new plays, and particularly for national attention; but in the early 1970s individual theatres were cooperating more with each other. Each leader, knowing that he was not going to be quickly outdistanced by another, seemed willing to share more of himself and to compete as an equal rather than as a potential superior. There was more philosophical security and more self-confidence among regional theatre people, and so there developed a new (if guarded) unity in the movement. Freed of the need to overcome one another, the theatres were once more able to run together.

One of the most healthy manifestations of the new unity was a fresh interest among regional theatres in the early 1970s in sharing not only ideas but even their work. Over the years, there had been frequent discussion of the possibility of exchanging productions, and there had

234

been a few isolated attempts at it (most notably, The Guthrie Theater's engagement at the Mark Taper Forum early in 1969, as part of
the same tour that took the company to New York), but usually the
discussions had no practical results because each theatre tended to fear
that its company might be bested by a visitor. This, of course, was competition at its fiercest. Now that the race for individual supremacy
was over, however, the way was cleared for exchange.

Like many key events in the movement, the exchange possibility
grew out of an accident. Early in 1972, Word Baker, then artistic director of Cincinnati's Playhouse in the Park, needed a production to open
his season (he could not mount one himself because he was scheduled
to direct an off-Broadway play that was taking him away from his
theatre). Baker mentioned his need to his friend Adrian Hall of Trinity Square in Providence, who happened to be concluding a very successful production of Molière's *School for Wives* and was seeking other
outlets for it. The two needs complemented each other, and the men
concluded that the Playhouse season could open with Trinity Square's
production. To round out the idea, Baker also invited Jon Jory to
bring the Actors Theatre of Louisville's production of *Dear Liar* to
Cincinnati at the same time, thereby creating a mini-festival of regional
theatre in one place. The experiment was very simply and neatly
arranged. Each visiting company was guaranteed a base fee plus a percentage of gross receipts, which made its participation risk-free (in fact,
Trinity Square realized a small profit on the arrangement); the host
theatre paid the fee (which allowed it to budget closely) and saved the
costs of mounting new productions of its own. The cooperation among
the three theatres proved very successful, and word spread quickly
through the movement about how easily the arrangement had been
made. Following up, Hall invited other regional theatre leaders to
Providence for a meeting to discuss informally how such an idea could
be extended. Significantly, the meeting was not an instance of small
theatres banding together for safety or strength in numbers; it included
representation from some of the largest (and previously most competitive) theatres in the country—Arena Stage, the Guthrie, and the Mark
Taper Forum. The group took pains not to formalize their idea into
a superstructure; they agreed simply to let similar arrangements happen naturally and to meet again a year later to decide whether the
original idea still seemed to have merit. The meeting showed that each

of the theatres was confident enough to consider the possibility that another's work might complement rather than compete with its own; as Zelda Fichandler noted, it showed that the theatres involved had become "old enough to share our toys."[1] Most of all, the meeting symbolized a hoped-for new era of cooperation and joint effort—a kind of "Spirit of Providence" which could not have happened a few short years earlier. Despite its generalizations, the meeting was a constructive and psychologically healthy occasion. Of course, the search for a revised national purpose hovered over the gathering. In announcing the original Cincinnati experiment, the three directors had made it clear that what they were doing was of national scope and importance; they called their experiment "the first step in the 'coming of age' of regional theatre, which in our view is a flourishing national theatre."[2] Whereas the phrase "National Theatre" earlier had meant a single company, better and more powerful than all others, the new "national theatre" implied a composite effort. The capital letters were gone, and the idea had changed from a specific one to a generic one. It was the idea of people who were realizing that perhaps they were not destined to save the world but that perhaps they might help to improve it.

Another manifestation of the new and more healthy climate was the willingness of regional theatre leaders to exchange ideas with leaders of other theatrical forms. In the 1960s, in organizations like Theatre Communications Group, the regional theatre had isolated itself from other facets of the American theatre—the commercial, the experimental, the academic, and the developing ethnic theatres. Part of the reason for this self-imposed isolation was the fact that the regional theatre was unique and that its special needs could not be adequately met by organizations which were designed to serve other forms of theatre as well. A less recognized part of the reason was the fact that in the 1960s the regional theatre was trying to divorce itself from the traditional forms (commercial and academic) while keeping its distance from the experimental and ethnic forms which could embarrass or even supersede it. With the new spirit and the new self-confidence of the 1970s, the regional theatre was ready to open itself up to the rest of the theatre. This was reflected even in Theatre Communications Group; with Peter Zeisler as its new executive director, TCG was restructured in 1972 to serve experimental and ethnic theatres as well as regional ones. While officially it remained as neutral as ever, TCG now had the potential to develop into a broader and more valuable forum.

The new self-confidence of the regional theatre is manifest in the artistic realm, too. For one thing, the attitude of theatres toward new plays has matured. In the late 1960s, new plays were seen at least privately as a way to extend theatres beyond their immediate regions and as a way to reach beyond (and perhaps get out of) the local situation. At present, with the thrust toward centrality behind them, theatres tend to see new plays as valuable in and of themselves, not as coattails on which to ride to New York. New plays now are mounted because the work deserves a hearing and because the companies want fresh stimuli (although of course theatres do not bar New York critics or producers from their premieres, hopes and dreams being what they are).

Ironically, the new spirit and self-confidence have developed at a time when Broadway has come to derive its power only from *where* it is rather than from *what* it is in itself. Throughout most of the regional theatre revolution, Broadway remained the ultimate expression of the American theatre—and that, of course, is what made it a citadel to storm. Yet in the last five years, the commercial theatre has entered a period of disarray and decline. The number of new productions presented on Broadway has dwindled steadily, season after season (from eighty-four in 1967–68 to fifty-three in 1971–72); the few serious works are almost exclusively importations from Europe and especially England; the high ticket prices and basic irrelevance of most offerings have driven young audiences out of the Broadway theatre; and the ludicrously high production costs have nearly ruled out the possibility of producing serious plays in the commercial theatre. It was partly the decline of Broadway's creativity that opened up the way to power for the New York Shakespeare Festival, which climaxed its ascension by moving to Broadway and besting it. Papp's theatre and smaller off-Broadway organizations like the American Place Theatre, the Chelsea Theater Center in Brooklyn, and Ellen Stewart's Cafe La Mama, have moved to fill the gap in imagination that has come with Broadway's decline. They have succeeded in moving the creative center of the New York theatre from Broadway to institutions.

The spirit of these New York institutions is akin to the spirit of the regional theatres, particularly in the emphasis on group effort while depending at the same time on the leadership of an individual. In all institutions, inside and outside New York, people believe that the decline of Broadway has come because artists have opted for institutions instead of for the commercial theatre, thus leaving Broadway decimated, isolated, and stranded. There is some truth in this, but it is not the only reason or even the major reason for Broadway's decline; the rise of institutionalism was parallel, not causal. The real reasons for the decline are economic, and it is Broadway's financial restrictions on art which have driven artists away from it into institutions. The commercial theatre is no longer where art is most possible, most often.

Yet while the creative decline has lessened Broadway's artistic influence, it has not reduced its power. It is still a magnet, and people remain all too ready to leave their institutions to try it. That is because even in decline Broadway is still the only theatrical context that can assure a national position. It is what most of the country still thinks of when they think of theatre, and, as critic Martin Gottfried has said, "what will appear to history as the American theatre."[3] Broadway remains the seat of power. The fact that it is no longer creatively strong makes its contextual power, for the first time, perverse; but the perversity has not yet diminished the power—and that is Broadway's special grotesquerie.

The belief that the center of power could be shifted was the fallacy that led to the national detour of the regional theatre. That detour kept hidden the really radical primary change that the regional theatre has effected—namely, the basic decentralization of the American theatre and the broadening of alternatives to include nonprofit institutions throughout the country. New York, because it boasts the widest and richest variety of theatrical fare, remains the most exciting place in America for a consumer of theatre; but it is no longer the only place in which to be a serious creator of theatre. That change in the last quarter century has altered the complexion of the American theatre significantly and probably permanently.* Part of the opportunity offered by

---

* The depth of the change that has been achieved is shown in the difficulties encountered by Lincoln Center with the Repertory Theater after Jules Irving resigned and before Joseph Papp's ascension-annexation. In 1965, after the departure of Elia Kazan and Robert Whitehead, the board of the Repertory Theater could find in Jules Irving and Herbert Blau two regional theatre leaders ready and eager to leave their outposts and assault the New York bastion. By 1972, when Irving resigned, it was hard to find any regional theatre leader who would consider deserting his opportunity at home

today's regional theatre is the possibility that for the first time in American history the contextual power of Broadway and the creative quality of the institutional theatre (inside and outside New York) can combine to create a truly superior expression of the art. It is a matter not of overthrowing Broadway's power but of using it. Already a significant number of talented artists are working alternately in both forms of theatre, moving easily from one to the other and enriching both. Coexistence is now possible.

Meanwhile, some of the very best work in the American theatre is being done in the regional context. For instance, much of the work of Zelda Fichandler in Washington, Arvin Brown in New Haven, Adrian Hall in Providence, William Ball in San Francisco, Gordon Davidson in Los Angeles, and Michael Langham (who became the artistic director of The Guthrie Theater in 1971) can hold its own against the best to be seen in New York. Most importantly, the work of these leaders is good not only on their stages but also within their institutions. In fact, the greatest success so far of the regional theatre has been its proof of the validity of theatrical *institutionalism*.

In taking the institutional approach, a theatre needs strong local roots to give it the psychological and financial support that can assure permanence and growth. The institutional approach is by definition a home-based one, and the theatre's attention must be focused primarily, if not exclusively, on its local world. There must be a marriage between the theatre and its community, not a marriage *plus* New York or *plus* the nation off to one side as the theatre's mistress. This is a very stringent rule to impose, and to some it may seem an unacceptable one. Nevertheless, it is absolutely essential because it is at the core of a new purpose for all regional theatres: that is, to become totally and deeply committed to their individual communities and to be at the service of those communities. In short, the regional theatre has passed through thrusts toward stability, toward quality, and toward centrality. It now

---

to suffer the frustrations of the capital scene. Lincoln Center officials did try to entice theatres to come to New York at least for short engagements at the Repertory Theater; their first thought was to arrange a season of guest productions much like the ANTA season of 1969–70. But there was very little interest among theatre leaders outside New York who well remembered earlier failures and mistreatment. (One of the largest theatres was approached regarding a guest engagement, and its disinterest reportedly left Lincoln Center officials amazed and incredulous.) Having forged a new alternative, the regional theatres needed the old New York one less.

needs a new, fourth thrust—toward community. That thrust is the more suitable dream.

It is significant that those theatres which are best supported and most solvent financially are often those which have concentrated in the recent past not on America but on their own communities, not on getting Clive Barnes to come out and unearth them and get them invited to New York but on serving their own communities with good theatre, responsibly presented. Among such theatres, the Actors Theatre of Louisville is a particularly dynamic example of the value of community commitment. As mentioned earlier, by the time Richard Block left the Actors Theatre of Louisville in 1969, the theatre's artistic development was at a standstill. Fortunately, the board of directors at the theatre engaged Jon Jory, co-creator of the Long Wharf Theatre in New Haven, as the new artistic director to replace Block. Jory accepted the position with the understanding that he would function not only as the artistic leader but also as his own producer. Actually, Jory was at least equally capable in the producing area (a fact that had not been evident at the Long Wharf, where he had been partnered with and overshadowed by a strong manager, Harlan Kleiman); when he took the helm of the Actors Theatre, his dual talent emerged. By adopting a more popular repertoire and by pursuing a much more colorful approach to promotion, Jory was able to turn the Actors Theatre around. For instance, when he arrived, the subscription rolls of the theatre had fallen from 5,000 to fewer than 2,000; within three seasons, they climbed to nearly 10,000—and the small theatre was almost sold out on subscription. A move to larger quarters was necessary in order to continue to accommodate all the people who wanted to see the Actors Theatre at work.

At the height of the "cultural explosion" days of the 1960s, such a need would have propelled a theatre into a gleaming new building which would probably have been chiefly an expression of artistic ego, out of proportion to the real needs and resources of the institution. Coming at a later time and out of Jon Jory's understanding of Louisville, the new Actors Theatre building was a more properly modest expression which more nearly suited the institution and its community. Jory did not plan a completely new building but a combination of new structure with renovation of an old one. In this way, the theatre saved something of value and also significantly lowered the construction costs. The new facility (designed by Arena Stage architect Harry Weese) was created for only $1,700,000, of which $1,200,000 was raised locally. Wisely, Jory chose to open the new theatre using only 575 of a possible 700 seats; thereby allowing for realistic and orderly growth when audience demand might justify it.

Still, the new building is not the most important example of the new community orientation of the Actors Theatre of Louisville. The main element is the immersion of the theatre's leadership in the total life of the city. For instance, the theatre sends out many speakers (including Jory himself) to address all kinds of community groups, explaining the theatre's program and encouraging listeners to come see for themselves. The search for the subscription audience has become a yearly renewal of contacts with all facets of the surrounding community. The theatre has a deliberate policy of not refusing requests for any service that the theatre or one of its people can perform for any group in the city. The Actors Theatre has been turned around by its leaders, who have committed themselves and their institution to community service; as Jory says, "Our primary responsibility is to the audience."[4] Hartney Arthur, formerly of Theatre Communications Group, has explained it more fully: "Jon has been marvellous. . . . I think he's part of the community, and I think he loves the community, and I think he's made it *his* community."[5] Clearly, Louisville and the Actors Theatre belong to each other—and that is an unbeatable combination.

Of course, it is worth noting that in turning itself toward its community the Actors Theatre of Louisville was not giving up any national opportunities; neither the theatre nor Jon Jory himself had yet been acclaimed at the center or even summoned to it.* In this, the Actors Theatre was typical of the smaller regional theatres with low visibility which have rarely needed to face a difficult and perhaps mutually exclusive choice between local and national emphases. Therefore, it is heartening to chronicle another situation in which that choice existed at least technically and in which a larger theatre chose the local course: The Guthrie Theater in Minneapolis.

As "granddaddy," The Guthrie Theater through the middle of the

---

* Increased national attention came to the Actors Theatre of Louisville after it had reoriented itself to its community. The theatre's production of *Tricks*, a musical version of Molière's *Scapin*, was remounted by Arena Stage in 1972 and then produced on Broadway by Herman Levin in 1973. Jon Jory made his Broadway directing debut with the Levin production.

1960s had been the measure for all others. Its foray into New York at the end of 1968 was seen as the centralization of the best of the form, and its failure there was the beginning of the defeat of the thrust for power. The disgrace suffered in New York also forced a change in the leadership of the company and fomented dissatisfaction in Minneapolis. Actually, the local disfavor had been building over several years; it was caused less by the New York failure than by the growing disregard for the community by the theatre's professional leadership. The Guthrie had started in 1963 with the most community-oriented philosophy of any regional theatre in the country; with the departure of most of its original leaders, the theatre turned its attention away from its home territory and toward the nation at large. This emphasis, which led to the New York excursion, seemed to be justified by the fact that the greatest support of the theatre at that point came from national sources rather than from local ones. By 1969 and 1970, the community began to realize that the Guthrie was no longer interested in it—and it returned the favor by becoming uninterested in the theatre. Subscriptions dropped to a new low of fewer than 10,000; at times during the 1970 season, the theatre attracted less than one-third of its potential capacity.[6] The operating deficit before contributions (income gap) was $683,000, and after contributions $187,000. The theatre was drifting, and its problems were being aired in public. *Minneapolis Tribune* critic Mike Steele summarized them: "It's a troubled institution. After seven years it has no artistic direction, no artistic continuity, no broad base of community support, and it's on the jittery end of increased sniping from critics and theatre professionals throughout the country. . . . What happens to the Guthrie is indicative of what will happen to other resident theatres and to a hefty portion of theater in America."[7] By the end of 1970, The Guthrie Theater was finally beginning to look like a cultural Edsel, but it was no longer funny.

If the board of directors of the Guthrie had been ruled only by logic, the members might have concluded that the theatre should be closed. Fortunately, however, they were ruled more by their own energy and that of their community. They hired a new artistic director, Michael Langham, who had succeeded Tyrone Guthrie at the helm of the Stratford Shakespearean Festival in Ontario and had led that theatre for twelve years. Also, rather than retrenching, the board agreed to arm Langham (and new managing director Donald Schoenbaum) with a large budget to mount an ambitious season, even though this approach assured an income gap of nearly $400,000 which the board would need to raise. This was particularly remarkable because 1971 was to be the first year in the Guthrie's history without major support from the Ford Foundation, until then the theatre's primary outside benefactor. If the 1971 season were to succeed and the theatre were to continue, it would have to be by finding most of its support at home. But the professional and lay leadership did not shy from this challenge; in fact, they chose to consider 1971 a year of "investment in the theatre's future."

The year 1971 saw the advent of the badly needed turn-around at the Guthrie. Langham mounted five productions which attracted more than 200,000 people. *Cyrano de Bergerac* was the most popular play in the theatre's history, and with *Taming of the Shrew* during the summer months it played to more than 90 percent of capacity in the large theatre. Equally impressive was the success of the theatre in raising money locally: $600,000, which covered both the 1971 income gap and the net deficit left over from 1970. Through a radical reversal of subscription philosophy and techniques, the theatre went to its audience, explained its financial need, and asked subscribers not only to buy their tickets at no discount but also to give contributions when they bought their tickets (a plan presented as "5 plays for the price of 6"); this brought in gifts from 2,665 Minnesotans—twenty-five times the number of people who had given to the theatre in any previous year.

Most importantly, the year 1971 was the one in which the Guthrie found its community again. And that one year was not an isolated phenomenon; in 1972, the community again responded to the theatre's interest in it by providing large audiences and full support—over 200,000 people in the theatre's seats and even a $43,000 surplus on the season. For the first time in the theatre's history, the subscription rolls were larger than the previous year. The "investment" was paying off in Minneapolis, an investment of energy, resources, and most important of all, faith in the community itself. The Guthrie had gained back its willingness to trust the people around it as supporters and as audiences. It had gained back its willingness to listen and to serve—its willingness to be *of* Minneapolis rather than merely in it.*

---

* The artist's role in this willingness, however, was put to a severe test early in 1973. After the success of *Cyrano de Bergerac* in 1971, Langham worked with adaptor Anthony Burgess on a new musical treatment of the Rostand play. When it was ready

Regional Theatre: The Revolutionary Stage

Theatres which turn back to their own communities are finding that the communities are more and more ready to support them. Generally, there is a new acceptance of regional theatres in individual cities, partly because the theatres have been absorbed into the Establishment, where fixtures are popular. But it is mostly because of the theatres' willingness and ability to serve more varied constituencies; because of the sheer staying power of most theatres; and even because of the growing number of new facilities, which tend to give an air of solidity. Indeed, the collapse of theatres that seemed so common in the late 1960s is now over; most of the unfit ones have been weeded out, and most of those remaining can be considered permanent.

Naturally, permanence depends heavily upon financial support, particularly with inflation pushing budgets and deficits ever higher. Here again, the future looks reasonably promising. While no theatre dares to assume that support is assured and while each must continue to strain and stretch and even plead for contributions, there is today a better climate for raising money for general support. Theatres are beginning to develop ways to raise funds on a regular and continuing basis, including annual "maintenance fund" drives like those of symphony orchestras, and there is significantly less reliance on support from national foundations and more reliance on local giving. For instance, the shift of both The Guthrie Theater and Arena Stage from almost total dependence on the Ford Foundation to dependence on their local communities was not only a financial change but a psychological change, and it is to be hoped that this kind of change will become more prevalent.

The Ford Foundation's role in this shift has been a basic and impor-

---

for production, the two men formed a relationship with producer Richard Gregson to try out the new musical at the Guthrie (with Christopher Plummer in the title role) and then to take it to Broadway. It was a complicated arrangement calling for the Guthrie to create the production and to share in its later assumed financial success; and in its apparent service of commercial interests and its concentration on Broadway opportunities, it seemed to run counter to the Guthrie's new philosophy. It was an awkward and potentially compromising situation. Ironically, it was righted in the end by an embarrassing turn: while the production was still playing on the Guthrie stage, Langham was replaced as the director of *Cyrano* by Broadway choreographer Michael Kidd. Langham was free once more to devote himself exclusively to the needs of his theatre. Certainly the absurdity of the outcome confirmed the differences between institutional and commercial theatre and proved the wisdom of the Guthrie's institutional approach.

tant one. From the start of its involvement, Ford insisted that no theatre should consider support from the foundation to be never-ending. The Ford approach was basically one of applying money to *demonstrations*, both of specific ideas and of the validity of the regional institutional form. Even in the late 1960s, when subsidy of deficits became acceptable, Ford's grants were usually couched in terms that underlined their function as experiments in validation. In this way, the foundation could maintain its rule that the basic financial responsibility was "properly the concern of communities supporting the companies."[8] In this, the foundation was a major influence in reorienting theatres to their own resources at home, just as it had been essential in legitimatizing and validating the form.

While the shift to community-based support made the Ford Foundation potentially less necessary, it freed the foundation to support the theatres much more imaginatively. In 1971, Ford announced a radical new approach, the "cash reserve" grant. It was designed for all performing arts groups, and it both matched community efforts to erase former deficits and provided money in advance for four consecutive years to be used by the groups for general expenses. To those theatres that could raise money to replace the "cash reserve" used each year, the foundation would grant an equal amount at the end of the four years to form an endowment for the future. McGeorge Bundy, president of the foundation, explained the idea: "The grants are designed to put the companies on an even keel financially by eliminating deficits, breaking the cycle of cash-flow crises, and alleviating the preoccupation with accumulating liabilities. Operating funds will have to be raised every year from other sources, but the groups that can meet the terms of the program will, in four years, have the working capital to set their sights on the future. That in itself will represent a major shift for performing arts groups in the United States."[9] Among the first regional theatres to receive "cash reserve" grants were Center Stage, the Cleveland Play House, the Hartford Stage Company, the Long Wharf, the Seattle Repertory Theatre, Stage/West, and Trinity Square—significantly, none of them (with the exception of the Cleveland Play House) theatres which had received major funding from Ford in earlier years.

The Ford "cash reserve" program was radical because it moved the foundation out of demonstrating and into supporting theatres for their own sake, into allowing theatres themselves to determine how they would use the money granted. For the first time, the foundation was saying simply, in effect, "You need money? Here—use ours." Through such imaginative funding and through increased support from local sources, the economics of regional theatre in the future can be more healthy. But there remain other challenges which will continue to test the validity of the regional theatre form and its ability to follow a new and more suitable dream.

The first challenge is the challenge of the audience—whether the audience can become truly adventurous and ready to experiment, to take chances, to go out on a limb with the unfamiliar. Certainly the growing emphasis on new plays indicates at least a partial willingness in the audience, but is it ready to become really open to a wide range of experiences on the stage? More important, are the theatre leaders ready to listen to their audiences and to learn from them without necessarily giving in to them on every issue?

The challenge of the audience is paralleled by the challenge of preservation—the job of maintaining and reinterpreting the classics of the theatre for each generation. After all, no matter how frequent new plays may become, the classics will remain the primary statement on the stages of most regional theatres, and I believe rightly so. Then, too, the institutional structure in itself is a form of preservation; institutions, by definition, accept the responsibility of maintaining the best of the past. With companies of actors accustomed to working together, with permanent stages and permanent staffs, with committed subscription audiences, and with the Establishment on their side, regional theatres today are ideally suited to preservation. They are the natural custodians of our dramatic heritage as Americans and as citizens of the world. The question is, Are they willing to concentrate on preservation, to amplify and ennoble it?

The third challenge is that of regionalism. In these pages, I have used the word "regional" to signify theatres outside New York and around the country; I have used it in a geographic sense and more especially in an anti-capital sense. But there is another, deeper sense of the word, in which a "regional" theatre is one growing out of a way of life in the broad area around it, and this is the sense in which regionalism is a new challenge. So far, there has been very little of this kind of regionalism. The Guthrie Theater, in its first years, made a deliberate attempt to relate to and serve people over a five-state area in the Upper Midwest, but the approach was really only a promotional one, used in the hope of finding audiences in those five states who would make pilgrimages to Minneapolis. I am suggesting a far deeper identification. Ideally, one should be able to identify the Seattle Repertory Theatre as northwestern, the Alley as southwestern, the Milwaukee Repertory Theater as midwestern—in outlook, in attitude, even in repertoire. For example, there could be a closer relationship with New England writers in New England theatres; more plays of political moment at Arena Stage in Washington; more hillbilly madness on the stage of the Actors Theatre of Louisville. There might be a musical about Paul Bunyan on the Guthrie stage in Minneapolis. In other words, a regional identity should be at the core of each theatre's character. Ultimately, the challenge of regionalism is the challenge to make each theatre *of its region* rather than of America.

Actually, regionalism should be seen as a further extension of decentralization. The creation of theatrical alternatives outside New York and throughout the country was the first goal of decentralization, and its achievement in recent years has resulted in a group of cities which are the cultural focal points of their areas. The second and equally important goal during the 1970s is to achieve the dissemination of the work of existing theatres from these centers out through the regions around them. This would constitute a new kind of centrifugal force and would allow the American theatre to serve all of America.

The challenge of regionalism is perhaps most applicable to theatres far away from New York, where regions are vaster and less crowded culturally. Already, there have been some modest but healthy efforts to provide regional services. The Seattle Repertory Theatre has often toured throughout the state of Washington, for example. The Milwaukee Repertory Theater has taken plays to high schools throughout Wisconsin, and Center Stage has regularly toured through Maryland. Most recently, the National Endowment for the Arts has provided major funding for touring full productions through wide regional areas without regard to state lines. Center Stage and The Guthrie Theater, in 1973, are the first to participate in this wider touring, and their experiences will serve as guides for more regional theatre touring in future years. One of the National Endowment's purposes in this new program is to bring high-quality theatre to people who do not usually get to see it, and of course this should be a goal of every regional theatre on its own. Indeed, if funds permitted, theatre companies headquartered in central cities within regions should perform short intensive seasons of plays (in rotating repertory) in up to half a dozen smaller cities throughout their area, with people traveling even long distances for weekends of plays. Naturally the schools throughout the region should play a pivotal role in such a program, with students being transported to the various cities to see the plays. Another smaller company of actors might travel exclusively to schools, performing for students and working with them in classrooms. In these activities, the wider regional role would be basically an extension of what many theatres now do on a metropolitan basis.

Again if funds permitted (and of course the lack of funds has been a major deterrent), a wider regional function should stress service by the theatre of the needs of its broad constituency. Part of this service should be improvement of the arts of the theatre. For example, amateur community theatre groups and theatre programs on college campuses should be able to use the professional regional theatre as a primary resource. Perhaps members of community theatres throughout the wide region could be invited to come to the professional theatre for weekend seminars in wig-making or makeup or the construction of scenery and stage properties. Perhaps the costumer of the professional theatre could be sent during a slack period to campus theatres to instruct students and faculty in costume cutting and fitting. Perhaps the promotion director could prepare a kit showing how to create a subscription brochure. (In fact, on its 1973 National Endowment tour, Center Stage will offer such seminars in backstage and administrative techniques to citizens in communities where their touring production is performed—again, a regional extension of the metropolitan function.) The ways in which regional theatres can be servers are many; and each time that a theatre helps people to do better nonprofessional theatre, it is also building its own constituency and ensuring support from that constituency.

All of these purposes would be valid if the money could be found (and indeed the provision of such funds appears to be a new major interest of the National Endowment). Still, such programs are oriented only to taking productions out from a central city—a one-way regionalism. The greater challenge is a regionalism going the other way—one

248

that defines the character of a theatre as a reflection of its region. Partly this could come about through a more regional repertoire, but primarily it would need to come from each theatre being a place in which the people of the region express *themselves*. And that leads to the fourth challenge, the challenge of training.

In America, young people have been trained for professional theatre careers primarily in colleges and universities and in acting schools in New York. The latter have taught techniques for the commercial Broadway stage and for films and television; the former, with few exceptions,* have simply perpetuated ancient anti-professional prejudices and have produced graduates suited not for the profession but rather only for teaching other people to teach other people, ad infinitum. The solution in training young people may well be for regional theatres (again, funds permitting) to function as trainers of all kinds of theatre talents—in acting, directing, and design and even in backstage and administrative disciplines. The regional theatre should serve as a laboratory (probably in conjunction with a university to provide academic training in the liberal arts outside theatre). Young people from throughout the region who wish to enter the professional theatre should be able to go to the cultural capital of their region for training at the professional theatre there. They would study, work, and absorb the professional atmosphere and the discipline necessary to take their places within the profession. In assuming this educator role, the regional theatre would be enlarging its service role within its wide region. It would also be developing talents which might tend to be distinctly regional in character. (Again, there are already modest training programs under way. Many regional theatres have formal relationships with local universities and provide professional training and experience for students. The Guthrie Theater, for instance, held auditions for its company in 1972 for aspirants from throughout the Upper Midwest; a total of 175 people participated in the audition, and several were hired for the season.)

---

* In the last few years, the exceptions have been notable. Under Robert Brustein, the Yale School of Drama has changed its philosophy and features a professional company in residence. At Wayne State University in Detroit, the Hilberry Classic Theatre provides jobs for its graduate students; similarly, Paul Baker's Dallas Theatre Center, allied with Trinity University, has a production program as full and various as most regional theatres. Several dozen universities now offer training on a professional level; they have recently banded together to form the University Resident Theatre Association, a TCG-like organization designed to serve their joint interests.

For the young people coming out of such training, there would be three possible avenues within the profession. The least talented would tend to go into other pursuits; they might return to their home communities, take unrelated jobs, and perhaps work with a local amateur theatre for enjoyment and the delight of their friends. Others who are more talented might still return home but might lead those community theatres (where they would be constantly frustrated by the lesser talent of the first group). Those who are considerably more talented might remain with the theatre where they received their training, working their way up through the ranks and replacing people who move on. In this way the theatre, through training young people, would also be developing talent for its own use.

Those few extraordinarily talented young people might also stay for a time at the theatre where they receive their training, but eventually some would leave to go on into a national context, there to seek a grander prize. Perhaps they would take with them all sorts of dreams about being involved in a National Theatre. Indeed, from a national point of view, we should hope that they would leave the regional context. After all, if there is a Laurence Olivier or a Peter Brook born in the Rocky Mountain states, he does have a certain national responsibility to get out of Denver and to present his talent in a situation from which it can serve and delight the nation as a whole.

Of course there is little danger of a new Laurence Olivier or a new Peter Brook devoting his talent finally and exclusively to Denver—not today, in fast-moving America. He may be willing to be on the periphery so long as he is testing his talent, but once he decides that his talent is a major one, he will yearn to move that talent into the center. America can count on that, and the regional theatre will have to live with it.

Yet while major talents may leave their regional theatres behind, that theatre will probably become more and more the primary provider of such talent. It is already the best forum in America for its identification, development, and testing. Over the years, the regional theatre has greatly stretched the horizons and capacities of a few key people whose talents have been honed to the point of readiness. Some of them have already left the regional theatre, and some of them may do so soon; but the fact that they leave "ready" is the other great success of the regional theatre and its special gift to the nation. Indeed, after institutionalism, the development of new talent is the second greatest achievement of the regional theatre.

However, these two achievements, the structural and the personal, may not be ultimately complementary. Together, it seems to me, they create a quandary for the regional theatre. Institutionalism, the structural achievement, appears to be the basis of the future. In it lies the more suitable dream—the institution as preserver, as trainer, and as server of the regional community. But it carries its own dangers, too: the danger of regionalism becoming parochialism, of preservation becoming stagnation, of service becoming servility. When it is good, institutionalism can be a cultural and social force; when it is bad, it is a dead end. The quandary comes from the natural reluctance of most major talents to express themselves exclusively or permanently only through institutions. For example, to see the development and then perhaps the relinquishing of new talent as a key function, the leaders of regional theatres would need to accept the idea that it is their responsibility to train other people to go beyond them, much as parents teach their children to live without them. They would need to accept the idea that the primary purpose of a regional theatre is not to save the American theatre but to serve its community. They would need to resolve the regional dilemma by accepting regionalism as an ultimate expression. Finally, to pursue all the new challenges, they would need to accept their own theatres as bourgeois. The new and more suitable dream, after all, is a bourgeois dream—wrapped up in preservation and service and putting one's hopes in the next generation.

True permanence may depend upon the acceptance and pursuit of such a dream, and such a dream may become acceptable as a new generation of leaders emerges—a generation which did not create the theatres but which will inherit them. Most theatres are still led by those who created them or who took them over soon after and defined them. The matter of their succession introduces a new wrinkle and another challenge. Whether the theatres will survive that succession remains to be seen; but those that do survive it probably will do so by becoming more bourgeois.

The new dream is worthy of both regional needs and the institutional form, and it will fit the new generation; but I suspect it may be now unattractive to those whose energy and commitment and egos forged the revolution. In the end, we return to those original creators and definers who are still at work. The quandary is especially theirs, for despite all their reliance on institutionalism, the primary statement of the regional theatre has been their personal one. The movement was built by individuals who discovered a new way through institutionalism but who still placed their primary faith in themselves as artists. Institutionalism was their means but not their end. The new and more suitable dream demands that they shift that faith from themselves to their institutions—which might be simply impossible because it would be completely unnatural for them. The person who *wills* something new may not be at all like a person who then makes it socially useful. The quandary, then, is finally the conflict between institutionalism and individualism, between the culture of the one and the art of the other.

This quandary will provide a new creative tension for the regional theatre's next stage. And yet, like other quandaries along the way, it need not overcome those who have survived so far. They are still extraordinarily resilient and persistent; and just as they have changed our American theatre, so they may be able to change themselves to meet the new challenge. They have found a new way, and its future looks promising. The past is prologue, and perhaps the best is yet to come.

Notes, Additional Reading, and Index

Notes

1. Defining a Revolution

1. W. McNeil Lowry, speech to the Association of Graduate Schools, reprinted in *Educational Theatre Journal,* XIV (May, 1962), p. 108.
2. Nan Martin, "A Two-Way River: The Journal of an Actress," *Theatre Arts,* XLVI (August, 1962), p. 65.
3. Tyrone Guthrie, *A New Theatre* (New York: McGraw-Hill, 1964), p. 178.
4. Zelda Fichandler, "Theatres or Institutions?" *Theatre 3* (New York: International Theatre Institute, 1970), p. 107.

2. Antecedents: A World Elsewhere

1. Howard Taubman, *The Making of the American Theatre* (New York: Coward-McCann, 1965), p. 126.
2. Norris Houghton, *Advance from Broadway* (New York: Harcourt-Brace, 1941; reprinted by Books for Libraries, 1971), pp. 129–130.
3. Hallie Flanagan, *Arena* (New York: Duell, Sloan, and Pearce, 1940; reprinted by Benjamin Blom, 1965), p. 22.
4. The official purposes of ANTA are quoted by Margo Jones in *Theatre-in-the-Round* (New York: McGraw-Hill, 1965), pp. 18–19.
5. Nan Martin, "A Two-Way River," p. 8.
6. Rex Partington, quoted in *Variety,* January 27, 1971.
7. "Cleveland Play House" (interview with Richard Oberlin), *Players,* XLVI (June–July, 1971), p. 206.
8. Margo Jones, *Theatre-in-the-Round* (New York: McGraw-Hill, 1965), p. 201.

3. Margo Jones: Legacy and Legend

1. Brooks Atkinson, quoted in an Arena Stage news release, March 4, 1972.
2. Margo Jones, *Theatre-in-the-Round,* p. 49.
3. *Ibid.,* pp. 55–56.
4. *Ibid.,* p. 8.
5. John Rosenfield, "Margo Jones '55," *Theatre Arts,* XXXIX (July, 1955), p. 94.
6. Adrian Hall, taped answers to questions submitted by the author, June, 1972.
7. Margo Jones, *Theatre-in-the-Round,* p. 3.
8. *Ibid.,* p. 47.
9. *Ibid.,* p. 192.
10. *Ibid.,* pp. 193–194.

Regional Theatre: The Revolutionary Stage

4. Acorns: Theatres before 1960

1. Martin Gottfried, *A Theater Divided: The Postwar American Stage* (Boston: Little-Brown, 1967), p. 95.
2. Zelda Fichandler, "Theatres or Institutions?" p. 106.
3. Alley Theatre, *Thresholds: The Story of Nina Vance's Alley Theatre* (Houston: Wall and Company, 1968), p. 22.
4. Nina Vance, quoted in "The View from the Alley," *Players*, XLIV (April–May, 1969), p. 139.
5. Alley Theatre, *Thresholds*, p. 34.
6. *Ibid.*, p. 23.
7. *Ibid.*, p. 19.
8. *Ibid.*, p. 62.
9. *Ibid.*, p. 23.
10. *Ibid.*, p. 54.
11. Theodore Hoffman, "Who the Hell Is Herbert Blau?" *Show*, V, 3 (April, 1965), p. 48.
12. Zelda Fichandler, quoted in an Arena Stage news release, March 4, 1972.
13. Richard L. Coe, "Washington's First Lady of the Theatre," *Theatre Arts*, XLVII (January, 1963), p. 23.
14. Zelda Fichandler, taped interview with the author, June, 1972.
15. Thomas Fichandler, quoted in "Arena Stage," *Players*, XLVII (December–January, 1972), p. 57.
16. Zelda Fichandler, "Theatres or Institutions?" p. 110.
17. Richard L. Coe, "Washington's First Lady of the Theatre," p. 24.
18. Mack Scism, quoted in "Mummers Theatre, Oklahoma City," *Players*, XLIV (June–July, 1969), p. 190.
19. *Ibid.*, p. 190.
20. *Ibid.*, p. 193.
21. *Ibid.*, p. 193.
22. News release from the Ford Foundation, October 10, 1962.
23. Mack Scism, "Mummers Theatre, Oklahoma City," p. 218.
24. Arthur Ballet, "The Theatre of Middle America," *Theatre 4* (New York: International Theatre Institute, 1972), p. 77.
25. Mary John, "Barn-Raising Spirit Produces an Arena-Type Theatre," *Theatre Arts*, XXXIX (March, 1955), p. 78.
26. *Ibid.*, p. 78.
27. News release from the Fred Miller Theater, June 1, 1959.
28. William J. Lacey, "A New Model for Professional Theatre," unpublished article.
29. Michael Murray, "The Regional Theatre: Four Views," *The Drama Review*, XIII (Fall, 1968), p. 26.
30. "Charles Playhouse Shutters in Boston," *Variety*, November 4, 1970.
31. Jack Conrad, "Profile of the Playgoer: A Study of a Theatre Audience," unpublished article, 1969, pp. 33–36.
32. *Ibid.*, p. 40.
33. News release from the Front Street Theatre, February, 1968.
34. Passage from material originally used for publicity purposes, quoted in Herbert Blau, *The Impossible Theater: A Manifesto* (New York: Collier, 1965), p. 113.
35. Herbert Blau, *The Impossible Theater*, p. 127.
36. *Ibid.*, p. 125.
37. *Ibid.*, p. 170.
38. *Ibid.*, p. 157.
39. *Ibid.*, p. 154.

40. Nan Martin, "A Two-Way River," p. 15.
41. Jules Irving, quoted in Julius Novick, *Beyond Broadway: The Quest for Permanent Theatres* (New York: Hill and Wang, 1968), p. 86.
42. Jules Irving, taped interview with the author, June, 1972.
43. Nan Martin, "A Two-Way River," p. 15.
44. Stanley Eichelbaum, "Actor's Workshop of San Francisco," *Theatre Arts*, XLVII (June, 1963), p. 69.
45. Herbert Blau, *The Impossible Theater*, p. 165.

5. Oak Trees: The Guthrie Theater and What Came After

1. John F. Kennedy, "The Arts in America," *Creative America* (New York: Ridge Press, 1962), p. 8.
2. Tyrone Guthrie, *A New Theatre*, p. 10.
3. *Ibid.*, p. 10.
4. *Ibid.*, pp. 41, 45.
5. *Ibid.*, p. 43.
6. *Ibid.*, p. 56.
7. *Ibid.*, pp. 36–37.
8. Louis Calta, "Stage Unit Slated outside of City," *New York Times*, September 30, 1959.
9. Tyrone Guthrie, *A New Theatre*, p. 47.
10. "The Rise of Rep," *Time*, LXXXIII (February 14, 1964), p. 61.
11. Stuart Vaughan, *A Possible Theatre* (New York: McGraw-Hill, 1969), p. 146.
12. News release from the Seattle Repertory Theatre, January 18, 1970.
13. Gordon Davidson, "Reflections on Beginnings," *Theatre 1* (New York: International Theatre Institute, 1968), p. 67.
14. Gordon Davidson, taped interview with the author, June, 1972.

6. Saplings: Small Theatres of the 1960s

1. Julius Novick, *Beyond Broadway*, pp. 167–168.
2. News release from the Long Wharf Theatre, April 5, 1967.
3. Arvin Brown, quoted in "A Director Named for the Long Wharf," *New York Times*, May 1, 1967.
4. Paul Weidner, taped answers to questions submitted by the author, June, 1972.
5. Peter Culman, quoted in "Center Stage," *Players*, XLVI (April–May, 1971), pp. 147–149.
6. President's Report released by Center Stage, March, 1971.
7. Davey Marlin-Jones, quoted in "The Washington Theatre Club," *Players*, XLV (August–September, 1970), p. 290.
8. *Ibid.*, p. 261.
9. Hugh Hardy, quoted in an undated news release from the Playhouse in the Park, 1968.
10. Arthur Ballet, "The Theatre of Middle America," p. 75.
11. Pirie MacDonald, "The Guest Director Is Come Hither," *Theatre Today*, III (Fall, 1970), pp. 7–8.
12. Jay Broad, quoted in "What Now Atlanta?" *Theatre Today*, II (Summer, 1969), p. 4.
13. André Gregory, "The Theatre of the Living Arts," *Tulane Drama Review*, XI (Summer, 1967), p. 20.
14. Adrian Hall, taped answers to questions submitted by the author, June, 1972.
15. *Ibid.*
16. Adrian Hall, quoted in "The Trinity Square Repertory Company," *Players*, XLIV (August–September, 1969), p. 237.

17. Adrian Hall, *Players*, p. 265.
18. Adrian Hall, taped answers to questions submitted by the author, June, 1972.

7. Stabs at a National Theatre

1. Tyrone Guthrie, *A Life in the Theatre* (New York: McGraw-Hill, 1959), p. 318.
2. Alice Griffin, "Summer Shakespeare," *Theatre Arts*, XXXIX (July, 1955), p. 28.
3. Michael Kahn, quoted in "Problems Abound at Stratford Fete," *New York Times*, July 26, 1971.
4. Robert Breen and Robert Porterfield, "Toward a National Theatre," *Theatre Arts*, XXIX (October, 1945), p. 599.
5. *Ibid.*, p. 601.
6. Irving Ives and Jacob Javits, "Toward a National Theatre," *Theatre Arts*, XXXIII (April, 1949), p. 13.
7. "ANTA's Forty-Theatre Circuit Plan," *Theatre Arts*, XXXIX (December, 1955), pp. 72, 82.
8. *Ibid.*, p. 76.
9. *Ibid.*, p. 75.
10. *Ibid.*, p. 82. ANTA set the cost of the venture at $5,000,000.
11. News release from APA-Phoenix, March 26, 1968.
12. T. Edward Hambleton, "Flight of the Phoenix," *Theatre 2* (New York: International Theatre Institute, 1970), pp. 79–80.

8. To Save the World:
The Actor's Workshop Moves East

1. Martin Gottfried, *A Theatre Divided*, p. 148.
2. Elia Kazan, quoted in "Setting the Stage for Lincoln Center," *Theatre Arts*, XLVIII (January, 1964), p. 13.
3. Martin Gottfried, *A Theatre Divided*, p. 154.
4. Herbert Blau, "Decentralization: New Frontiers and Old Dead Ends," *Tulane Drama Review*, VII (Summer, 1963), p. 78.
5. Herbert Blau, *The Impossible Theater*, p. 30.
6. *Ibid.*, p. 43.
7. Jules Irving, taped interview with the author, June, 1972.

9. Up against the Marble Wall:
The Loss of The Actor's Workshop

1. Herbert Blau, quoted in " 'The New Establishment'? Fragments of the TDR Theatre Conference," *Tulane Drama Review*, X (Summer, 1966), p. 124.
2. Theodore Hoffman, "Who the Hell Is Herbert Blau?" p. 39.
3. Jules Irving, quoted in "In the Words of Jules Irving," *Cue*, July 17, 1970, p. 15.
4. Howard Taubman, review of *Danton's Death, New York Times*, October 22, 1965.
5. Howard Taubman, "Lincoln Center: Improve It Must," *New York Times*, December 19, 1965.
6. Jules Irving, "In the Words of Jules Irving," p. 15.
7. Clive Barnes, review of *The Miser, New York Times*, May 9, 1969.
8. Jules Irving, quoted in "They All Wear Clothes in This Play of Ideas," *Boston Sunday Herald Traveller Show Guide*, November 16, 1969.
9. Lewis Funke, "Lincoln Repertory: Busy and Collected," *New York Times*, December 9, 1969.
10. News release from the Repertory Theater of Lincoln Center, January 21, 1971.
11. Jules Irving, quoted in "Lincoln Center Group Survives on 'Insanity,' Jules Irving Asserts," *Variety*, March 1, 1972.

Notes

12. Herbert Blau, taped interview with the author, May, 1972.
13. Jules Irving, "In the Words of Jules Irving," p. 15.
14. Jules Irving, "Diary of a Madman, or How to Build a Classical Theater on $5 a Day," *New York Times*, July 16, 1972.
15. Clarke Coggeshall, quoted in "Lincoln Center Forum Curtailing Season, and Jules Irving Resigns," *New York Times*, October 27, 1972.
16. Amyas Ames, quoted in "Repertory Theater Battles Deficit Woes," *New York Times*, November 22, 1972.

10. The Establishment Theatre

1. Douglas Campbell, quoted by Bradley G. Morison and Kay Fliehr in *In Search of an Audience* (New York: Pitman, 1968), p. 121.
2. Opinion quoted by Gordon Davidson in "Davidson of Los Angeles," *Theatre Today*, II (Summer, 1969), p. 16.
3. Jack Conrad, "Profile of the Playgoer," pp. 92–100.
4. *Ibid.*, pp. 85, 105.
5. *Ibid.*, pp. 122–123.
6. Ford Foundation Annual Report, Humanities and the Arts Program, 1962, p. 1.
7. Bradley G. Morison and Kay Fliehr, *In Search of an Audience*, p. 186.
8. Nan Martin, "A Two-Way River," p. 7.
9. W. McNeil Lowry, quoted in "Two Theater Groups Get Ford Grants," *New York Times*, May 19, 1967.
10. W. McNeil Lowry, quoted in a news release from Studio Arena Theatre, May 1, 1967.
11. Ford Foundation Annual Reports, 1962 through 1971.
12. Peter Zeisler, letter to the *New York Times*, published in the *Times*, October 26, 1969.
13. Zelda Fichandler, "Theatres or Institutions?" p. 113.
14. Theodore Hoffman, "A Hard Times Letter to the TCG," *The Drama Review*, XII (Winter, 1968), p. 22.
15. *Ibid.*, p. 26.
16. Michael Murray, "The Regional Theatre," pp. 25–26.

11. New Plays and New Ploys

1. Allen Fletcher, "A Broad Spectrum," *Theatre Today*, III (Spring, 1970), p. 7.
2. The story of *Futz* at the Guthrie is told more fully by Jack Poggi in *Theater in America: The Impact of Economic Forces, 1870–1967* (Ithaca: Cornell University Press, 1968), pp. 236–237.
3. Edwin Sherin, quoted in "In the Words of Edwin Sherin," *Cue*, May 24, 1969, p. 15.
4. Henry Hewes, review of *The Great White Hope*, *Saturday Review*, December 30, 1967, p. 18.
5. Zelda Fichandler, taped interview with the author, June, 1972.
6. *Ibid.*
7. Zelda Fichandler, "Theatres or Institutions?" p. 111.
8. Martin Gottfried, "What Shall It Profit a Theatre If . . . ?" *New York Times*, August 23, 1970.
9. Gordon Davidson, taped interview with the author, June, 1972.
10. Clive Barnes, review of *Indians* at Arena Stage, *New York Times*, May 27, 1969.

12. The Regional Dilemma

1. Herbert Blau, *The Impossible Theater*, pp. 157–158.
2. Arvin Brown, interview with the author, January, 1970.

259

3. "Puppet Shows" (a review of the American Conservatory Theatre appearance at the ANTA Theatre in New York), *Time*, October 17, 1969, p. 72.

4. Herbert Blau, "Decentralization: New Frontiers and Old Dead Ends," *Tulane Drama Review*, VII (Summer, 1963), p. 78.

5. "What Makes a City Great?" *Time*, November 14, 1969, pp. 47–48.

6. Alvin Toffler, "New York Faces Future Shock," *New York*, July 27, 1970, p. 25.

7. Rene Dubos, "Reports of the Death of New York Are Greatly . . ." *Intellectual Digest*, II (June, 1972), p. 67.

8. "Down with Provincialism, Long Live Regionalism," *Time*, October 21, 1966, p. 37.

9. Michael Murray, "The Regional Theatre," p. 27.

10. William Gibson, quoted by Herbert Blau in *The Impossible Theater*, pp. 34–35. Blau, of course, disagrees with Gibson.

11. Rene Auberjonois, "The Regional Theatre: Four Views," *The Drama Review*, XIII (Fall, 1968), p. 24.

13. Storming the Citadel:
The Theatres Go to New York

1. Barton Emmet, letter to the *New York Times*, published in the *Times*, November 9, 1969.

2. Auberjonois, "The Regional Theatre," p. 24.

3. Walter Kerr, "Why Revive *Mourning Becomes Electra?*" *New York Times*, September 7, 1969.

4. Arvin Brown, interview with the author, January, 1970.

5. Advertisement in the *New York Times*, May 21, 1969, p. 42.

6. Dan Sullivan, review of *The House of Atreus*, *New York Times*, July 24, 1967.

7. Walter Kerr, review of *The House of Atreus*, *New York Times*, September 10, 1967.

8. Clive Barnes, review of *The House of Atreus*, *New York Times*, December 18, 1968.

9. *Variety*, December 25, 1968, through January 15, 1969.

10. Walter Kerr, "Why This Grass? Rosemary Asked," *New York Times*, January 29, 1967.

11. For an official report on this step, see *The Arts*, 1969 Annual Report of the National Endowment for the Arts and the National Council on the Arts (Washington: U. S. Government Printing Office, 1970), p. 35.

12. *Ibid.*

13. Gottfried made his case in "What Shall It Profit a Theatre If . . . ?" *New York Times*, August 23, 1970.

14. Walter Kerr, "Why Revive *Mourning Becomes Electra?*" *New York Times*, September 7, 1969.

15. Clive Barnes, "Theatre Season: Strange and Tough," *New York Times*, December 30, 1971.

16. Norris Houghton, *Advance from Broadway*, p. 292.

17. Mel Gussow, "Papp's Troupe to Replace Lincoln Center Repertory," *New York Times*, March 7, 1973.

14. A More Suitable Dream

1. Zelda Fichandler, taped interview with the author, June, 1972.

2. Joint news release from the Playhouse in the Park, Trinity Square, and the Actors Theatre of Louisville, March 13, 1972.

3. Martin Gottfried, *A Theatre Divided*, p. 4.

4. Jon Jory, taped answers to questions submitted by the author, June, 1972.

Notes

5. Hartney Arthur, taped interview with the author, May, 1972.

6. *Variety*, September 23, 1970.

7. Mike Steele, "Guthrie Theatre Has Its Troubles," *Minneapolis Tribune*, January 18, 1970.

8. Ford Foundation president McGeorge Bundy, quoted in a news release from the foundation, October 18, 1971.

9. *Ibid.*

Suggestions for Additional Reading

Books

Baumol, William J., and William G. Bowen. *Performing Arts: The Economic Dilemma*. New York: Twentieth Century Fund, 1966.

Beeson, William, editor. *Thresholds: The Story of Nina Vance's Alley Theatre*. Houston: Wall and Company, 1968.

Blau, Herbert. *The Impossible Theater: A Manifesto*. New York: Macmillan, 1964.

Flanagan, Hallie. *Arena*. New York: Duell, Sloan, and Pearce, 1940.

Gard, Robert E., Marston Blach, and Pauline Temkin. *Theater in America: Appraisal and Challenge*. New York: Theatre Arts Books, 1968.

Gottfried, Martin. *A Theater Divided*. Boston: Little-Brown, 1967.

Guthrie, Tyrone. *A Life in the Theatre*. New York: McGraw-Hill, 1959.

_____. *A New Theatre*. New York: McGraw-Hill, 1964.

Houghton, Norris. *Advance from Broadway*. New York: Harcourt-Brace, 1941.

Jones, Margo. *Theatre-in-the-Round*. New York: Rinehart and Company, 1951.

Morison, Bradley G., and Kay Fliehr. *In Search of an Audience: How an Audience Was Found for the Tyrone Guthrie Theatre*. New York: Pitman, 1968.

Novick, Julius. *Beyond Broadway: The Quest for Permanent Theatres*. New York: Hill and Wang, 1968.

Rockefeller Brothers Fund. *The Performing Arts: Problems and Prospects*. New York: McGraw-Hill, 1965.

Taubman, Howard. *The Making of the American Theatre*. New York: Coward-McCann, 1965.

Toffler, Alvin. *The Culture Consumers: A Study of Art and Affluence in America*. New York: St. Martin's Press, 1964.

Vaughan, Stuart. *A Possible Theatre*. New York: McGraw-Hill, 1969.

Articles

"ANTA's Forty-Theatre Circuit Plan: ANTA's First Step in the Creation of a National Theatre." *Theatre Arts*, XXXIX, 12 (December, 1955), pp. 67–82.

Ballet, Arthur. "The Theatre of Middle America." *Theatre 3*. New York: International Theatre Institute, 1970, pp. 76–87.

_____. "The Theatre of Middle America." *Theatre 4*. New York: International Theatre Institute, 1972, pp. 72–81.

Blau, Herbert. "Decentralization: New Frontiers and Old Dead Ends." *Tulane Drama Review*, VII, *4* (Summer, 1963), pp. 55–85.

Breen, Robert, and Robert Porterfield. "Toward a National Theatre." *Theatre Arts*, XXIX, *10* (October, 1945), pp. 599–601.

Coe, Richard L. "Washington's First Lady of the Theatre." *Theatre Arts*, XLVII, *1* (January, 1963), pp. 22–24.

Davidson, Gordon. "Reflections on Beginnings." *Theatre 1*. New York: International Theatre Institute, 1969, pp. 64–67.

Eichelbaum, Stanley. "Actor's Workshop of San Francisco." *Theatre Arts*, XLVII, *6* (June, 1963), pp. 34–36, 68–69.

Fichandler, Zelda. "Theatres or Institutions?" *Theatre 3*. New York: International Theatre Institute, 1970, pp. 104–117.

Ford Foundation Annual Reports, 1962–1971. *Humanities and the Arts.*

Gregory, André. "The Theatre of the Living Arts." *Tulane Drama Review*, XI, *4* (Summer, 1967), pp. 18–21.

Hambleton, T. Edward. "Flight of the Phoenix." *Theatre 2*. New York: International Theatre Institute, 1970, pp. 70–81.

Hoffman, Theodore, "A Hard Times Letter to the TCG." *The Drama Review*, XII, *2* (Winter, 1968), pp. 21–27.

_____. "Who the Hell Is Herbert Blau?" *Show*, V, *3* (April, 1965), pp. 38–49, 88.

Ives, Irving, and Jacob Javits. "Toward a National Theatre." *Theatre Arts*, XXXIII, *4* (April, 1949), pp. 10–13.

John, Mary. "Barn-Raising Spirit Produces an Arena-Type Theatre." *Theatre Arts*, XXXIX, *3* (March, 1955), pp. 77–78, 89.

"Joe Papp: Populist and Imperialist." *Time*, July 3, 1972, pp. 69–70.

Kazan, Elia. "Look, There's the American Theatre!" *Tulane Drama Review*, IX, *2* (Winter, 1964), pp. 61–83.

Kleiman, Harlan. "Is There an Audience in the House?" *Theatre 1*. New York: International Theatre Institute, 1969, pp. 22–26.

Kupferberg, Herbert. "New York Shakespeare Festival." *Theatre 3*. New York: International Theatre Institute, 1970, pp. 118–131.

_____. "The Repertory Theater of Lincoln Center." *Theatre 4*. New York: International Theatre Institute, 1972, pp. 130–149.

Martin, Nan. "A Two-Way River: The Journal of an Actress." *Theatre Arts*, XLVI, *8* (August, 1962), pp. 6–15, 64–66.

Meyer, Richard D., and Nancy Meyer. "Setting the Stage for Lincoln Center." *Theatre Arts*, XLVIII, *1* (January, 1964), pp. 12–16, 69.

Michener, Charles. "Papp's Universal Theater." *Newsweek*, July 3, 1972, pp. 52–56.

Novick, Julius. "The Great Beyond." *Theatre 2*. New York: International Theatre Institute, 1970, pp. 90–107.

Pasolli, Robert. "The New Playwrights' Scene of the Sixties: Jerome Max Is Alive and Well and Living in Rome." *The Drama Review*, XIII, *1* (Fall, 1968), pp. 150–162.

"The Rise of Rep." *Time*, February 14, 1964, pp. 54–61.

Rosenfield, John. "Margo Jones '55." *Theatre Arts*, XXXIX, 7 (July, 1955), pp. 78–79, 94–95.

Schechner, Richard, "Blau and Irving at Lincoln Center." *Tulane Drama Review*, IX, *4* (Summer, 1965), pp. 15–18.

_____. "Ford, Rockefeller, and Theatre." *Tulane Drama Review*, X, *1* (Fall, 1965), pp. 23–49.

_____. "The Regional Theatre: Four Views." *The Drama Review*, XIII, *1* (Fall, 1968), pp. 21–28.

Regional Theatre: The Revolutionary Stage

✓ _____, editor. "Federal Aid and Regional Theatre." *Tulane Drama Review*, XI, 2 (Winter, 1966), pp. 23–28.

_____, editor. " 'The New Establishment'? Fragments of the TDR Theatre Conference." *Tulane Drama Review*, X, 4 (Summer, 1966), pp. 109–129.

✓ Schmidt, Sandra. "The Regional Theatre: Some Statistics." *Tulane Drama Review*, X, 1 (Fall, 1965), pp. 50–61.

Schneider, Alan. "The Theatre: Does It Exist?" *Arts in Society*, VIII (1971), pp. 608–625.

Southern, Hugh. "The Great Mail Fraud." *Theatre 3*. New York: International Theatre Institute, 1970, pp. 98–103.

Sullivan, Dan. "The West Coast." *Theatre 4*. New York: International Theatre Institute, 1972, pp. 82–93.

Theatre Today. Quarterly published by AIDART (Advanced Institute for the Development of American Repertory Theatre), I–IV (1968–1971). Various articles.

Treanor, Aline Jean. "Oklahoma's Mummers Theatre." *Theatre Arts*, XLVII, 12 (December, 1963), pp. 55–58.

Zeisler, Peter. "Leave the Driving to Us." *Theatre 1*. New York: International Theatre Institute, 1969, pp. 60–63.

_____. "The East Coast." *Theatre 4*. New York: International Theatre Institute, 1972, pp. 56–71.

Index

Aaron, Stephen, 98
Abbey Theatre, 19
Actors' Equity Association, 1, 32, 48, 54, 59, 82, 104, 105, 109, 138
Actors' Studio, 10, 96
Actors Theatre of Louisville, 103–105, 183, 235, 240–241, 247
Actor's Workshop, The, 46, 52–61, 69, 74, 99, 100, 111, 121, 128, 136, 138, 139, 141, 142–155, 156–169, 170, 172, 179, 181, 183, 189, 200, 230
Advance from Broadway, 6, 231, 234
After the Fall, 106, 144, 145
Ah, Wilderness!, 114
Ahmanson Theatre, 82, 84
Albee, Edward, 2, 107, 137, 196
Alchemist, The, 68, 160, 163
Aldrich, Richard, 126
Alexander, Jane, 124, 212
Alexander, Ronald, 189
Alfred, William, 100
Alice in Wonderland, 177
All Summer Long, 189, 211
Alley Theatre, 24, 26–31, 32, 33, 35, 40, 41, 42, 43, 46, 50, 51, 53, 60, 116, 128, 136, 141, 154, 174, 182, 183, 185 n, 189, 190, 213, 247
Alliance Theatre, 86, 87, 106
All's Well That Ends Well, 119
Altfeld, Robert, 26, 28, 32
Altfeld, Vivien, 26, 28
American Conservatory Theatre, 45, 95, 130, 136–141, 146, 182, 183, 185, 196, 213, 217, 224, 225, 230
American Institute of Architects, 30, 42
American National Theatre and Academy (ANTA), 10–12, 15, 125–128, 129, 143, 222–226, 239 n
American Place Theatre, 237

American Repertory Theatre, 10
American Shakespeare Festival, 78, 82, 95, 121–125, 132, 142, 154, 172, 183, 212, 213, 217, 224, 225
Ames, Amyas, 169
And Things That Go Bump in the Night, 193
Anderson, Judith, 66, 142
Anderson, Maxwell, 19
Anderson, Robert, 92, 189, 215
Angel Street, 42, 105
Anniversary Waltz, 27
Another Part of the Forest, 26
Anouilh, Jean, 39, 46, 110, 112
ANTA Theatre, 135, 222–226
ANTA–Washington Square Theatre, 115, 143
Antigone, 39, 46
Antioch Shakespeare Festival, 121
Antony and Cleopatra, 121, 124, 140, 211
APA-Phoenix, 130–136, 183, 185 n
Applause, 212
Arbuzov, Aleksei, 139
Architect and Emperor of Assyria, The, 139
Arden, John, 99
Ardrey, Robert, 77
Arena, 18
Arena Stage, 5, 25, 31–38, 43, 45, 46, 50, 51, 53, 55, 56, 59, 60, 73, 85, 95, 97, 98, 98 n, 99, 107, 112, 116, 128, 136, 141, 154, 154 n, 174, 182, 183, 185 n, 189, 192, 193–197, 198, 211, 212, 213, 216, 217, 230, 235, 241, 241 n, 244, 247
Aristophanes, 57, 58
Arms and the Man, 13
Arrabal, Fernando, 139
Art Institute of Chicago, 109, 110
Arthur, Hartney, 241

Arturo Ui, 73, 218–220
As You Like It, 82, 123
Assassination, 1865, 110
Association of Producing Artists (APA), 43, 130–136, 154, 230
Atkinson, Brooks, 17, 67
Atlanta Arts Alliance, 86
Atlanta Constitution, 106
Atlanta Memorial Cultural Center, 85, 86, 105, 106
Atlanta Municipal Theatre, 85
✓Atlanta Repertory Theatre, 85–87
Atlanta Symphony, 85
Auberjonois, Rene, 137, 208, 210, 213–214

Babes in Arms, 48
Bacall, Lauren, 212
Baker, Paul, 249 n
Baker, Word, 103, 174, 235
Balanchine, George, 143
Ball, William, 29, 136–141, 146, 213, 224, 239
Ballet, Arthur, 41, 102, 193
Bancroft, Anne, 163, 164, 211
Bankhead, Tallulah, 102
Barnes, Clive, 2, 165, 198, 202, 214, 220, 228, 240
Barr, Richard, 223, 224
Barter Theatre, 12, 43, 95, 125
Basehart, Richard, 12
Basic Training of Pavlo Hummel, The, 100
Baumol, William, 63, 182
Beckett, Samuel, 2, 54, 101
Beclch, 111, 191, 196
Bedford, Brian, 136
Beethoven, Ludwig van, 52
Behrman, S. N., 144
Bergman, Ingrid, 19, 82
Berliner Ensemble, 5, 59
Bernhardt, Sarah, 6, 212
Bernstein, Leonard, 82–83, 143, 216
Beyond Broadway, 90, 111
Beyond the Fringe, 138, 213
Billy Budd, 115
Billy Rose Foundation, 218
Billy Rose Theatre, 218, 219, 220, 222, 224
Birds, The, 57–58, 160
Birthday Party, The, 57
Bishop, David, 86
Bissinger, Tom, 112
Blau, Herbert, 24, 52–61, 64, 71, 100, 142–

155, 156–163, 167, 174, 189, 200, 203, 211, 221, 222, 232, 238 n
Blithe Spirit, 39
Block, Richard, 103–104, 174, 240
Blood Wedding, 54
Bond, Edward, 46
Bos, John, 112
Boston Symphony Orchestra, 45
Bowen, William, 63, 182
Bowmer, Angus, 121
Box, 107, 196
Boy Friend, The, 48
Boyle, Ray, 43
Brecht, Bertolt, 2, 34, 46, 57, 59, 73, 77, 111, 160, 191
Breen, Robert, 125, 126
Bristol Old Vic, 92
Broad, Jay, 105–107, 195
Bromberg, Conrad, 57, 152
Brook, Peter, 250
Brother to Dragons, 115
Brown, Arvin, 91–93, 202, 214, 215–216, 217, 234, 239
Brown, Gilmor, 18
Brown, Harry, 26
Brubeck, Dave, 58
Brussels World's Fair, 55
Brustein, Robert, 91, 249 n
Büchner, Georg, 158
Bundy, McGeorge, 245
Burdick, Elizabeth, 11
Burgess, Anthony, 243 n
Burke, Michael, 145
Bus Stop, 142
Bush, Geoffrey, 100
Bushnell, William, 95
But For Whom Charlie, 144, 145
Bye Bye Birdie, 48

Caesar and Cleopatra, 106
Cafe La Mama, 223, 237
Calderón de la Barca, Pedro, 105
Caldwell, Zoe, 121, 211–212, 214
California Theatre Foundation, 139
Call, Edward Payson, 73, 219
Call Me Madam, 48
Camino Real, 54, 79
Campbell, Douglas, 73, 84, 109, 119, 172
Canadian Broadcasting Company, 120
Candida, 13
Candide, 83
Capote, Truman, 136
Captain Brassbound's Conversion, 82
Career, 189

Index

Caretaker, The, 48, 57, 112
Carey, Denis, 122
Cariou, Len, 212
Carnovsky, Morris, 82, 92, 123, 124
Caro, Warren, 126, 223
Caroline, 26
Cartier, Jacques, 81, 93–94
Casals, Pablo, 62
Cassidy, Frank, 100
Cat on a Hot Tin Roof, 39, 48
Caucasian Chalk Circle, The, 34, 57, 58–59, 73, 158, 159, 160, 211
Center Stage, 95–97, 107, 108, 109, 112, 183, 196, 245, 247, 248
Center Theatre Group, 81–82
Chalk Garden, The, 39
Chamberlain, Richard, 79
Champion, Gower, 139, 224
Chandler, Mrs. Norman, 83
Changeling, The, 145
Changing Room, The, 92
Chapin, Schuyler, 145
Chaplin, Charles, 7
Charles Playhouse, 45–47, 51, 99, 100, 107, 108, 112, 175, 187, 192, 212
Charley's Aunt, 86, 105, 138, 192, 213
Chekhov, Anton, 12, 99, 191, 197
Chelsea Theater Center, 237
Cherry Orchard, The, 73, 77, 132, 133, 135, 224
Chicago Lyric Opera, 177
Chichester Festival, 121
Christie, Agatha, 33
City Center of Music and Drama, 166–167, 224
Civic Playhouse, 105
Civic Repertory Theatre, 10
Clandestine on the Morning Line, 189
Clash by Night, 26
Cleveland Play House, 12–15, 19, 34, 43, 68, 94, 190, 196, 245
Clurman, Harold, 10, 83–84, 143
Cobb, Lee J., 164, 213
Cock-a-Doodle Dandy, 133
Cocktail Party, The, 133
Coco, 213
Coe, Peter, 15, 216
Coe, Richard L., 37
Coggeshall, Clarke, 168
Cohan, George M., 131
Colicos, John, 119
Collection, The, 152
Columbia Broadcasting System, 145, 227, 229

Come Blow Your Horn, 48, 108
Comédie Française, 5, 197
Comedy of Errors, The, 130
Condemned of Altona, The, 158, 163, 164
Conflict of Interest, A, 106–107, 195
Connelly, Marc, 219
Conrad, Jack, 176, 177
Copeau, Jacques, 19
Coppola, Francis Ford, 140
Coriolanus, 16, 226
Corn is Green, The, 42
Cornell, Katherine, 122
Cornett, Ewel, 103
Count of Monte Cristo, The, 6
Country People, 92, 214
Country Scandal, A, 99
Country Wife, The, 93, 158, 159, 163, 172
Coward, Noel, 129, 215
Cowles, John, 70
Cowles, John, Jr., 70
Craig, Gordon, 19
Crawford, Cheryl, 10
Crest Theatre (Toronto), 120
Cresta Run, The, 103–104
Cretan Woman, The, 189
Criss, Louis, 46
Cromwell, James, 94
Cronyn, Hume, 72, 73, 75, 84, 131, 211, 213
Crucible, The, 54, 60, 90, 139
Cry of Players, A, 164
Culman, Peter, 95–96, 107
Culture Consumers, The, 63
Cyrano de Bergerac, 107, 163, 164, 243, 243 n–244 n

Daley, Richard, 109
Dallas Theater Center, 249 n
Dalrymple, Jean, 224–225
Daly, James, 107
Dames at Sea, 47
Danton's Death, 155, 158
Dark at the Top of the Stairs, 20
Dark of the Moon, 39
Davidson, Gordon, 82–85, 87, 135, 165, 175, 198, 216, 217, 223, 224, 239
Dear Liar, 235
Death of a Salesman, 29, 54, 72, 96, 135, 143
Deeter, Jasper, 12
Defense of Taipei, The, 57
Dekker, Albert, 29
deLiagre, Alfred, 224–225

Delicate Balance, A, 139
Dell, Jeffrey, 26
Deputy, The, 82
Design for Living, 44, 82
Devil and the Good Lord, The, 99
Devil's Disciple, The, 86, 139
Devils, The, 83, 211
Dewell, Michael, 129
Dewhurst, Colleen, 107, 109, 227
Disenchanted, The, 32
Disney, Walt, 162
Don Carlos, 68
Don Juan, 135
Don Juan in Hell, 48
Donnelly, Peter, 79
Don't Shoot Mable It's Your Husband, 196
Dougherty, Frances Ann, 129
Douglas, Melvyn, 189
Drake, Alfred, 123
Drama Review, The, 88, 170, 199, 210, 213
Drexler, Rosalyn, 112
Dryden, John, 86
Dubos, Rene, 203
DuBrock, Neal, 107–108, 175
Dumbwaiter, The, 99
Dunaway, Faye, 144
Dunnock, Mildred, 92, 123, 215
Durrenmatt, Friedrich, 84
Dwarfs, The, 99
Dysart, Richard, 137

East Wind, The, 160, 164
Eastern States Exposition, 94
Edinburgh Festival, 92, 115, 121
Edith Stein, 195
Effect of Gamma Rays on Man-in-the-Moon Marigolds, The, 191, 196
Ehrlanger, Abraham, 6
Eichelbaum, Stanley, 61
Eisenhower, Dwight, 62
Elementary and Secondary Education Act, 172
Emery, John, 123
Emmet, Barton, 210
Endgame, 54, 57, 103, 111
Enemies, 136
Enemy of the People, An, 140
Enters, Warren, 108
Entertainer, The, 112
Epitaph for George Dillon, 32
Equity Library Theatre, 97
Esso Repertory Series, 75

Ethel Barrymore Theatre, 163
Exit the King, 47, 132, 133
Expo '67, 121, 132

Fairbanks, Douglas, 7
Fairfield, Robert, 119
Fallen Angels, 48
Fantasticks, The, 48, 101
Farther Off from Heaven, 20
Faulkner, William, 200
Federal Theatre Project, 9–10, 14, 15, 18
Feiffer, Jules, 84
Ferlinghetti, Lawrence, 55
Ferrer, José, 11, 15
Fervent Years, The, 10
Feydeau, Georges, 46
Fichandler, Thomas, 34, 37, 95
Fichandler, Zelda, 4–5, 24, 25, 31–38, 43, 48, 50, 64, 71, 98, 186, 189, 194–197, 217, 223, 224, 236, 239
Fire, 213
Firebugs, The, 57, 77
Firehouse Theatre, 192
Flanagan, Hallie, 9, 18
Flea in Her Ear, A, 46, 49, 79, 139, 224
Fletcher, Allen, 78–79, 80, 124, 140, 174, 191
Fliehr, Kay, 62, 178–180
Foch, Nina, 123, 129
Folksbiene Playhouse, 131
Fonda, Henry, 225
Fontanne, Lynn, 44
Forbes-Robertson, J., 6
Ford Foundation, 3, 13, 29, 30, 33, 34, 36, 37, 39, 40, 41, 46, 50, 51, 54, 55, 60, 61, 63–65, 74, 94, 96, 98, 102, 109, 113, 116, 124, 132, 141, 147, 162, 177, 180–185, 189, 190, 192, 231, 243, 244–246
Ford's Theatre, 130
Forget-Me-Not Lane, 92
Forty-Theatre Circuit Plan (ANTA), 126–128, 129
Forum Theatre, 158, 160, 164, 166, 168
Foster, Donald, 78
Fourposter, The, 48
Francis, Arlene, 11
Franzen, Ulrich, 30
Fred Miller Theater, 42–43, 44, 45, 131, 174, 183
Friedman and Son, 157
Frisch, Max, 57, 77
Frohman, Charles, 6
Front Street Theatre, 47–50, 51, 176, 185 n
Frost, Robert, 62

Index

Fry, Christopher, 15
Funke, Lewis, 165, 167
Funny Thing Happened on the Way to the Forum, A, 108
Future Shock, 203
Futz, 193

Gagliano, Frank, 190, 193
Galileo, 77, 111, 160, 163
Galphin, Bruce, 106
Gam, Rita, 72, 79
Garfield, John, 11
Gargoyle Cartoons, 112
Garson, Greer, 82
Gascon, Jean, 121
Getting Gertie's Garter, 14
Ghelderode, Michel de, 132
Ghosts, 13, 215
Gibson, William, 164, 207
Gigi, 48
Gilbert and Sullivan, 119
Gill, Brendan, 215
Gingham Dog, The, 98, 196
Girl on the Via Flaminia, The, 57
Giron, Arthur, 195
Glass Menagerie, The, 19, 32, 73
Globe Theatre, 197
Glory, Hallelujah!, 139
Godfather, The, 100, 140
Godspell, 140
Golden, Edward J., 95
Goldoni, Carlo, 93
Goldwater, Barry, 14
Goodman Theatre, 64, 109–110, 138, 185 n
Gordone, Charles, 228
Gorky, Maxim, 92, 131, 136, 214
Gottfried, Martin, 24, 143, 145, 170, 197, 224, 238
Goulet, Robert, 82
Granger, Farley, 129
Grass Harp, The, 136
Great Depression, 7, 8, 9, 89
Great God Brown, The, 135
"Great Society," 172, 179
Great White Hope, The, 193–195, 196, 197, 198, 200, 203, 212, 216, 217, 224
Greenberg, Stanley, 195
Greene, William, 14
Greenfeld, Josh, 189
Greenwich Mews Theatre, 113
Gregory, André, 77, 111–112, 113, 174, 191
Gregson, Richard, 244 n

Grey, Joel, 13
Grimes, Tammy, 136
Grizzard, George, 32, 72, 73, 107, 189, 211
Grotowski, Jerzy, 115
Group Theatre, 9, 10, 12, 15, 59
Guare, John, 84, 112, 193
Guinness, Alec, 119
Gunn, Moses, 124
Guthrie, Tyrone, 4, 66–76, 77, 83, 94, 118–119, 120, 129, 131, 156, 172, 188, 211, 218, 220, 242
Guthrie Theater, The, 4, 65–76, 81, 84, 87, 88, 89, 90, 100, 105, 106, 109, 116, 117, 118, 119, 122, 132, 135, 139, 141, 142, 154, 170, 172, 178, 182, 183, 185 n, 191, 192, 193, 207, 210, 211, 212, 218–221, 222, 226, 230, 235, 239, 241–243, 243 n–244 n, 244, 246, 247, 249
Guys and Dolls, 48
Gypsy, 48

Habimah Theatre, 13
Hadrian VII, 140
Hagen, Uta, 131, 132
Hair, 108, 140, 228
Hall, Adrian, 21, 44, 113–116, 223, 225, 235, 239
Hambleton, T. Edward, 131–135, 216
Hamlet, 68, 72, 77, 133, 139, 212
Hancock, John, 154 n
Happy Time, The, 82
Harding, Ann, 12
Hardy, Hugh, 102
Harris, Julie, 81, 119, 142, 227
Harris, Mark, 55, 57, 157, 189
Harris, Rosemary, 131, 132, 133
Harry, Noon, and Night, 112
Hart, Moss, 39, 92, 132
Hartford Stage Company, 93–94, 96, 97, 183, 193, 245
Harvey, 135, 225
Hasso, Signe, 29, 129
Hasty Heart, The, 32
Havoc, June, 81, 86, 123
Hawkes, John, 100, 190
Hay Fever, 79, 215
Haydon, Julie, 42
Hayes, Helen, 132, 135, 225
Hays, David, 41
Hays, Stephen, 94–95
Hedda Gabler, 13, 57, 129
Hedgerow Theatre, 12
Heflin, Van, 12
Hellman, Lillian, 26, 82

269

Henry IV, Part 1, 48
Henry V, 73, 124, 212, 224, 225
Hepburn, Katharine, 123
Herakles, 132
Hewes, Henry, 194
Hilberry Classic Theatre, 249 n
Hingle, Pat, 123
Hirsch, John, 121, 160, 163
Hochhuth, Rolf, 110
Hoffman, Dustin, 99, 212
Hoffman, Theodore, 62, 75, 88, 157, 186
Hogan's Goat, 100
Hoguet, Mrs. Robert L., Jr., 146
Hoguet, Robert L., Jr., 142, 145
Holbrook, Hal, 144
Holland, Norman, 115
Holm, Celeste, 108
Holt, Stella, 113
Homecoming, The, 175, 176
Hostage, The, 90
Houghton, Norris, 6, 7, 8, 12, 13, 131, 231, 234
House of Atreus, The, 74, 203, 218, 219–220
House of Bernarda Alba, The, 11
Houseman, John, 10, 82, 123, 124, 131, 132, 135
Houston Community Players, 18, 22, 26, 149
Houston Endowment, 30
Houston Federal Theatre, 18
Houston Recreation Department, 18
Howard, Michael, 85–86
Huddle, Elizabeth, 159
Hughes, Glenn, 18
Hunt, H. L., 105
Hutt, William, 120

I Am a Camera, 48, 57
"I Left My Heart in San Francisco," 155
I Remember Mama, 108
Ibsen, Henrik, 215
Iceman Cometh, The, 46
Idiot's Delight, 82
Imaginary Invalid, The, 78, 129
Importance of Being Earnest, The, 32, 77, 93, 112, 191
Impossible Theater, The, 24, 53, 142, 146, 147, 148
Impromptu at Versailles, The, 131
Improvisational Theatre Project (Mark Taper Forum), 85
In Search of an Audience, 62, 178
In the Jungle of Cities, 46

In the Matter of J. Robert Oppenheimer, 84, 164, 165, 203, 216
In Three Zones, 47, 160, 161
In White America, 139
Incident at Vichy, 145
Indian Wants the Bronx, The, 46
Indians, 79, 195, 196, 198, 212
Inge, William, 20
Inherit the Wind, 20, 21
Inquest, 196
Ionesco, Eugene, 47, 132
Irving, Henry, 77
Irving, Jules, 24, 52–61, 64, 71, 100, 142–155, 156–169, 172, 211, 221, 222, 232, 238 n
Isaacs, Edith, 8
Ivanov, 136
Ives, Irving, 126

Jackson, Nagle, 45
Jacques Brel Is Alive and Well and Living in Paris, 47
Janus, 224
Javits, Jacob, 126
J.B., 143, 224
Jeffers, Robinson, 189
Jefferson, Joseph, 6
Jellicoe, Ann, 99
Joan of Lorraine, 19, 39
Joe Egg, 92
Johansen, John, 41
John, Mary, 42–44
John Brown's Body, 130
John Fernald Company, 224
John Loves Mary, 26
Johnson, Jack, 194
Johnson, Lyndon Baines, 223
Jones, Brooks, 101–103
Jones, James Earl, 195, 227
Jones, Margo, 16, 17–23, 24, 25, 26, 27, 28, 31, 38, 42, 113, 118, 127, 149, 188, 189, 230
Jones, Robert Edmund, 10
Jory, Jon, 90–91, 104–105, 174, 188, 191, 235, 240–241, 241 n
Jory, Victor, 90
Juilliard School, 135, 213
Julius Caesar, 77, 82, 122, 124, 146, 152

Kahn, Michael, 124
Kaplan, Abbott, 82
Kaufman, George S., 92, 132, 219
Kazan, Elia, 10, 142–145, 159, 174, 238 n
Keach, Stacy, 92, 212, 215, 227

Index

Kean, Norman, 134, 136
Kelly, George, 132
Kennedy, John F., 62
Kennedy, Keith, 49
Kennedy Center for the Performing Arts, 79, 216
Kerr, Walter, 132, 214, 220, 222, 226
Kidd, Michael, 244 n
Killing of Sister George, The, 175
King and I, The, 49
King Arthur, 86
King John, 123
King Lear, 57, 77, 82, 124, 164, 213, 217
Kirstein, Lincoln, 122
Kiss Me Kate, 177
Kitch, Kenneth, 154 n
Kleiman, Harlan, 90–91, 95, 191, 240
Knack, The, 99
Knacker's ABC, 49
Kopit, Arthur, 79, 195
Krasna, Norman, 26
Kreeger, David Lloyd, 36

La Guardia, Fiorello, 166
La Turista, 112
Lahr, Bert, 123
Lampert, Zohra, 144
Landa, Harvey, 49
Landau, Jack, 123, 124
Langham, Michael, 119, 121, 239, 242–243, 243–244 n
Langner, Lawrence, 122, 123
Last Analysis, The, 111
Latent Heterosexual, The, 140
Law, John Philip, 144
Lawrence, Jerome, 20
Leach, Wilford, 47, 160
League of New York Theatres, 133
Lee, Eugene, 116
Lee, Frania, 105, 106
Lee, James, 189
Lee, Robert E., 20
Left-Handed Liberty, 99
Le Gallienne, Eva, 10, 42, 129, 132
Leighton, Margaret, 163, 211
Lemmon, Jack, 82
Lemon Sky, 108, 196
Lerman, Leo, 160
Levin, Herman, 195, 196, 216, 241 n
Library Raid, The, 190
Life Is a Dream, 105
Light Up the Sky, 32, 39
Lincoln, Abraham, 130

Lincoln Center for the Performing Arts, 62, 170, 232
Line of Least Existence, The, 112
Little Blue Light, The, 11
Little Foxes, The, 86, 107, 163
Little Mary Sunshine, 90
Little Murders, 139
Little Theatre movement, 8, 9, 12, 15, 16, 25, 27
Live Like Pigs, 99
Living Stage (Arena Stage), 36, 85
Living Theatre, 14
Lloyd, Norman, 123
Local Stigmatic, The, 99
Loden, Barbara, 144
Loeb Drama Center, 100
Long Day's Journey into Night, 91–92, 93, 215
Long Wharf Theatre, 90–93, 94, 104, 182, 191, 196, 202, 212, 214, 215, 240, 245
Loot, 47
Lorca, Frederico Garcia, 54, 160
Los Angeles County Board of Supervisors, 83
Los Angeles Music Center, 81, 83
Los Angeles Times, 83
Louder, Please!, 39
Lovecraft's Follies, 115, 225
Lowe, K. Elmo, 13, 14
Lowell, Robert, 99
Lower Depths, The, 131
Lowry, W. McNeil, 3, 64, 65, 109, 162, 180–184
Lunney, David, 111, 112
Lunt, Alfred, 44
Lust for Life, 82
Luther, 75
Lyceum Theatre, 131–135
Lysistrata, 54

Mabry, Michael, 184
Macbeth, 123
Macbird, 106
McCallum, Charles, 44–45
McCallum, David, 79
McCarter Theatre, 101, 131
McCarthy, Joseph, 53
McConnell, Frederic, 12, 13, 14
MacDonald, Pirie, 104
McDowall, Roddy, 122
McGaw, Charles, 110
MacLaine, Shirley, 189
MacLeish, Archibald, 132
McNally, Terrence, 193

271

McQuiggan, Jack, 43–44
Mademoiselle Colombe, 32
Mailer, Norman, 58, 157
Major Barbara, 86
Making of the American Theatre, The, 7
Man for All Seasons, A, 41, 142
Man in the Glass Booth, The, 110
Mandell, Alan, 60, 146
Mangum, Edward, 32, 43
Manitoba Theatre Center, 160
Manos, Christopher, 85, 86
Mansfield, Richard, 6
Manson, Charles, 115
Marat/Sade, 206, 207
Marathon 33, 86
Marco Millions, 144, 145
Margo Jones Award, 20, 84, 98, 115, 191, 196
Mark Taper Forum, 82–85, 87, 135, 165, 182, 183, 185 n, 192, 196, 213, 216, 218, 219, 224, 235
Marks, David, 189
Marlin-Jones, Davey, 97–98
Marriage of Mr. Mississippi, The, 84
Marshall, E. G., 163
Martin, Dean, 189
Martin, Mary, 171
Martin, Nan, 3, 14, 56, 60, 181
Mary, Mary, 57
Mary Stuart, 129
Maryland State Arts Council, 96
M.A.S.H., 213
Mason, James, 119
Mass, 216
Massey, Raymond, 120, 122
Massey, Vincent, 120
Maugham, W. Somerset, 26
Mayleas, Ruth, 11, 182, 222
Measure for Measure, 119, 123
Medea, 66, 142
Meeker, Ralph, 144
Mein Kampf, 148
Melfi, Leonard, 193
Member of the Wedding, 42, 66, 106, 142
Memphis State University, 49
Merchant of Venice, The, 123, 136
Mercury Theatre, 10, 82
Merrick, David, 136
Merry Wives of Windsor, The, 211
Merton of the Movies, 219
Metropolitan Opera, 94, 143
Michaels, Sidney, 189
Midsummer Night's Dream, A, 114, 123
Mielziner, Jo, 143

Milk Train Doesn't Stop Here Anymore, The, 154 n
Miller, Arthur, 33, 143, 144, 145
Miller, Jason, 229
Milwaukee Repertory Theater, 42–45, 51, 181, 183, 185 n, 192, 196, 247
Minneapolis Star, 70
Minneapolis Tribune, 70, 242
Minnesota Theatre Company, 65, 71
"Miracle in Minnesota," 70
Misalliance, 91
Misanthrope, The, 133, 134, 135
Miser, The, 72, 73, 79, 84, 164, 165, 213, 218
Moiseiwitsch, Tanya, 119
Molière, 93, 129, 131, 135, 191, 197, 235, 241 n
Monroe, Marilyn, 144
Moon for the Misbegotten, A, 49, 107
Moonchildren, 195
More Stately Mansions, 82, 84
Morison, Bradley, 62, 178–180
Morris, Chester, 29
Moscow Art Theatre, 5, 13, 14, 19, 197
Moses, Robert, 227
Moss, Arnold, 123
Mother Courage, 57
Mourning Becomes Electra, 68, 124
Mousetrap, The, 33, 48
Mozart, Wolfgang Amadeus, 52
Mrs. McThing, 47
Much Ado about Nothing, 86, 123, 229
Mulhare, Edward, 41
Mummers Theatre, 38–42, 45, 51, 183, 185 n
Murderous Angels, 135, 216
Murphy, Thomas, 92, 215
Murray, Michael, 45–46, 71, 100, 112, 170, 186, 199, 205
Muzeeka, 112
My Fair Lady, 195
My Sweet Charlie, 98
Myers, Kenneth, 110

Naked, 47
Narrow Road to the Deep North, 46
National Educational Television, 75
National Endowment for the Arts, 34–35, 80, 113, 128, 129, 140, 182, 194, 218, 222–224, 247–248
National Repertory Theatre, 128–130
National Theatre (England), 5, 161, 164
National Theatre for America, 5, 21, 22, 25, 76, 87, 116, 117, 118, 125, 126, 128,

135, 136, 137, 141, 142, 143, 145, 149, 154, 156, 158, 162, 165, 170, 185, 200, 205, 206, 209, 221, 226, 231, 232, 233, 234, 236, 250
National Theatre for the Deaf, 193
National Theatre School of Canada, 79, 120
National Theatre Service, 11, 222
Needles, William, 120
New Haven Register, 234
New Theatre, A, 66, 188
New Theatre for Now, 84, 192
New York City Ballet, 122, 143, 166
New York City Opera, 136, 166
New York Philharmonic, 143
New York Shakespeare Festival, 34, 76, 121, 212, 223, 227–232, 237
New York Times, 2, 67, 68, 74, 75, 132, 157, 158, 165, 167, 185 n, 198, 200, 202, 203, 206, 210, 214, 215, 219, 220, 222, 226
New Yorker, 215
Newman, Danny, 177–178, 180, 184, 185
Newman, Paul, 13
Newsweek, 229
Nichols, Luther, 54
Nichols, Mike, 99, 163
Nichols, Peter, 92
Night of the Dunce, 190
Night of the Iguana, 57
Nightwatch, 212
No Place to Be Somebody, 228
Novick, Julius, 90, 111
Nye, Carrie, 47

Oberlin, Richard, 14–15
O'Casey, Sean, 113, 133
O'Connor, Sara, 100
Odets, Clifford, 10, 26, 140
Oedipus Rex, 14, 119, 212
Of Mice and Men, 212
Office for Advanced Drama Research, 192–193
Oh! Calcutta!, 136
Oklahoma!, 48
Old Globe Theatre, 78, 121, 212
Old Vic, 19, 66, 79
Olivier, Laurence, 161, 164, 250
Olson and Johnson, 58
O'Neill, Eugene, 6, 10, 68, 82, 129, 135, 144, 191
O'Neill, James, 6
O'Neill Foundation, 192–193
Oresteia, The, 74

Orestes, 68
Osborne, John, 112
O'Sullivan, Michael, 137
Ostrow, Stuart, 223
Othello, 48, 93, 123, 124
Our Town, 105, 225
Owen, Paul, 28
Owens, Rochelle, 111, 193

Pacino, Al, 100
Padula, Edward, 106
Page, Geraldine, 42, 109
Palance, Jack, 122
Pantagleize, 132, 133, 135
Papp, Joseph, 34, 76, 121, 223, 224, 227–232, 237, 238 n
Paradise Lost, 140
Park, 96, 196
Parone, Edward, 84
Partington, Rex, 14
Pasadena Playhouse, 18, 19
Pastime of Monsieur Robert, The, 139
Patchett and Tarses Stage a Spontaneous Demonstration, 112
Patterson, Tom, 118–119
Paxinou, Katrina, 11
Payment Deferred, 26
Payne, Virginia, 29
Peer Gynt, 11
Performing Arts: Problems and Prospects, The, 63
Performing Arts: The Economic Dilemma, 34, 63, 182
Period of Adjustment, 48
Peter Pan, 48
Petit Théâtre de Vieux Carré, 80
Phaedra, 99
Phoenix Theatre, 76, 129, 131–136, 216, 225
Pickford, Mary, 7
Pilgrimage Theatre, 85
Pinter, Harold, 2, 57, 99, 112, 152, 175
Pirandello, Luigi, 47, 131, 191
Piscator, Erwin, 131
Pittsburgh Playhouse, 136, 137, 154 n
Playboy of the Western World, The, 57
Players, 199
Playhouse in the Park, 101–103, 183, 185 n, 193, 235
Playwrights Unit, 223, 225
Plummer, Christopher, 119, 121, 123, 211, 244 n
Plumstead Playhouse, 225
Poor Bitos, 110, 111

Porter, Stephen, 135
Porterfield, Robert, 12, 125, 126
Possible Theatre, A, 76
Price, The, 79
Prime of Miss Jean Brodie, The, 211
Prince, Harold, 135, 212
Private Ear, The, 90
Private Lives, 47, 136, 140, 177
Project Discovery, 114, 115
Promise, The, 139
Provincetown Players, 10
Public Eye, The, 90
Pueblo, 195
Pulitzer Prize, 190, 195, 200, 228

Quayle, Anthony, 163
Quintero, José, 107, 144
Quotations from Chairman Mao Tse-Tung, 107

Rabb, Ellis, 43, 130–136
Rabe, David, 229
Rainmaker, The, 43
Ravinia Festival, 138
Rea, Oliver, 66–76, 101, 109, 142, 218
Recruiting Officer, The, 112
Red Roses for Me, 113
Red, White, and Maddox, 106, 107, 196
Reed, Joseph Verner, 122, 124
Rehearsal, The, 112
Reich, John, 64, 109–110
Reid, Kate, 119, 211
Reinhart, Ray, 137
Remarkable Mr. Pennypacker, The, 32
Repertory Theater of Lincoln Center, 115, 136, 137, 142–155, 154 n, 156–169, 185 n, 211, 213, 216, 221, 222, 229, 232, 238–239 n
Repertory Theatre New Orleans, 80–81, 114
Rexroth, Kenneth, 55
Richard II, 79
Richard III, 73, 119
Richardson, Ralph, 136
Riddle of Lester Maddox, The, 106
Right You Are, 131
Ritchard, Cyril, 123
Rivals, The, 81, 129
Riverwind, 113
Robards, Jason, 119, 144
Roberts, Pernell, 32, 123
Rockefeller, John D., 142
Rockefeller Brothers Fund, 63

Rockefeller Foundation, 19, 44, 63, 84, 99, 137, 164, 176, 192, 231
Rodgers and Hammerstein, 171
Romeo and Juliet, 49
Room Service, 32, 139
Rooming House, The, 152
Rope's End, 39
Rose Tattoo, The, 47
Rosencrantz and Guildenstern Are Dead, 139
Rosenfield, John, 21
Ross, Duncan, 79
Roth, Philip, 190
Royal Hunt of the Sun, The, 106, 224
Royal Shakespeare Company, 5, 82, 140
Ryan, Robert, 82, 123

Saarinen, Eero, 143
Sackler, Howard, 193–197
Sadler's Wells, 66
St. Denis, Michel, 79
Saint Joan, 68, 73, 114, 163
San Francisco Chronicle, 54
San Francisco Examiner, 61
San Quentin Drama Workshop, 55
Sands, Diana, 106, 163
Sartre, Jean-Paul, 99, 158
Saturday Review, 194
Scaffold for Marionettes, A, 112
Scapin, 131, 241 n
Schevill, James, 55, 57, 115, 189, 225
Schiller, Friedrich von, 129
Schneider, Alan, 29, 32, 33, 34, 72, 107, 132, 154, 189, 211
Schoenbaum, Donald, 242
School for Scandal, The, 131, 132, 135
School for Wives, The, 235
Scism, Mack, 38–42, 50, 53, 64
Scott, George C., 163, 227
Scott, Harold, 103
Sea Gull, The, 129, 131
Seale, Douglas, 95, 96, 109, 124
Season with Ginger, 189
Seattle Repertory Theatre, 76–80, 111, 140, 183, 185 n, 191, 245, 247
Seattle World's Fair, 55, 76
Selling of the President, The, 136
Separate Tables, 142
Servant of Two Masters, The, 93
Seven-Year Itch, The, 177
Sevilla, José, 158
Shadow and Substance, 42
Shadow of Heroes, 77

Index

Shakespeare, William, 2, 12, 48, 118, 123, 125, 191, 197, 227
Shapiro, Mel, 73
Shaw, George Bernard, 12, 82, 191
Shaw, Robert, 85
She Stoops to Conquer, 32, 78, 129, 130
Shepard, Sam, 112
Sherin, Edwin, 194, 195, 216–217
Show, 62, 75, 157
Showboat, 49
Show-Off, The, 132, 133, 134, 135
Shubert, John, 126
Shubert Alley, 8, 152, 157
Shubert brothers, 6, 171
Shubert Theatre, 91
Shyre, Paul, 44
Sidney, Sylvia, 42, 129
Silvera, Frank, 217
Simon, Neil, 175
Simpson, N. F., 103
Six Characters in Search of an Author, 112, 136, 137, 138
Skin of Our Teeth, The, 68
Slapstick Tragedy, 211
Sleuth, 136
Slow Dance on the Killing Ground, 96, 103
Smith, Maggie, 82
Smith, Oliver, 223
Soldiers, 110
Solid Gold Cadillac, The, 48
Solitaire, Double Solitaire, 92, 215
Son of Man and the Family, 115
Sound of Hunting, A, 26
Sound of Music, The, 68
South Pacific, 48
Stage/West, 94–95, 245
"Stagehands" (The Guthrie Theater), 71–72
Staircase, 139
Stanford University Summer Festival, 138
Stanislavski, Constantin, 19
Star-Spangled Girl, The, 175
Steele, Mike, 242
Steiger, Rod, 160, 163
Stevens, Roger, 80, 122, 128 n, 222–224
Stewart, Ellen, 223, 224, 237
Stewart, James, 135, 225
Stewart, William, 93
Sticks and Bones, 229
Stix, John, 95–96
Stop the World—I Want to Get Off, 49
Storey, David, 92
Strasberg, Lee, 10, 11

Stratford Festival (England), 122
Stratford Shakespearean Festival (Ontario), 66, 118–121, 122, 123, 125, 132, 154, 160, 211, 212, 242
Streetcar Named Desire, A, 47, 143
Student Prince, The, 48, 177
Studio Arena Theatre, 107–109, 175, 183, 196
Subber, Saint, 163
Sudden and Accidental Re-Education of Horse Johnson, The, 196
Sugrue, Frank, 45–47, 107, 112
Summer and Smoke, 20, 39, 42
Summer of the Seventeenth Doll, 32
Survival of St. Joan, The, 108
Susskind, David, 75
Swan, Jon, 78
Swanson, Gloria, 11
Symonds, Robert, 60, 146, 159, 160, 164, 211

Taming of the Shrew, The, 57, 82, 123, 243
Tandy, Jessica, 72, 73, 75, 123, 131
Tartuffe, 136, 137, 138, 146
Taubman, Howard, 7, 158, 160, 185 n, 202
Tavern, The, 131
Tea and Sympathy, 143, 189
Tempest, The, 122, 123
Tender Trap, The, 27, 47
Terry, Megan, 84, 193
That Championship Season, 229
Theater Divided, A, 170
Theatre Arts, 8, 21, 125, 126, 128
Theatre Atlanta, 105–106, 196
Theatre Communications Group, 184–185, 231, 236–237, 241, 249 n
Theatre Company of Boston, 97, 98–100, 192, 193, 212
Theatre for Tomorrow, 44, 192
Theatre Group, UCLA, 82, 183
Theatre Guild, 10, 122, 126
Theatre-in-the Round, 16, 17, 19–20, 118, 188
Theatre of the Living Arts, 110–113, 175, 191, 196
Theatre St. Paul, 105
Theatre 3, 24
Theatre Today, 188
Thieves' Carnival, 73
Thomas, Augustus, 8
Thompson, Sada, 124
Three Men on a Horse, 32

Three Sisters, The, 36, 72, 91, 114, 139, 211, 218, 224
Threepenny Opera, The, 86
Thresholds, 24, 29
Tiger at the Gates, 82, 163
Time, 75, 202–204, 204–205
Time of Your Life, The, 49, 164
Time Out for Ginger, 189
Tiny Alice, 137, 138, 224
Tobacco Road, 105
Toffler, Alvin, 63, 203
Tolstoy, Leo, 131
Tonight at 8:30, 129
Tony Awards, 133, 211, 212, 213, 229
Touch of the Poet, A, 129
Touliatos, George, 47–50, 64
Trial of the Catonsville Nine, The, 84, 96, 135, 216
Tricks, 241 n
Trinity Square Repertory Company, 44, 113–116, 143, 183, 185 n, 210, 224, 225, 235, 245
Troilus and Cressida, 123
Trojan Women, The, 129
Twelfth Night, 77, 86, 123, 136, 191, 213, 218
Twentieth Century, 11
Twentieth Century Fund, 34, 63, 182
Two Blind Mice, 39
Two for the Seesaw, 48
Two Gentlemen of Verona, 229
Tynan, Kenneth, 161

Ulmer, John, 94
Un-American Activities Committee, 9, 229
Uncle Vanya, 83, 138, 153, 192
United States Congress, 126
United States Department of State, 225
United States Department of the Interior, 130
United States Office of Education, 80, 114, 173
University Resident Theatre Association, 249 n

van Itallie, Jean-Claude, 84
van Zandt, Roland, 115
Vance, Milton, 26
Vance, Nina, 26–31, 32, 33, 38, 48, 50, 64, 199
Variety, 1, 8, 139, 195, 196
Vaughan, Stuart, 76–81, 111, 114, 174, 191, 227

Venturi, Robert, 94
View from the Bridge, A, 33
Visit, The, 73
Vivian Beaumont Theater, 143, 157, 158, 163, 166–167, 222
Voice of the Turtle, The, 224
Voight, Jon, 212
Volpone, 68, 73

Waiting for Godot, 48, 55, 57, 168, 176
Walker Foundation, 70
Wallach, Eli, 131
Waltz of the Toreadors, The, 106
War and Peace, 131, 132, 135
Warren, Robert Penn, 115
Washington Drama Society, 35
Washington Square Players, 10
Washington Theatre Club, 97–98, 183, 192, 196
Waters, Ethel, 42, 142
Way of the World, The, 73, 211
Wayne, David, 82, 144
We Bombed in New Haven, 196
We Comrades Three, 32
Weaver, Fritz, 123
Weber, Carl, 59, 159, 163
Weese, Harry, 33, 36, 241
Weidner, Paul, 93–94
Weiler, Berenice, 124
Weller, Michael, 195
Welles, Orson, 10, 82
Wentworth, Hazel, 97
Wentworth, John, 97
Westport Country Playhouse, 122
Wheeler, David, 99–100
Where's Charley? 48
Whistle in the Dark, A, 92, 196, 215
White, George, 193
Whitehead, Robert, 142–145, 159, 174, 211, 223, 238 n
Whiting, John, 83
Whitman, Walt, 132
Who's Afraid of Virginia Woolf?, 78, 135, 177
Who's Happy Now?, 196
Wilde, Oscar, 114
Wilder, Thornton, 191
Williams, Emlyn, 152
Williams, Heathcote, 99
Williams, Tennessee, 18, 19, 20, 47, 68, 154 n, 191, 200, 211
Wilson, Edmund, 11
Wilson, Lanford, 84, 98, 108, 193, 196

Index

Wilson in the Promised Land, 115, 224, 225

Winter, Edward, 211

Winter's Tale, The, 123

Woman in the Dunes, 15

Women, The, 81

Wood, Audrey, 223

Works Progress Administration, 9, 12

Worth, Irene, 119

Wright, Bagley, 77–80

Wright, Frank Lloyd, 44

Wright, Teresa, 92

Yale Repertory Theatre, 91, 196

Yale School of Drama, 34, 44, 86, 90, 91, 92, 93, 193, 249 n

Yalman, Tunc, 44–45

Yard of Sun, A, 15

Years of the Locust, 114–115

Yerma, 160

You Can't Take It with You, 86, 92, 132, 135, 136, 176

You Touched Me, 39

Young, Stark, 8

You're a Good Man, Charlie Brown, 108

Zeisler, Peter, 66–76, 184, 207, 218–221, 223, 224, 236

Zindel, Paul, 84, 190